SPEECH PERCEPTION AND SPOKEN WORD RECOGNITION

Speech Perception and Spoken Word Recognition features contributions from the field's leading scientists. It covers recent developments and current issues in the study of cognitive and neural mechanisms that take patterns of air vibrations and turn them 'magically' into meaning. The volume makes a unique theoretical contribution in linking behavioural and cognitive neuroscience research, cutting across traditional strands of study, such as adult and developmental processing.

The book:

- Focuses on the state of the art in the study of speech perception and spoken word recognition.
- Discusses the interplay between behavioural and cognitive neuroscience evidence and between adult and developmental research.
- Evaluates key theories in the field and relates them to recent empirical advances, including the relationship between speech perception and speech production, meaning representation and real-time activation, and bilingual and monolingual spoken word recognition.
- Examines emerging areas of study, such as word learning and time course of memory consolidation, and how the science of human speech perception can help computer speech recognition.

Overall this book presents a renewed focus on theoretical and developmental issues, as well as a multifaceted and broad review of the state of research in speech perception and spoken word recognition. The book is ideal for researchers of psycholinguistics and adjoining fields, as well as advanced undergraduate and postgraduate students.

M. Gareth Gaskell is Professor of Psychology at the University of York, UK.

Jelena Mirković is Senior Lecturer in Psychology at York St John University, UK, and an Honorary Fellow at the University of York, UK.

Current Issues in the Psychology of Language
Series Editor: Trevor A. Harley

Current Issues in the Psychology of Language is a series of edited books that will reflect the state of the art in areas of current and emerging interest in the psychological study of language.

Each volume is tightly focused on a particular topic and consists of seven to ten chapters contributed by international experts. The editors of individual volumes are leading figures in their areas and provide an introductory overview.

Example topics include language development, bilingualism and second language acquisition, word recognition, word meaning, text processing, the neuroscience of language, and language production, as well as the interrelations between these topics.

Visual Word Recognition Volume 1
Edited by James S. Adelman

Visual Word Recognition Volume 2
Edited by James S. Adelman

Sentence Processing
Edited by Roger van Gompel

Speech Perception and Spoken Word Recognition
Edited by M. Gareth Gaskell and Jelena Mirković

SPEECH PERCEPTION AND SPOKEN WORD RECOGNITION

*Edited by M. Gareth Gaskell
and Jelena Mirković*

Routledge
Taylor & Francis Group

LONDON AND NEW YORK

First published 2017
by Routledge
2 Park Square, Milton Park, Abingdon, Oxon OX14 4RN

and by Routledge
711 Third Avenue, New York, NY 10017

Routledge is an imprint of the Taylor & Francis Group, an informa business

British Library Cataloguing in Publication Data

A catalogue record for this book is available from the British Library

Library of Congress Cataloging-in-Publication Data
Names: Gaskell, M. Gareth, editor. | Mirkovic, Jelena, editor.
Title: Speech perception and spoken word recognition / edited by
     M. Gareth Gaskell and Jelena Mirkoviâc.
Description: Abingdon, Oxon ; New York, NY : Routledge, 2016. |
     Series: Current issues in the psychology of language | Includes
     bibliographical references and index.
Identifiers: LCCN 2016000884 (print) | LCCN 2016009488 (ebook) |
     ISBN 9781848724396 (hardback) | ISBN 9781848724402 (pbk.) |
     ISBN 9781315772110 (ebook)
Subjects: LCSH: Speech perception. | Word recognition. | Psycholinguistics.
Classification: LCC BF463.S64 S64 2016 (print) | LCC BF463.S64
     (ebook) | DDC 401/.95—dc23
LC record available at http://lccn.loc.gov/2016000884

ISBN: 978-1-84872-439-6 (hbk)
ISBN: 978-1-84872-440-2 (pbk)
ISBN: 978-1-315-77211-0 (ebk)

Typeset in Bembo
by Apex CoVantage, LLC

CONTENTS

CONTRIBUTORS

Heather Bortfeld
Department of Psychology
University of Connecticut
406 Babbidge Road, Unit 1020
Storrs, CT 06269 USA

Bradley R. Buchsbaum
Rotman Research Institute
Baycrest, Toronto
Ontario M6A 2E1 Canada

Peiyao Chen
Department of Communication Sciences and Disorders
Northwestern University
2240 Campus Drive
Evanston, IL 60208 USA

Matthew H. Davis
Medical Research Council
Cognition & Brain Sciences Unit
15 Chaucer Road
Cambridge CB2 7EF UK

M. Gareth Gaskell
Department of Psychology
University of York
York YO10 5DD UK

Ingrid S. Johnsrude
Brain and Mind Institute
Department of Psychology
University of Western Ontario
London
Ontario N6A 5B7 Canada

Efthymia C. Kapnoula
Department of Psychological and Brain Sciences
University of Iowa
Iowa City, IA 52245 USA

Breanna I. Krueger
Department of Speech-Language-Hearing
University of Kansas
1000 Sunnyside Ave
Lawrence, KS 66045 USA

James Magnuson
Department of Psychology
Connecticut Institute for Brain and Cognitive Sciences
University of Connecticut
406 Babbidge Road, Unit 1020
Storrs, CT 06269 USA

Viorica Marian
Department of Communication Sciences and Disorders
Northwestern University
2240 Campus Drive
Evanston, IL 60208 USA

Sven L. Mattys
Department of Psychology
University of York
York YO10 5DD UK

Bob McMurray
Department of Psychological and Brain Sciences
University of Iowa
Iowa City, IA 52245 USA

Jelena Mirković
Department of Psychology
York St John University
York YO31 7EX UK

Daniel Mirman
Department of Psychology
Drexel University
3141 Chestnut Street
Philadelphia, PA 19104 USA

Thierry Nazzi
Laboratoire Psychologie de la Perception, CNRS
Université Paris Descartes
45 rue des Saint-Pères
75006 Paris, France

Silvana Poltrock
Laboratoire Psychologie de la Perception, CNRS
Université Paris Descartes
45 rue des Saint-Pères
75006 Paris, France

Odette Scharenborg
Centre for Language Studies
Radboud University
6500 Nijmegen, Netherlands

Sophie K. Scott
University College London
17 Queen Square
London WC1N 3AR UK

Holly L. Storkel
Department of Speech-Language-Hearing
University of Kansas
1000 Sunnyside Ave, 3001 Dole
Lawrence, KS 66045 USA

INTRODUCTION

M. Gareth Gaskell and Jelena Mirković

Perhaps the most crucial accomplishment of humankind is the ability to communicate through language. This volume discusses the key mechanisms that represent the perceptual "front end" of this process: mechanisms that take patterns of air vibration and somehow – spectacularly – transform these into meaning.

Putting together a volume of just ten relatively short, accessible chapters on this process was a demanding task, and we had to make some tough decisions. Looking back at the field over the last ten years or so, there has been both steady progress and also rather more dramatic shifts of scope. Steady progress has been made in understanding the cognitive and perceptual mechanisms that assist us in speech perception, where we are building on 30 or 40 years of increasingly elegant empirical behavioural paradigms. At the same time, cognitive neuroscience has made more extensive advances in identifying the neural mechanisms that support speech perception, and these advances are now beginning to contribute to cognitive theory. Here, the research base is much newer, with almost all the significant advances taking place within the last decade.

Given this multidimensional progress, we decided not to request long, historical reviews from our authors; other volumes do a good job of that. Instead we asked our authors to describe the state of the art in their area and at the same time to write about relevant interplay between behavioural and cognitive neuropsychological evidence, as well as between adult and developmental research. This is one of the aspects of the field that make it exciting for us. In many ways, we do not yet have "joined-up" cognitive neuroscientific models of speech perception and spoken word recognition across the lifespan, and, as will become clear, there are some areas of research where good progress has been made towards this goal and others where the majority of the hard work is yet to be done. In short, this volume describes the current state of affairs in the linking process and, we hope, also provides some useful hints as to where the research stars of the future should focus their efforts.

The authors of the individual chapters have done a superb job of addressing this challenging brief. In Chapter 1, **Johnsrude** and **Buchsbaum** describe the very first stage of the perceptual system dedicated to speech: the identification of perceptual units that can make extraction of words from the speech stream possible. They answer questions such as, "How do we deal with variability in speech?" and "What kinds of units are extracted?" The cognitive neuroscience evidence base here is in fact quite revealing, and substantial recent progress has been made in answering these questions.

Johnsrude and Buchsbaum end with a brief discussion of the involvement of speech production units in speech perception, and this issue is taken up in greater detail by **Scott** in Chapter 2. Her chapter covers an issue of great debate in recent years: to what extent do the perceptual and production systems for speech make use of shared resources? Interest in the "mirror neuron" system and the development of new empirical neuroscience methods, such as transcranial magnetic stimulation (TMS), have led to a renewed interest in this question. Previously, researchers assessed the issue of shared resources in cognitive terms, but now one can also ask whether, for example, speech production areas of the brain are recruited to help us understand speech. Scott's review points to an asymmetry in the role of perception and production systems for speech, with perceptual systems playing a dominant role in production but production systems not having a similar involvement in perception.

Chapter 3 addresses the development of speech perception mechanisms. **Nazzi** and **Poltrock** discuss the acquisition of phonetic categories in infant speech perception and specifically focus on the link between phonological and lexical development. They assess the observation that consonants tend to be given more weight than vowels in the early stages of word learning and lexical development. They evaluate three explanations for the source of this bias and, on the basis of recent cross-linguistic evidence, argue that it reflects learned acoustic-phonetic differences in variability and reliability of consonants compared with vowels.

In Chapter 4, **Mattys** and **Bortfeld** shift the focus to the segmentation of the continuous speech stream in order to identify likely word beginnings or ends. Traditionally, solutions to this problem have fallen into two categories. Lexical solutions use acquired knowledge about the phonological composition of words to identify likely junctures between those words. This type of solution contrasts with non-lexical solutions that rely on the identification of informative cues in the speech stream that might help identify word boundaries from the bottom up. Mattys and Bortfeld review the evidence for these two types of segmentation process in a wide range of circumstances, in both development and adulthood. The model they propose stresses the flexibility of the system to adapt to a wide range of circumstances (e.g., conversing in a crowded room or listening to a speaker with a strong accent). Nonetheless, they argue that there is, above all, an intrinsic priority given to lexical information in word boundary identification.

Speech perception has no value if it does not lead to meaning. In Chapter 5, **Magnuson** first evaluates the key theories of how meanings can be represented and then relates them to the empirical advances in spoken word recognition. Given the volume's emphasis on recent developments, much of the data in this chapter exploits the visual world paradigm. This method has been particularly fruitful in assessing real-time meaning activation by analysing listeners' eye movement patterns to pictures on a screen as they listen to spoken language. As well as being an effective method of assessing the time course of meaning activation when listeners hear isolated words, the visual world paradigm has also helped us to understand how this process changes when words are heard in a conversational context. Although these contexts can make a substantial difference to the way in which the meanings of words are extracted, nonetheless, Magnuson argues that the human system remains heavily constrained by the details of the speech signal. This is the so-called bottom-up priority that helps us to understand words properly even in highly unlikely sentence contexts.

In Chapter 6, **Mirman** reviews the state of the art in computational models of spoken word recognition. As described in his chapter, two types of models have been particularly successful over recent decades: the TRACE interactive activation network model and the simple recurrent network (SRN) models that learn structure from their input. These models have remained relevant because of their astonishing success in capturing and, indeed, predicting a wide range of empirical observations. Mirman describes the recent advances that have been made, for example in understanding the nature of individual differences in lexical competition. Such advances have broadened the scope of the models, but Mirman argues that much more can be done in the future to expand their relevance to traditionally separate adjoining fields. These "zones of proximal development" include higher-level processes (e.g., syntactic influences), lower-level processes (e.g., the acoustic front end), cognitive control, and learning and memory.

Chapter 7 takes up the last of these challenges and describes recent research towards a better link between lexical processes and our wider understanding of learning and memory. Whereas the traditional view of the adult speech system stressed "fixed" mechanisms, recent studies have shifted the focus to plasticity and learning. **McMurray**, **Kapnoula** and **Gaskell** examine a key area in which plasticity is important: the incorporation of new words into the mental lexicon. The chapter describes an emerging literature in which multiple time courses for word learning have been identified. Some properties of new words can be available immediately, suggesting that word learning is an encoding problem, whereas other aspects emerge over a longer period, implying consolidation. In part, this division of labour can be explained in terms of complementary learning systems applied to the lexicon, but McMurray and colleagues also argue for incorporating a broader perspective on learning and consolidation to explain the full range of lexical properties and their emergence in vocabulary acquisition.

The great majority of research in speech perception and spoken word recognition has assumed, for the sake of simplicity, that the listener knows a single language. This of course is often not the case, with many people fluent in two languages and sometimes in three or more. **Chen** and **Marian** examine the consequences of bilingual fluency on spoken word recognition. Their starting point is the observation that in many situations words from both languages will be mentally activated during the perception of speech from either language. However, the extent to which this competition between languages is balanced depends on many factors, and Chapter 8 reviews the latest research on how these factors interact and considers both linguistic (e.g., phonological and lexical similarity between the languages) and cognitive factors (e.g., language proficiency, age of acquisition). Chen and Marian also examine the consequences of the interlanguage activation. For example, they argue that a cost of knowing two languages is the impaired ability to understand speech in adverse conditions, such as in a noisy environment. On the other hand, the enhanced need to resolve competition between as well as within two languages may also have benefits, such as an enhanced cognitive flexibility that may operate beyond the linguistic domain.

All the chapters in this volume have incorporated as a central concept the notion of a phonological representation of speech. Chapter 9 addresses and augments this centrality from a different angle by looking at how the developing language system operates in cases where the phonological representation may be weaker or impaired in some way. **Krueger** and **Storkel** review current research on developmental phonological disorders (DPDs), in which delayed speech production is observed in the absence of any obvious external cause (e.g., deafness, motor impairments). The authors review the wide-ranging effects of this delay and describe how the consequences of DPD can help elucidate the mechanisms of speech processing in development. They also critically evaluate DPD treatment options, and with relevance to the theme of the volume, discuss the potential for eyetracking and neuroimaging methods to further enhance our understanding of DPD and its consequences for the language system.

Finally, in Chapter 10, **Davis** and **Scharenborg** relate our understanding of the human speech system to the automatic speech recognition (ASR) literature. The latter is another area in which substantial progress has been made over the last few years, with ASR systems now a mainstream component of consumer devices such as tablets and smartphones. Although ASR remains less effective than its human equivalent, the narrowing gap in accuracy between these two systems makes the comparison of their mechanisms ever more interesting. The authors take a bold approach and argue that now is the time for some of the "tricks" that humans use to maximise recognition efficiency to be incorporated into automatic systems.

When we initially assembled a structure for this volume, we faced a difficult selection task, and several possible topics could have strengthened the book but in the end did not make the cut. Nonetheless, we think that the ten selected chapters provide a multifaceted and broad review of the state of research in speech perception and spoken word recognition. Furthermore, we are thrilled by the quality and academic rigour of the chapters that we received. We hope that the reader will find the volume revealing and that the reviews here will help to shape the research agenda for the future.

1

REPRESENTATION OF SPEECH

Ingrid S. Johnsrude and Bradley R. Buchsbaum

Introduction

To comprehend a spoken utterance, listeners must map a dynamic, variable, spectrotemporally complex continuous acoustic signal onto discrete linguistic representations in the brain, assemble these so as to recognize individual words, access the meanings of these words, and combine them to compute the overall meaning (Davis & Johnsrude, 2007). Words or their elements do not correspond to any invariant acoustic units in the speech signal: the speech stream does not usually contain silent gaps to demarcate word boundaries, and dramatic changes to the pronunciation of words in different contexts arise due to variation both between and within talkers (e.g., coarticulation). Despite the continuous nature and variability of speech, native speakers of a language perceive a sequence of discrete, meaningful units. How does this happen? What are the linguistic representations in the brain, and how is the mapping between a continuous auditory signal and such representations achieved? Given that speaking is a sensorimotor skill, is speech perceived in terms of its motor or auditory features? Does processing occur on multiple linguistic levels simultaneously (e.g., phonemes, syllables, words), or is there a single canonical level of representation, with larger units (like words) being assembled from these elemental units? How is acoustic variability – among talkers, and within talkers across utterances, dealt with, such that acoustically different signals all contact the same representation? (In other words, how do you perceive that Brad and Ingrid both said "I'd love lunch!" despite marked variability in the acoustics of their productions?)

These questions are fundamental to an understanding of the human use of language and have intrigued psychologists, linguists, and others for at least 50 years. Recent advances in methods for stimulating and recording activity in the human brain permit these perennial questions to be addressed in new ways. Over the last 20 years, cognitive-neuroscience methods have yielded a wealth of data related to the organization of speech and language in the brain. The most important methods include functional magnetic resonance imaging (fMRI), which is a non-invasive method used to study brain activity in local regions and functional interactions among regions. Pattern-information analytic approaches to fMRI data, such as multi-voxel pattern analysis (Mur, Bandettini, & Kriegeskorte, 2009), permit researchers to examine the information that is represented in different brain regions. Another method is transcranial magnetic stimulation (TMS), which is used to stimulate small regions on the surface of the brain, thereby reducing neural firing thresholds or interrupting function.

Recently, intracranial electrocorticography (ECoG) has re-emerged as a valuable tool for the study of speech and language in the human brain. Intracranial electrodes are implanted in some individuals with epilepsy who are refractory to drug treatment and so are being considered for surgical resection. ECoG electrodes, placed on the surface of the brain or deep into the brain, record neural activity with unparalleled temporal and spatial resolution. The hope is that the person with epilepsy will have a seizure while implanted: electrodes in which seizure activity is first evident are a valuable clue to the location of abnormal tissue giving rise to the seizures (resection of this tissue is potentially curative). Patients can be implanted for weeks at a time and often agree to participate in basic-science research (i.e., on speech and language) during their seizure-free periods.

In this chapter, we will first review what the cognitive psychological literature reveals about the nature of the linguistic representations for speech and language (What are the units? Are representations auditory or vocal gestural?) and about how speech variability is handled. We then turn to the cognitive-neuroscience literature, and review recent papers using fMRI, TMS, and ECoG methods that speak to these important questions.

The nature of the linguistic representations for speech and language: Cognitive considerations

What are the units?

The generativity and hierarchical structure of language appears to strongly imply that there must be units in speech; these units are combined in different ways to create an infinite number of messages. Furthermore, speech is not heard as the continuous signal that it physically is; instead, listeners perceive speech sounds in distinct categories, along one or more linguistic dimensions or levels of analysis (such as articulatory gestures or features, or phonemes, syllables, morphemes, or words). Experience shapes perception to permit such analysis by highlighting and accentuating meaning*ful* variability while minimizing meaning*less* variability (see Davis & Johnsrude, 2007; Diehl, Lotto, & Holt, 2004, for reviews). Furthermore, we can repeat and imitate what someone else has said; such imitation requires that we parse another's behaviour into components and then generate the motor commands to reproduce those behaviours (Studdert-Kennedy, 1981). Finally, we expect 'core' representations of language to be abstract since they must be modality independent: the spoken word [kaet] and the written form CAT must contact the same representations. What are the dimensions to which listeners are sensitive and which permit classification, imitation, and abstraction? What level or levels of analysis are 'elemental' in speech perception? What are the representational categories to which speech is mapped and that are used to retrieve the meaning of an utterance?

It is often assumed that the phoneme is the primary unit of perceptual analysis of speech (Nearey, 2001). The search for invariants in speech perception began with the observation that acoustically highly variable instances (variability caused in part by coarticulation and allophonic variation) were all classified by listeners as the same phoneme (Liberman, Cooper, Shankweiler, & Studdert-Kennedy, 1967; Liberman, Harris, Hoffman, & Griffith, 1957). Such perceptual constancy for phonemic identity can be viewed either as a natural outcome of perceptual systems that are maximizing sensitivity to change (see Kluender & Kiefte, 2006, pp. 171–177, for discussion) or as evidence that speech perception is a modular, specialized function and that phonemes have some cognitive reality within an efficient and restricted inventory of speech events represented in the brain.

Although patterns of speech errors during sentence planning and execution are compatible with the psychological reality of phonemes as a unit of representation in the brain (Fromkin, 1971; Klatt, 1981), awareness of the phonemes in speech is generally restricted to users of alphabetic written languages, and phonemic awareness may in fact be a *result* of recognizing individual words rather than a prerequisite (Charles-Luce & Luce, 1990; Marslen-Wilson & Warren, 1994). Another objection to the phoneme as the primary unit in speech perception is that subphonemic acoustic information – fine phonetic detail – has important and systematic effects on speech perception (Hawkins, 2003; McMurray, Tanenhaus, & Aslin, 2009; see also Port, 2007). Listeners may use abstract prelexical, subphonemic representations, but it is still not clear what the 'grain size' of these units is (Mitterer, Scharenborg, & McQueen, 2013). Alternatively, several researchers have argued that listeners map relatively low-level information about the speech signal (phonetic features) directly onto words (or their meanings) without the need for a separate "phoneme recognition" stage (Gaskell & Marslen-Wilson, 1997; Kluender & Kiefte, 2006; Marslen-Wilson & Warren, 1994).

Another possible category of representation is the morpheme; theories of spoken language production and recognition generally posit that words like *brightness* are assembled out of smaller morphemic units (in this case, *bright* and *ness*; Dell, 1986; Levelt, Roelofs, & Meyer, 1999; Marslen-Wilson, Tyler, Waksler, & Older, 1994) and that morphological representations may be somewhat independent of phonological representations and appear to be recruited at a relatively early stage of processing, before phonological representations are computed in detail (Cohen-Goldberg, Cholin, Miozzo, & Rapp, 2013). Furthermore, the fact that morphologically related words prime one another in the absence of priming for word form, or meaning, across different psycholinguistic paradigms suggests that morphology plays an independent role in the organization and processing of words (Bozic, Marslen-Wilson, Stamatakis, Davis, & Tyler, 2007).

Intriguingly, languages differ in terms of the evidence for prominence of a particular kind of speech unit. For example, the syllable appears to play a prominent role in speech perception in French, Spanish, Italian, Dutch, and Portuguese but not necessarily in English (Bien, Bölte, & Zwitserlood, 2015; Floccia, Goslin, Morais, & Kolinsky, 2012; Goldinger & Azuma, 2003).

The cognitive literature on speech perception is now shifting away from a preoccupation with the question of which particular linguistic unit is most important and towards a more domain-general account in which the statistics of the input are used discover the structure of natural sounds (Kluender & Kiefte, 2006; Port, 2007). Perceptual inferences can then be made in a Bayesian fashion, using probability distributions defined on structured representations. This brings theorizing about the mechanisms of auditory and speech perception in line with what is known about visual perception (Kersten, Mamassian, & Yuille, 2004; Yuille & Kersten, 2006).

Are representations auditory or gestural?

In their seminal 1959 paper, "What the Frog's Eye Tells the Frog's Brain," Jerry Lettvin and colleagues (Lettvin, Maturana, McCulloch, & Pitts, 1959) identified optic nerve fibers from the retina of the frog that were sensitive to small, dark convex objects that enter the receptive field, stop, and then move about in the field intermittently. They were tempted to call these bug detectors, since it is hard to imagine a system better equipped "for detecting an accessible bug" (Lettvin et al., 1959). Before these studies, retinal cells were viewed as light sensors, which relayed a copy of the local distribution of light to the brain in an array of impulses. This study demonstrated that, in fact, information is already highly organized and interpreted by the time it leaves the retina, providing the frog with precisely the information that is most relevant and useful to it. This is highly consistent with the direct-perception or direct-realist account of perception, as put forward by James Gibson (Gibson, 1966) and others; this account emphasized that the objects of perception are not patterns of light or sound but environmental events that provide opportunities for interaction and behaviour.

Carol Fowler at Haskins Laboratories has put forward a direct-realist account of speech perception (Fowler, 1986), arguing that listeners directly perceive articulatory gestures, which are reflected in the sounds of speech. This position is similar to that held by proponents of the motor theory of speech perception, also developed at Haskins (Galantucci, Fowler, & Turvey, 2006; A.M. Liberman et al., 1967; A.M. Liberman & Mattingly, 1985), who suggested that speech is primarily a motoric phenomenon. In a series of investigations aimed at understanding the acoustic signatures of phonemes, Liberman's group demonstrated that the spectrotemporal sound pattern of a given consonant is not invariant but that coarticulation gives every consonant (and vowel) multiple acoustic realizations. For example, when the identical consonant /d/ is spoken in different vowel contexts (e.g., *dih*, *dee*, and *dar*), the formant transition patterns during the articulation of the stop consonant change in each case. Despite the variation in the acoustic properties of the consonant, however, the observer hears the same /d/ sound. The way in which /d/ is articulated is the same in each case, with the tip of the tongue pressing against the alveolar ridge; this articulatory invariance led Liberman and colleagues to suggest that the goal of the speech perception system is not to perceive sounds but rather to recover the invariant articulatory gestures produced by the speaker.

More recent behavioural work makes it clear that articulation itself is not as invariant as previously believed. Although the goal of articulation can be relatively constant (i.e., upper lip contacting lower lip), the actual movements required to achieve such a goal vary substantially (Gracco & Abbs, 1986). It is possible that abstract movement goals are invariantly represented but that the actual motor commands to achieve those movements probably are not.

As in other domains of motor control, speech may rely on forward internal models (Webb, 2004; Wolpert & Ghahramani, 2000), which allow a talker to predict the sensory (acoustic) consequences of their (articulatory) actions, based on the current state of the articulatory apparatus and the motor commands that have been issued. Articulatory commands are altered based on feedback mechanisms that use both proprioceptive and auditory information (Munhall, MacDonald, Byrne, & Johnsrude, 2009; Nasir & Ostry, 2006). This suggests that the representations of goal states must be multimodal and somehow incorporate movement, proprioception, and acoustics.

What has cognitive neuroscience taught us about how the brain is organized for speech perception?

Brain organization supporting speech and language

Much of the brain's cortex appears to be involved in the processing of speech information. Current evidence from fMRI suggests that much of the superior and middle temporal gyri bilaterally, as well as the angular and supramarginal gyri, bilateral inferior frontal cortex, medial frontal cortex, and precuneus region are routinely involved when people hear and understand naturalistic narrative spoken language (Adank, 2012; Davis & Johnsrude, 2007; Peelle, 2012; Regev, Honey, Simony, & Hasson, 2013).

The pattern of activity observed in the human brain using fMRI (Adank, 2012; Regev et al., 2013) is quite similar to that observed in response to auditory stimulation in macaque monkeys (Poremba et al., 2003), despite macaque monkeys relying far less than humans on audition for communication. In the macaque, a primary auditory cortical *core* of areas projects to a surrounding *belt*, which in turn connects with lateral *parabelt* fields (Hackett, 2011). The core, belt and parabelt areas are strikingly hierarchical in their connections and are functionally distinct, suggesting at least three discrete levels of processing (Hackett, 2011; Kaas & Hackett, 2000; Kaas, Hackett, & Tramo, 1999; Rauschecker, 1998). Connections within the macaque auditory system are topographically organized (see Figure 1.1), radiating out from core auditory regions and interconnecting multiple temporal and frontal regions, converging in lateral frontal cortex (Frey, Mackey, & Petrides, 2014; Petrides & Pandya, 1988, 2009; Romanski, Bates, & Goldman-Rakic, 1999; Romanski, Tian et al., 1999; Seltzer & Pandya, 1989). These routes may be functionally specialized (Hackett, 2011; Rauschecker, 1998; Romanski, Tian et al., 1999; Tian, Reser, Durham, Kustov, & Rauschecker, 2001). Projection zones in frontal, temporal and

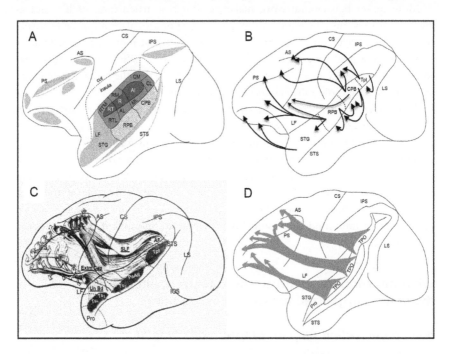

FIGURE 1.1 Auditory cortex: levels of processing and frontotemporal connectivity in the macaque monkey. (A) The anatomical organization of the auditory cortex in the nonhuman primate is consistent with at least four levels of processing, including core regions (darkest shading) belt regions (lighter shading), parabelt regions (stripes), and temporal and frontal regions that interconnect with belt and parabelt regions (lightest shading). Dotted lines indicate sulci that have been opened to show auditory regions. (Adapted from Kaas et al., 1999.) (B) Connectivity of auditory belt and parabelt regions with lateral frontal and temporal cortex. (Adapted from Hackett, 2011.) Regions along the length of both the (C) superior temporal gyrus and (D) dorsal bank of the superior temporal sulcus connect with prefrontal regions in a topographically organized anterior-to-posterior fashion. (C adapted from Petrides & Pandya, 1988, p. 64; D adapted from Seltzer & Pandya, 1989.)

Key Abbreviations: A1 = Auditory area 1; AF = arcuate fasciculus; AS = arcuate sulcus; CPB = Caudal parabelt area; CS = central sulcus; Extm Cap = Extreme Capsule; IOS = inferior occipital sulcus; IPS = intraparietal sulcus; LF = lateral fissure; LS = lunate sulcus; PaAlt = lateral parakoniocortex; Pro = Proisocortical area; PS = principal sulcus; R = Rostral Area; RPB = Rostral parabelt area; RT = Rostrotemporal area; SLF = superior longitudinal fasciculus; STG = superior temporal gyrus; STS = superior temporal sulcus; TPO = polymodal cortex; Tpt = Temporal parietotemporal area; Ts 1/2/3 = three subdivisions of rostral superior temporal gyrus; Un Bd = Uncinate Bundle.

parietal cortex may constitute a fourth (or higher) level of processing (Hackett, 2011; Kaas et al., 1999).

In humans, core auditory cortex has been identified on the first transverse temporal gyrus of Heschl (Celesia, 1976; Howard et al., 2000; Morosan et al., 2001) and is surrounded by many other anatomically differentiable regions (Chiry, Tardif, Magistretti, & Clarke, 2003; Hackett, Preuss, & Kaas, 2001; Rivier & Clarke, 1997; Wallace, Johnston, & Palmer, 2002), many of which share characteristics with macaque belt areas. Although the organization of the human auditory system is considered to be largely homologous with that in macaques (Frey, Campbell, Pike, & Petrides, 2008; Hackett, 2011; Hall, Hart, & Johnsrude, 2003; Petrides & Pandya, 1994, 2009; Petrides, Tomaiuolo, Yeterian, & Pandya, 2012; Rauschecker, 1998), this homology is limited since macaques do not have a middle temporal gyrus. In humans, the superior temporal sulcus (delimiting superior and middle temporal gyri) is very long and deep, comprising substantial cortical territory; the cortical region of the middle temporal gyrus (MTG) is also large and probably anatomically highly diverse (Morosan, Schleicher, Amunts, & Zilles, 2005). Many of these brain regions appear to play a role in the comprehension of spoken language (Adank, 2012; Davis & Johnsrude, 2007; Liebenthal, Desai, Humphries, Sabri, & Desai, 2014; Regev et al., 2013).

An important goal of a cognitive neuroscience of language is to functionally parcellate the vast region of speech-sensitive cortex in order to discover how different parts of this large region differentially subserve the cognitive processes and representations required for transformation of acoustic signals into language. We now briefly examine some examples of how cognitive neuroscience methods, including fMRI, EcoG, and TMS, have been productively employed to begin to address this goal. fMRI tools, such as adaptation paradigms and multi-voxel pattern analysis, allow researchers to ask questions related to the representation of information in the brain. ECoG permits similar inferences, by virtue of the very high temporal and spatial resolution of this technique and the sophisticated methods that are used to analyze neural activity measured by it. Both fMRI and ECoG reveal correlated activity, which may not be critical for cognition and behaviour. TMS transiently interrupts local brain function and so reveals areas that are not simply correlated with but that are critically involved in the cognitive process of interest.

What are the units?

Much attention has been paid in the cognitive neuroscience literature to how stimuli that differ acoustically can be mapped into a distinct category of speech unit, such as a particular phoneme class. What are the neural mechanisms underlying perceptual invariance in the face of so much acoustic variability in speech? Chang and colleagues (Chang et al., 2010) used intracranial recording (ECoG) in four patients and the classic paradigm of Liberman and colleagues (Liberman et al., 1957; Liberman et al., 1967) (a synthetic [ba] to [da] to [ga] continuum in which the second formant was systematically manipulated) in order to demonstrate that neural response patterns in the posterior superior temporal gyrus reflected phonetic category rather than the linear changes in acoustics. Several other neuroimaging investigations have also implicated posterior brain regions in the left hemisphere, such as the posterior superior temporal gyrus (STG), supramarginal gyrus, and angular gyrus, in categorical phoneme perception (see Lee, Turkeltaub, Granger, & Raizada, 2012; Turkeltaub & Coslett, 2010).

Other experiments highlight a role for left inferior frontal regions in the computation of phonetic invariants. For example, Myers and associates (Myers, Blumstein, Walsh, & Eliassen, 2009) studied brain sensitivity to acoustic changes in voice onset time that fell either on one side of a phonetic boundary (i.e., both stimuli perceived as [da] or as [ta]) or fell across the phonetic boundary (i.e., one stimulus perceived as [da] and the other as [ta]). They used a short-interval adaptation paradigm (Grill-Spector & Malach, 2001; Henson, 2003), which takes advantage of the assumption that neural tissue sensitive to a particular stimulus dimension will adapt, demonstrating less activity, to repeated presentations (within a short time) of a given value along that dimension. If two different values along the dimension are presented, then greater activity, reflecting release from adaptation, is observed. According to this reasoning, brain regions sensitive to the phonetic category ought to show adaptation when stimuli that are perceived as the same phonetic category are heard (even if these differ acoustically) and to release from adaptation when stimuli that are perceived as phonetically distinct are heard (even if these differ acoustically by the same amount). Myers and colleagues (2009) observed a region in left dorsal pars opercularis (according to gross anatomical criteria, a region that is considered to be part of Broca's area) that appeared to be uniquely sensitive to phonetic category, since release from adaptation was observed in this region only when acoustic differences resulted in perceptually different phonetic categories. Acoustic differences that did not result in phonetic category differences were processed much like stimuli that were identical acoustically. The authors conclude that phonetic categorization is computed by this region of left frontal cortex.

Another way to study invariant perception with variable acoustics is to use pattern-information approaches to fMRI data analysis, which allow spatially distinct patterns of activity within a local region to be discriminated (Mur et al., 2009). For example, Raizada and colleagues (Raizada, Tsao, Liu, & Kuhl, 2010) used a multi-voxel pattern analytic (MVPA) approach to evaluate where in the brain the statistical separability of fMRI patterns predicted the ability of native speakers of English and Japanese to discriminate the syllables [ra] and [la]. In conventional analyses of fMRI data, activation is averaged over a brain region, and differences between stimuli or tasks are assessed by comparing the regional-average magnitude of activity for one stimulus (or task) to that for another. This enhances signal-to-noise ratio but obliterates any differences in spatial pattern of activity within an area. MVPA can be used to detect stimulus-specific (or task-specific) changes in the pattern of fMRI activity within a brain region, even if the regional-average change across the region (which is the dependent variable in conventional fMRI analysis) is unchanged. MVPA thus has great potential as a tool to probe brain specialization for perceptually invariant representations (Ley, Vroomen, & Formisano, 2014; but see Davis & Poldrack, 2013). Indeed, Raizada and associates (2010) observed that the statistical distinctness of activity patterns for the two stimulus types in right auditory cortex predicted perception, not just across groups (Japanese speakers find the discrimination more difficult than English speakers) but also across individuals within the Japanese group. This suggests that phonemic or syllabic category perception depends to some degree on the right auditory region.

In another paper, Lee and colleagues (Lee et al., 2012) used MVPA analyses and individual listeners' own category boundaries for [ba] and [da] syllables. They observed, in two separate sets of data, that left dorsal pars opercularis exhibited distinct neural activity patterns between the two perceptual categories, in a region very similar to that observed by Myers et al. (2009). The reasons for the distinction between these results, implicating left inferior frontal cortex in computation of invariant phonetic categories, and other results (reviewed by Lee et al., 2012 and Turkeltaub & Coslett, 2010), highlighting more posterior locations in the superior temporal and inferior parietal regions, are not yet clear.

Another strand of cognitive-neuroscience literature, by Marslen-Wilson, Tyler, and colleagues, has investigated the degree to which the morphological structure of words might be distinctly represented in the brain (Bozic et al., 2007; Marslen-Wilson & Tyler, 2007; Szlachta, Bozic, Jelowicka, & Marslen-Wilson, 2012; Tyler, Randall, & Marslen-Wilson, 2002; Tyler, Stamatakis, Post, Randall, & Marslen-Wilson, 2005). For example, considerable attention has been paid to the distinction between regular and irregular past tense verb forms in English: regular forms are the product of a predictable, rule-based process (stem + affix [-d]; e.g., *preach – preached*) whereas irregular forms are not very predictable and must be learned individually by rote (*teach – taught*). One prediction is that regular past-tense items might be processed differently from irregulars, that regular past-tense items are decomposed into their constituent morphemes whereas irregulars are processed as whole forms. Evidence consistent with this idea comes from an event-related fMRI study (Tyler et al., 2005) that demonstrated that English regular and irregular past tense verb forms differentially activate a fronto-temporal network. Specifically, the evidence (from this and other neuropsychological studies reviewed by Marslen-Wilson and Tyler [2007]; also see Ullman et al., 2005) is that a decompositional parsing process, tuned to the properties of English inflectional morphemes and dependent on left inferior frontal gyrus, appears to be more active not only for regular past-tense items than for irregulars but also for pseudo regular past-tense items (*tray – trade*) compared to pseudo irregular forms (*peach – port*) and even for non-words with a past-tense affix (*snay – snayed*), compared to non-words with an extra phoneme (*blay – blayn*). These latter two comparisons indicate that the decompositional process does not depend on the lexical status of the stem. This left-hemispheric decomposition process may be specific to inflectional morphology, whereas derivational morphology (e.g., *happy + ness = happiness*) seems to result in stems that function as new lexical items and that are processed as whole forms, similarly to morphological simple items (Bozic, Szlachta, & Marslen-Wilson, 2013).

These studies so far have been concerned more with cognitive processes, within implications for representation (i.e., inflectionally complex items are represented as stems + affixes, whereas derivationally complex items may be represented as whole forms) rather than with representations themselves.

Are representations auditory or gestural?

In the early 1990s, a potential neurophysiological mechanism for the motor theory of speech perception came in the form of neurons discovered using single-unit recordings in monkeys. Recording from neurons in area F5 of ventral premotor cortex, Rizzolatti and colleagues (Rizzolatti, Fogassi, & Gallese, 2001) identified cells that discharged both when the monkey grasped an object and when the monkey merely observed the experimenter grasp an object. These "mirror neurons" were doing double duty: firing vigorously during both the perception and motor performance of the same abstract gesture. The discovery of mirror neurons seemed to give credence to the idea that the recognition of motor actions was the proper domain of the motor system. The so-called direct-matching hypothesis, proposed by Rizzolatti and colleagues (2001), argues that we perceive an action by mapping the visual representation of the observed action onto our internal motor representation of that same action. According to this view, an action is fully understood when observing it causes the motor system of the observer to resonate. Of course, speech can also be viewed as an "action" – one that happens to emanate from a speaker's motor act and travels through the air as acoustic vibrations; the basic premise of the direct-matching hypothesis is essentially fully compatible with that of the motor theory of speech perception. Before long, "mirror neurons" were proposed as a possible physiological basis for a gesture-based form of speech perception located in the premotor cortex of humans.

Evidence from fMRI studies provided early support for the role of premotor cortex in human speech perception. Buchsbaum, Hickok, and Humphries (2001) showed, in an fMRI study, overlap between areas active during the perception and silent repetition of multisyllabic pseudo words in the premotor cortex. Wilson, Saygin, Sereno, and Iacoboni (2004) also showed that the dorsal portion of the ventral premotor cortex was active both when subjects passively listened to and when they overtly produced meaningless monosyllables. Pulvermüller and colleagues (2006) showed furthermore that activation in the motor and premotor cortex during speech perception was somatotopic. This was demonstrated by first localizing somatotopic areas of motor cortex by having subjects make lip-and-tongue movements during fMRI scanning. In the same experiment, subjects then passively listened to spoken syllables, including [p] and [t] sounds that movements of the lips and tongue produce, respectively. Activation of the lip area of motor cortex showed more activation when subjects listened to [p] sounds, whereas activation in the tongue area of motor cortex activated more when subjects listened to [t] sounds. These results not only showed that premotor cortex was active during speech perception but that the spatial topography of the activation pattern mapped on to the somatotopic layout of motor cortex in a way that would be predicted by a motor-theoretic view of speech perception.

TMS has also been used to examine motor cortical involvement during speech perception (Devlin & Watkins, 2007). For example, Fadiga, Craighero, Buccino, and Rizzolatti (2002) showed that when subjects passively listened to words involving strong tongue movements (the Italian double *r* as in *terra*), there was an increase in the motor-evoked potential recorded from the listener's tongue muscles as TMS was applied to the tongue region of motor cortex. Watkins and Paus (2004) used simultaneous TMS and PET to show that the intensity of TMS-induced motor-evoked potentials correlated with trial-to-trial variation in regional blood flow in the posterior portion of the IFG (part of Broca's area).

D'Ausilio and colleagues (2009) examined the role of the motor cortex in the discrimination of speech sounds by measuring the impact of TMS pulses to motor cortex on performance on a speech perception task. Subjects were presented with lip and tongue syllables ([b], [p] and [d], [t]) embedded in white noise, and on each trial they had to identify the presented syllable. On some trials, TMS pulses were delivered to the lip area of motor cortex and on other trials to the tongue area coincident with syllable presentation. The authors found that subjects responded faster and more accurately when TMS pulse was administered to the motor cortical ROI (region of interest) associated with production of the perceived syllable. In other words, TMS applied to the lip area improved performance for [b] and [p] sounds but not for [d] and [t] sounds, and vice versa. Schomers and associates (2015) have shown that the RT (response time), but not accuracy, effect extends to studies using whole words that are presented in silence (although at low volume), thus generalizing the finding beyond the somewhat artificial syllable identification tasks that have typically been used to investigate motor cortex contributions to speech perception. Using a similar task, however, Krieger-Redwood, Gaskell, Lindsay, and Jefferies (2013) showed that TMS applied to dorsal premotor cortex disrupted phonological judgements about whether a word started with [p] or [t] but did not disrupt decisions about the meaning of the word (e.g., is the object "large" or "small"). Thus, there is still some conflicting evidence about the extent to which the motor system is important for understanding speech when the goal of the listener is not to make decisions about how words *sound* but rather to understand their meaning.

Although numerous studies such as those just reviewed show that the motor system contributes in some way to speech perception, there is a still considerable debate as to whether "motor codes" are the fundamental basis of speech perception (see, e.g., Lotto, Hickok, & Holt, 2009; Wilson, 2009). For example, it can be argued that stimulation of the motor cortex with TMS leads to a spreading of activation to auditory cortex, which in turn disrupts or biases auditory speech processing. In this view, the role of motor cortex is to modulate the processing of speech in adverse listening conditions (e.g., high noise, accented speech, at a cocktail party) or during complex speech-processing tasks (Davis & Johnsrude, 2007; Hickok, 2010). Consistent with this idea is the finding that applying TMS to motor cortex is most disruptive when speech is presented in background noise that makes speech discrimination difficult and unreliable (D'Ausilio, Bufalari, Salmas, & Fadiga, 2012; Sato, Tremblay, & Gracco, 2009). For example, Du, Buchsbaum, Grady, and Alain (2014) have shown with fMRI that multivariate patterns of activity during a phoneme identification task are more robust to acoustic background noise than the multivariate patterns seen in the STG. These results reinforce the view that motor cortical contributions to speech perception are most evident in noisy conditions or in tasks requiring explicit categorization of speech sounds. Möttönen, van de Ven, and Watkins (2014) also showed that the top-down modulatory effect of motor cortex on auditory sensory processing is enhanced when subjects must explicitly attend to phonemic stimuli. They stimulated motor cortex with TMS while concurrently measuring auditory responses with high temporal resolution magnetoencephalography and showed that a modulatory effect was observed only when subjects were required to attend to an incoming stream of phonetic stimuli.

Perhaps the clearest evidence, however, in support of a modulatory role of motor cortex in speech perception is gained from examining patients with acquired lesions to motor cortex who have severe impairments in speech production. Motor theories of speech perception predict that these also would have equally severe deficits in speech comprehension. However, this is not typically the case (Hickok & Poeppel, 2004). Patients with left inferior frontal lesions resulting in non-fluent aphasia show only subtle deficits on speech perception tasks. For example, Baker, Blumstein, and Goodglass (1981) reported that such patients were ~97% accurate on a speech perception task that required subjects to determine whether two words that differed by a single phoneme (e.g., *bear* and *pear*) are the same or different. A recent study (Stasenko et al., 2015) showed moreover that a patient (AD) who had a large lesion to the left motor cortex and apraxia of speech, nevertheless showed a normal phonemic categorical boundary when discriminating two non-words that differ by a minimal pair (e.g., ADA–AGA). In addition, AD's overall speech perception was relatively intact, scoring over 90% on the comprehension subtest of the Boston Diagnostic Aphasia Examination. However, when this patient was asked to identify or label the non-word speech sounds (ADA–AGA) presented in isolation, he showed a profound impairment. Thus, it appears, then, that motor cortical contributions to speech perception are especially important in tasks requiring the categorization or explicit identification of the speech sounds. These motor speech regions might instantiate top-down models that influence sensory processing in auditory cortex, particularly acoustically degraded conditions (Davis & Johnsrude, 2007; Wilson & Iacoboni, 2006). This functionality is not merely an artefact of the laboratory but is relevant to everyday language where suboptimal auditory input is a common element of life (also, see Scott, Chapter 2 of this volume).

Conclusion

Cognitive theories of speech perception and processing are increasingly turning away from a speech-specific, modular approach focused on serial, discrete stages of processing. Current approaches emphasize the importance of experience and learning to the formation and extraction of perceptually invariant representations, in speech as in other domains of human perception (Davis & Johnsrude, 2007; Guediche, Blumstein, Fiez, & Holt, 2014; Kluender & Kiefte, 2006; Port, 2007). Cognitive neuroscience is exploring functional specialization within the multiple, parallel, hierarchically organized systems in the brain that appear to support speech perception (and production). The powerful methods available in cognitive neuroscience, particularly newer methods that allow us to address questions about representation, are also productively informing cognitive theory.

References

Adank, P. (2012). Design choices in imaging speech comprehension: an Activation Likelihood Estimation (ALE) meta-analysis. *NeuroImage*, *63*(3), 1601–13.

Baker, E., Blumstein, S., & Goodglass, H. (1981). Interaction between phonological and semantic factors in auditory comprehension. *Neuropsychologia*, *19*(1), 1–15.

Bien, H., Bölte, J., & Zwitserlood, P. (2015). Do syllables play a role in German speech perception? Behavioral and electrophysiological data from primed lexical decision. *Frontiers in Psychology*, *5*.

Bozic, M., Marslen-Wilson, W. D., Stamatakis, E. A., Davis, M., & Tyler, L. K. (2007). Differentiating morphology, form, and meaning: neural correlates of morphological complexity. *Journal of Cognitive Neuroscience*, *19*(9), 1464–75.

Bozic, M., Szlachta, Z., & Marslen-Wilson, W. D. (2013). Cross-linguistic parallels in processing derivational morphology: evidence from Polish. *Brain and Language*, *127*(3), 533–8.

Buchsbaum, B., Hickok, G., & Humphries, C. (2001). Role of left posterior superior temporal gyrus in phonological processing for speech perception and production. *Cognitive Science*, *25*(5), 663–78.

Celesia, G. G. (1976). Organization of auditory cortical areas in man. *Brain*, *99*(3), 403–14.

Chang, E. F., Rieger, J. W., Johnson, K., Berger, M. S., Barbaro, N. M., & Knight, R. T. (2010). Categorical speech representation in human superior temporal gyrus. *Nature Neuroscience*, *13*(11), 1428–32.

Charles-Luce, J., & Luce, P. A. (1990). Similarity neighbourhoods of words in young children's lexicons. *Journal of Child Language*, *17*(1), 205.

Chiry, O., Tardif, E., Magistretti, P. J., & Clarke, S. (2003). Patterns of calcium-binding proteins support parallel and hierarchical organization of human auditory areas. *European Journal of Neuroscience*, *17*(2), 397–410.

Cohen-Goldberg, A. M., Cholin, J., Miozzo, M., & Rapp, B. (2013). The interface between morphology and phonology: exploring a morpho-phonological deficit in spoken production. *Cognition*, *127*(2), 270–86.

D'Ausilio, A., Bufalari, I., Salmas, P., & Fadiga, L. (2012). The role of the motor system in discriminating normal and degraded speech sounds. *Cortex*, *48*(7), 882–7.

D'Ausilio, A., Pulvermüller, F., Salmas, P., Bufalari, I., Begliomini, C., & Fadiga, L. (2009). The motor somatotopy of speech perception. *Current Biology*, *19*(5), 381–5.

Davis, M., & Johnsrude, I. (2007). Hearing speech sounds: top-down influences on the interface between audition and speech perception. *Hearing Research*, *229*(1–2), 132–47.

Davis, T., & Poldrack, R. A. (2013). Measuring neural representations with fMRI: practices and pitfalls. *Annals of the New York Academy of Sciences*, *1296*, 108–34.

Dell, G. S. (1986). A spreading-activation theory of retrieval in sentence production. *Psychological Review*, *93*(3), 283–321.

Devlin, J. T., & Watkins, K. E. (2007). Stimulating language: insights from TMS. *Brain: A Journal of Neurology, 130*(Pt 3), 610–22.

Diehl, R. L., Lotto, A. J., & Holt, L. L. (2004). Speech perception. *Annual Review of Psychology, 55*, 149–79.

Du, Y., Buchsbaum, B. R., Grady, C. L., & Alain, C. (2014). Noise differentially impacts phoneme representations in the auditory and speech motor systems. *Proceedings of the National Academy of Sciences of the United States of America, 111*(19), 7126–31.

Fadiga, L., Craighero, L., Buccino, G., & Rizzolatti, G. (2002). Speech listening specifically modulates the excitability of tongue muscles: a TMS study. *The European Journal of Neuroscience, 15*(2), 399–402.

Floccia, C., Goslin, J., Morais, J. J. De, & Kolinsky, R. (2012). Syllable effects in a fragment-detection task in Italian listeners. *Frontiers in Psychology, 3*, 140.

Fowler, C. A. (1986). An event approach to a theory of speech perception from a direct-realist perspective. *Journal of Phonetics, 14*, 3–28.

Frey, S., Campbell, J. S. W., Pike, G. B., & Petrides, M. (2008). Dissociating the human language pathways with high angular resolution diffusion fiber tractography. *Journal of Neuroscience, 28*(45), 11435–44.

Frey, S., Mackey, S., & Petrides, M. (2014). Cortico-cortical connections of areas 44 and 45B in the macaque monkey. *Brain and Language, 131*, 36–55.

Fromkin, V. (1971). The non-anomalous nature of anomalous utterances. *Language, 47*, 27–52.

Galantucci, B., Fowler, C. A., & Turvey, M. T. (2006). The motor theory of speech perception reviewed. *Psychonomic Bulletin & Review, 13*(3), 361–77.

Gaskell, M. G., & Marslen-Wilson, W. D. (1997). Integrating form and meaning: a distributed model of speech perception. *Language and Cognitive Processes, 12*, 613–56.

Gibson, J. J. (1966). *The senses considered as perceptual systems.* Boston, MA: Houghton Mifflin.

Goldinger, S. D., & Azuma, T. (2003). Puzzle-solving science: the quixotic quest for units in speech perception. *Journal of Phonetics, 31*(3–4), 305–20.

Gracco, V. L., & Abbs, J. H. (1986). Variant and invariant characteristics of speech movements. *Experimental Brain Research, 65*(1), 156–66.

Grill-Spector, K., & Malach, R. (2001). fMR-adaptation: a tool for studying the functional properties of human cortical neurons. *Acta Psychologica, 107*(1–3), 293–321.

Guediche, S., Blumstein, S. E., Fiez, J. A., & Holt, L. L. (2014). Speech perception under adverse conditions: insights from behavioral, computational, and neuroscience research. *Frontiers in Systems Neuroscience, 7*, 126.

Hackett, T. (2011). Information flow in the auditory cortical network. *Hearing Research, 271*(1–2), 133–46.

Hackett, T., Preuss, T. M., & Kaas, J. (2001). Architectonic identification of the core region in auditory cortex of macaques, chimpanzees, and humans. *Journal of Comparative Neurology, 441*(3), 197–222.

Hall, D. A., Hart, H. C., & Johnsrude, I. (2003). Relationships between human auditory cortical structure and function. *Audiology & Neuro-Otology, 8*(1), 1–18.

Hawkins, S. (2003). Roles and representations of systematic fine phonetic detail in speech understanding. *Journal of Phonetics, 31*, 373–405.

Henson, R. N. A. (2003). Neuroimaging studies of priming. *Progress in Neurobiology, 70*(1), 53–81.

Hickok, G. (2010). The role of mirror neurons in speech and language processing. *Brain and Language, 112*(1), 1–2.

Hickok, G., & Poeppel, D. (2004). Dorsal and ventral streams: a framework for understanding aspects of the functional anatomy of language. *Cognition, 92*(1–2), 67–99.

Howard, M. A., Volkov, I. O., Mirsky, R., Garell, P. C., Noh, M. D., Granner, M., . . . Brugge, J. F. (2000). Auditory cortex on the human posterior superior temporal gyrus. *Journal of Comparative Neurology*, *416*(1), 79–92.

Kaas, J., & Hackett, T. (2000). Subdivisions of auditory cortex and processing streams in primates. *Proceedings of the National Academy of Sciences of the United States of America*, *97*(22), 11793–9.

Kaas, J., Hackett, T., & Tramo, M. J. (1999). Auditory processing in primate cerebral cortex. *Current Opinion in Neurobiology*, *9*(2), 164–70.

Kersten, D., Mamassian, P., & Yuille, A. (2004). Object perception as Bayesian inference. *Annual Review of Psychology*, *55*, 271–304.

Klatt, D. (1981). Lexical representations for speech production and perception. In T. Myers, J. Laver, & J. Anderson (Eds.), *The cognitive representation of speech* (pp. 11–32). Amsterdam: North-Holland Publishing Company.

Kluender, K., & Kiefte, M. (2006). Speech perception within a biologically realistic information-theoretic framework. In M. A. Gernsbacher & M. Traxler (Eds.), *Handbook of Psycholinguistics* (pp. 153–99). London: Elsevier.

Krieger-Redwood, K., Gaskell, M. G., Lindsay, S., & Jefferies, E. (2013). The selective role of premotor cortex in speech perception: a contribution to phoneme judgements but not speech comprehension. *Journal of Cognitive Neuroscience*, *25*(12), 2179–88.

Lee, Y.-S., Turkeltaub, P., Granger, R., & Raizada, R. D. S. (2012). Categorical speech processing in Broca's area: an fMRI study using multivariate pattern-based analysis. *The Journal of Neuroscience: The Official Journal of the Society for Neuroscience*, *32*(11), 3942–8.

Lettvin, J. Y., Maturana, H. R., McCulloch, W. S., & Pitts, W. H. (1959). What the frog's eye tells the frog's brain. *Proceedings of the Institute of Radio Engineers*, *49*, 1940–51.

Levelt, W. J., Roelofs, A., & Meyer, A. S. (1999). A theory of lexical access in speech production. *The Behavioral and Brain Sciences*, *22*(1), 1–38; discussion 38–75.

Ley, A., Vroomen, J., & Formisano, E. (2014). How learning to abstract shapes neural sound representations. *Frontiers in Neuroscience*, *8*, 132.

Liberman, A. M., Cooper, F. S., Shankweiler, D. P., & Studdert-Kennedy, M. (1967). Perception of the speech code. *Psychological Review*, *74*(6), 431–61.

Liberman, A., Harris, K., Hoffman, H., & Griffith, B. (1957). The discrimination of speech sounds within and across phoneme boundaries. *Journal of Experimental Psychology*, *54*, 358–68.

Liberman, A. M., & Mattingly, I. G. (1985). The motor theory of speech perception revised. *Cognition*, *21*(1), 1–36.

Liebenthal, E., Desai, R. H., Humphries, C., Sabri, M., & Desai, A. (2014). The functional organization of the left STS: a large scale meta-analysis of PET and fMRI studies of healthy adults. *Frontiers in Neuroscience*, *8*, 289.

Lotto, A. J., Hickok, G. S., & Holt, L. L. (2009). Reflections on mirror neurons and speech perception. *Trends in Cognitive Sciences*, *13*(3), 110–4.

Marslen-Wilson, W. D., & Tyler, L. K. (2007). Morphology, language and the brain: the decompositional substrate for language comprehension. *Philosophical Transactions of the Royal Society of London: Series B, Biological Sciences*, *362*(1481), 823–36.

Marslen-Wilson, W. D., & Warren, P. (1994). Levels of perceptual representation and process in lexical access: words, phonemes, and features. *Psychological Review*, *101*(4), 653–75.

Marslen-Wilson, W. D., Tyler, L. K., Waksler, R., & Older, L. (1994). Morphology and meaning in the English mental lexicon. *Psychological Review*, *101*, 3–33.

McMurray, B., Tanenhaus, M. K., & Aslin, R. N. (2009). Within-category VOT affects recovery from "lexical" garden-paths: evidence against phoneme-level inhibition. *Journal of Memory and Language*, *60*(1), 65–91.

Mitterer, H., Scharenborg, O., & McQueen, J. M. (2013). Phonological abstraction without phonemes in speech perception. *Cognition, 129*(2), 356–61.

Morosan, P., Rademacher, J., Schleicher, A., Amunts, K., Schormann, T., & Zilles, K. (2001). Human primary auditory cortex: cytoarchitectonic subdivisions and mapping into a spatial reference system. *NeuroImage, 13*(4), 684–701.

Morosan, P., Schleicher, A., Amunts, K., & Zilles, K. (2005). Multimodal architectonic mapping of human superior temporal gyrus. *Anatomy and Embryology, 210*(5–6), 401–6.

Möttönen, R., van de Ven, G. M., & Watkins, K. E. (2014). Attention fine-tunes auditory-motor processing of speech sounds. *The Journal of Neuroscience: The Official Journal of the Society for Neuroscience, 34*(11), 4064–9.

Munhall, K., MacDonald, E. N., Byrne, S. K., & Johnsrude, I. (2009). Talkers alter vowel production in response to real-time formant perturbation even when instructed not to compensate. *Journal of the Acoustical Society of America, 125*(1), 384–90.

Mur, M., Bandettini, P. A., & Kriegeskorte, N. (2009). Revealing representational content with pattern-information fMRI – an introductory guide. *Social Cognitive and Affective Neuroscience, 4*(1), 101–9.

Myers, E. B., Blumstein, S. E., Walsh, E., & Eliassen, J. (2009). Inferior frontal regions underlie the perception of phonetic category invariance. *Psychological Science, 20*(7), 895–903.

Nasir, S. M., & Ostry, D. J. (2006). Somatosensory precision in speech production. *Current Biology: CB, 16*(19), 1918–23.

Nearey, T. M. (2001). Phoneme-like units and speech perception. *Language and Cognitive Processes, 16*, 673–81.

Peelle, J. E. (2012). The hemispheric lateralization of speech processing depends on what "speech" is: a hierarchical perspective. *Frontiers in Human Neuroscience, 6*, 309.

Petrides, M., & Pandya, D. (1988). Association fiber pathways to the frontal cortex from the superior temporal region in the rhesus monkey. *Journal of Comparative Neurology, 273*, 52–66.

Petrides, M., & Pandya, D. N. (1994). Comparative architectonic analysis of the human and macaque frontal cortex. In F. Boller & J. Grafman (Eds.), *Handbook of neuropsychology (Vol. 9)* (pp. 17–58). Amsterdam: Elsevier.

Petrides, M., & Pandya, D. N. (2009). Distinct parietal and temporal pathways to the homologues of Broca's area in the monkey. *PLOS Biology, 7*(8), e1000170.

Petrides, M., Tomaiuolo, F., Yeterian, E. H., & Pandya, D. N. (2012). The prefrontal cortex: comparative architectonic organization in the human and the macaque monkey brains. *Cortex, 48*(1), 46–57.

Poremba, A., Saunders, R. C., Crane, A. M., Cook, M., Sokoloff, L., & Mishkin, M. (2003). Functional mapping of the primate auditory system. *Science, 299*(5606), 568–72.

Port, R. (2007). What are words made of?: beyond phones and phonemes. *New Ideas in Psychology, 25*, 143–70.

Pulvermüller, F., Huss, M., Kherif, F., Moscoso del Prado Martin, F., Hauk, O., & Shtyrov, Y. (2006). Motor cortex maps articulatory features of speech sounds. *Proceedings of the National Academy of Sciences of the United States of America, 103*(20), 7865–70.

Raizada, R. D. S., Tsao, F.-M., Liu, H.-M., & Kuhl, P. K. (2010). Quantifying the adequacy of neural representations for a cross-language phonetic discrimination task: prediction of individual differences. *Cerebral Cortex, 20*(1), 1–12.

Rauschecker, J. P. (1998). Parallel processing in the auditory cortex of primates. *Audiology & Neuro-Otology, 3*(2–3), 86–103.

Regev, M., Honey, C. J., Simony, E., & Hasson, U. (2013). Selective and invariant neural responses to spoken and written narratives. *The Journal of Neuroscience: The Official Journal of the Society for Neuroscience, 33*(40), 15978–88.

Rivier, F., & Clarke, S. (1997). Cytochrome oxidase, acetylcholinesterase, and NADPH-diaphorase staining in human supratemporal and insular cortex: evidence for multiple auditory areas. *NeuroImage, 6*(4), 288–304.

Rizzolatti, G., Fogassi, L., & Gallese, V. (2001). Neurophysiological mechanisms underlying the understanding and imitation of action. *Nature Reviews Neuroscience, 2*(9), 661–70.

Romanski, L. M., Bates, J. F., & Goldman-Rakic, P. S. (1999). Auditory belt and parabelt projections to the prefrontal cortex in the rhesus monkey. *Journal of Comparative Neurology, 403*(2), 141–57.

Romanski, L. M., Tian, B., Fritz, J., Mishkin, M., Goldman-Rakic, P. S., & Rauschecker, J. P. (1999). Dual streams of auditory afferents target multiple domains in the primate prefrontal cortex. *Nature Neuroscience, 2*(12), 1131–6.

Sato, M., Tremblay, P., & Gracco, V. L. (2009). A mediating role of the premotor cortex in phoneme segmentation. *Brain and Language, 111*(1), 1–7.

Schomers, M. R., Kirilina, E., Weigand, A., Bajbouj, M., & Pulvermüller, F. (2015). Causal Influence of articulatory motor cortex on comprehending single spoken words: TMS evidence. *Cerebral Cortex, 25*(10), 3894–902.

Seltzer, B., & Pandya, D. N. (1989). Frontal lobe connections of the superior temporal sulcus in the rhesus monkey. *Journal of Comparative Neurology, 281*(1), 97–113.

Stasenko, A., Bonn, C., Teghipco, A., Garcea, F. E., Sweet, C., Dombovy, M., . . . Mahon, B. Z. (2015). A causal test of the motor theory of speech perception: a case of impaired speech production and spared speech perception. *Cognitive Neuropsychology, 32*(2), 38–57.

Studdert-Kennedy, M. (1981). Perceiving phonetic segments. In T. Myers, J. Laver, & J. Anderson (Eds.), *The cognitive representation of speech* (pp. 3–10). Amsterdam: Elsevier.

Szlachta, Z., Bozic, M., Jelowicka, A., & Marslen-Wilson, W. D. (2012). Neurocognitive dimensions of lexical complexity in Polish. *Brain and Language, 121*(3), 219–25.

Tian, B., Reser, D., Durham, A., Kustov, A., & Rauschecker, J. P. (2001). Functional specialization in rhesus monkey auditory cortex. *Science, 292*(5515), 290–3.

Turkeltaub, P. E., & Coslett, H. B. (2010). Localization of sublexical speech perception components. *Brain and Language, 114*(1), 1–15.

Tyler, L. K., Randall, B., & Marslen-Wilson, W. D. (2002). Phonology and neuropsychology of the English past tense. *Neuropsychologia, 40*(8), 1154–66.

Tyler, L. K., Stamatakis, E. A., Post, B., Randall, B., & Marslen-Wilson, W. (2005). Temporal and frontal systems in speech comprehension: an fMRI study of past tense processing. *Neuropsychologia, 43*(13), 1963–74.

Ullman, M. T., Pancheva, R., Love, T., Yee, E., Swinney, D., & Hickok, G. (2005). Neural correlates of lexicon and grammar: evidence from the production, reading, and judgment of inflection in aphasia. *Brain and Language, 93*(2), 185–238; discussion 239–42.

Wallace, M. N., Johnston, P. W., & Palmer, A. R. (2002). Histochemical identification of cortical areas in the auditory region of the human brain. *Experimental Brain Research, 143*(4), 499–508.

Watkins, K., & Paus, T. (2004). Modulation of motor excitability during speech perception: the role of Broca's area. *Journal of Cognitive Neuroscience, 16*(6), 978–87.

Webb, B. (2004). Neural mechanisms for prediction: do insects have forward models? *Trends in Neurosciences, 27*(5), 278–82.

Wilson, S. M. (2009). Speech perception when the motor system is compromised. *Trends in Cognitive Sciences, 13*(8), 329–30; author reply 330–1.

Wilson, S. M., & Iacoboni, M. (2006). Neural responses to non-native phonemes varying in producibility: evidence for the sensorimotor nature of speech perception. *NeuroImage, 33*(1), 316–25.

Wilson, S. M., Saygin, A. P., Sereno, M. I., & Iacoboni, M. (2004). Listening to speech activates motor areas involved in speech production. *Nature Neuroscience*, 7(7), 701–2.

Wolpert, D. M., & Ghahramani, Z. (2000). Computational principles of movement neuroscience. *Nature Neuroscience*, 3 Suppl, 1212–7.

Yuille, A., & Kersten, D. (2006). Vision as Bayesian inference: analysis by synthesis? *Trends in Cognitive Sciences*, 10(7), 301–8.

2

PERCEPTION AND PRODUCTION OF SPEECH: CONNECTED, BUT HOW?

Sophie K. Scott

Introduction

Behaviourally, speech production and perception are or have been considered to be linked in many different ways. These range from the possibility of shared phonetic representations (Pulvermüller et al., 2006), to a candidate unifying role of Broca's area in language processing (Hagoort, 2005), through to notions of a centrality of motor representations in speech perception and embodied perception and cognition (e.g., Zwaan & Kaschak, 2009). Others have argued for a contrasting perspective that links perception and production in a different direction, whereby motor control (in speech as well as in other actions) is essentially dependent on perceptual processing (e.g., Darainy, Vahdat, & Ostry, 2013). In this chapter I will outline the evidence for and against arguments that motor processes are critical to the understanding of speech and also argue for a functional role for motor cortices in the priming and alignment of behavioural responses. I will not be addressing the ways that motor representations form part of a more distributed semantic processing system (e.g., Patterson, Nestor, & Rogers, 2007).

Behavioural evidence for links between perception and action in speech and language is manifold. Silent mouthing of a word primes later lexical decision (Monsell, 1987). The phonetic limitations of the language we learn to speak also affect the nature of the phonetic distinctions that we can hear (e.g., Kuhl et al., 2008). Learning to talk is critically dependent on intact hearing; even moderate hearing loss will affect how speech production develops (Mogford, 1988). However, there is also evidence for a distinction between speech production and perception; in development, speech production skills and speech perception skills are not correlated (at age two) and are predicted by distinctly different factors (speech production skills being predicted by other motor skills and speech perception skills being predicted by factors that affect how the parents talk to the child (Alcock & Krawczyk, 2010). There is considerable individual difference in the ability to acquire nonnative phonetic contrasts in adulthood, and within this variability, perception and production skills do not correlate strongly, though there is a moderate relationship (Hattori & Iverson, 2009). How do these links and these dissociations relate to the neuroanatomy of spoken language? In the next section I will review the development of our understanding of the ways that speech is processed in the human brain.

Speech production

In the 1800s, there was a growing consensus that left inferior frontal areas in the human brain had a central role in speech production, a view that was supported and consolidated by Paul Broca's work (1861). A wealth of data has now confirmed the importance of the posterior third of the left inferior frontal gyrus (IFG) in speech production. Notably, however, damage limited to Broca's area results in transient mutism, rather than Broca's aphasia, with halting, effortful, agrammatic speech (Mohr, 1976). To see full Broca's aphasia, more widespread damage is required, with a particular involvement of the white matter tracts underlying BA 44/45 (Mohr, 1976) (Figure 2.1). More recent work in functional imaging has confirmed a role for the left posterior IFG in speech production but not simple articulation (e.g., word repetition), which seems to rely principally on the left anterior insula (Dronkers, 1996; Wise, Greene, Büchel, & Scott, 1999). Other functional imaging studies have confirmed that the left posterior IFG is associated with a wide variety of (apparently) non-linguistic tasks (Thompson-Schill, D'Esposito, Aguirre, & Farah, 1997).

While neuropsychology has focused on the left inferior frontal gyrus and speech production, other cortical fields are essentially involved in the voluntary control of

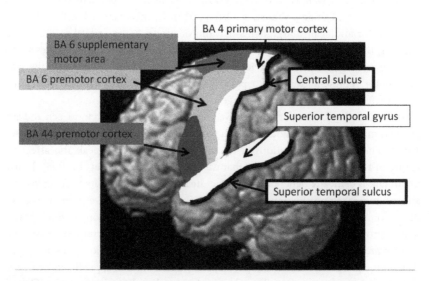

FIGURE 2.1 Auditory and motor fields (BA = Broadmann area).

speech production (Simonyan & Horwitz, 2011). These fields are implicated in the direct control of the respiratory, laryngeal, and articulatory movements that are essential to speech. These fields have direct connections to the activation of skeletal muscles (e.g., Dum & Strick, 1991). Another cortical field strongly associated with the control of articulation is the supplementary motor area (SMA) (Penfield & Welch, 1951), which has been consistently activated in functional imaging experiments that require articulation and verbal rehearsal (e.g., Blank, Scott, Murphy, Warburton, & Wise, 2002). Unlike the left IFG and left anterior insula, these laryngeal motor areas and SMA are bilaterally implicated in speech production.

In terms of functional cortical anatomy of speech production, therefore, Broca's area seems to be associated with higher-order control (e.g., response selection and planning) in speech, while the motor control of speech is dependent on a complex network including lateral primary motor areas, premotor cortex (extending into posterior Broca's area), and midline supplementary motor cortex, as well as basal ganglia, periaqueductal grey and cerebellar loops (Blank et al., 2002; Simonyan & Horwitz, 2011; Wise et al., 1999). Recruitment of these fields in both production and perception gives an anatomical basis to explore the functional role of motor areas in perception and vice versa.

Shortly after Broca's paper was published, Carl Wernicke (1874) described patients with complementary problems: they had a specific problem with the reception of spoken language. Wernicke specifically associated these speech perception deficits with damage to the left superior temporal gyrus. However, by the 1970s this was refined by further research to the left posterior temporal sulcus (Bogen & Bogen, 1976). It has since become clear that this emphasis on posterior auditory fields was a consequence of the cardiovascular accidents that led to the deficits being observed in clinical cases: most of the patients had suffered strokes, and strokes follow vascular anatomy. The vasculature of the dorsolateral temporal lobes runs in a posterior-anterior direction, which has been argued to lead to a dominance of strokes affecting posterior superior temporal regions and few leading to anterior superior temporal gyrus (STG) damage (Wise, 2003) (Figure 2.1). Studies in non-human primates and humans have now demonstrated that there is considerable complexity in the functional anatomy of auditory cortex, with a concomitant effect on the neural pathways associated with the perception of speech. Critically, these auditory systems involve cortical fields running posteriorially, laterally, and anteriorally to primary auditory cortex. In non-human primates, at least two distinct functional and anatomical streams of processing have been described within auditory cortex (Kaas & Hackett, 1999). Anatomically, the first stream is associated with a lateral and anterior stream, running along the STG to the anterior superior temporal sulcus (STS) and then to prefrontal cortex. The second stream is associated with posterior auditory areas, projecting to inferior parietal and premotor cortex. The two streams project to adjacent but non-overlapping fields in prefrontal cortex. The posterior stream provides a clear link between perceptual and production fields (Rauschecker, 2011; Rauschecker & Scott, 2009). Functionally, the two streams show somewhat distinct response profiles, with the anterior stream showing a stronger response to the identification of sounds and posterior fields being implicated in both the spatial representation of sounds in the environment and in the sensory guidance of actions. Thus several studies have implicated anterior STS fields in the early perceptual processing of intelligibility in speech (Scott, Blank, Rosen, & Wise, 2000), while posterior auditory fields show a clear response to articulation – even silent articulation (Wise, Scott, Blank, Mummery, & Warburton, 2001). These studies suggest that auditory perceptual processing may comprise a variety of distinctly different subsets of kinds of processing and that processing heard speech for meaning may require different kinds of acoustic engagement from the kinds of acoustic information used to control and guide speech production.

The motor theory of speech perception and mirror neurons

Historically, theories of speech perception fall into one of two opposing positions. The first, which is seldom graced with being a philosophical or theoretical position, takes the view that speech perception is a product of auditory processing and that speech perception can be understood within an auditory perceptual framework (e.g., Stilp, Rogers, & Kluender, 2010). The second holds the perspective that speech perception necessarily entails the processing of the talker's intended articulations and that this requires the processing of motor representations (e.g., Liberman & Mattingly, 1985). Instead of positing that these motor constraints might directly determine the nature of the auditory representations, this approach typically requires that the perceptual process engages motor systems. This motor theory of speech perception also views speech perception as being qualitatively different from its earliest encoded entry into the cortex. In other words, the motor theory of speech specifies that speech is processed in a way that is distinctly and qualitatively different from the perceptual processing of other sounds from the earliest stages in auditory processing.

The motor theory of speech perception has generally enjoyed somewhat limited appeal but has received a great deal of support from recent developments in neuroscience, specifically the discovery of mirror neurons (Galantucci, Fowler, & Turvey, 2005). These neurons respond to both the perception and production of an action and have led to a great deal of interest in their possible role in the recognition of actions, as well as in the evolution of empathy and language. In turn, a theoretical basis for a role of motor cortex in speech perception has been enthusiastically adopted in neuroscience, with many studies arguing for a central role of motor representations in speech and sound processing (e.g., Pulvermüller & Fadiga, 2010).

Motor vs. auditory perceptual processing of speech

Two largely independent functional imaging literatures have now evolved around speech perception (Scott, McGettigan, & Eisner, 2009). The first approach is based on an auditory processing view of speech. This approach tends to emphasize and examine the patterns of activations to speech and sound that are found within the dorsolateral temporal lobes and relates such processing to models of auditory stream of processing (Rauschecker & Scott, 2009) or to different candidate auditory processing capabilities in the left and right temporal lobes (McGettigan & Scott, 2012). In other words, this approach focuses on the ways that speech is processed in auditory fields. Occasionally, these studies find activation in the left inferior frontal gyrus, and this is often ascribed to higher-order factors implicated in speech perception (e.g., contextual processing, perceptual difficulty, adaptation to a novel form of intelligible speech) (Scott et al., 2009). These auditory studies of speech perception often do not use any overt task, preferring to delineate the obligatory, automatic speech perception system in the absence of controlled processes associated with overt task requirements, which do not typically probe the same computations as those needed for speech comprehension.

The second kinds of studies, addressing the motor theory of speech, tend not to focus on activations within auditory areas and instead address activations seen in motor and premotor fields, which are considered to perform computations that are critical to speech perception (Pulvermüller & Fadiga, 2010). In contrast, studies that target motor representations and their role in speech perception very frequently use overt tasks, such as phoneme categorization, phoneme discrimination, phoneme matching (Scott et al., 2009). Arguably, such active tasks are not tapping the same resources as speech perception; many people who have never learnt to read struggle with these tasks, but they can understand speech without difficulty. It is also the case that using such active tasks may also overemphasize the role of motor representations and processes (McGettigan, Agnew, & Scott, 2010; Scott et al., 2009). There is now good evidence that placing working memory demands on a speech task leads to significant enhancement of motor and premotor activations. We directly interrogated this in an fMRI study in which we contrasted activation seen to the perception of non-words that varied in length and consonant cluster complexities (McGettigan et al., 2011), while varying whether participants were listening passively or actively rehearsing the non-words. During passive listening, the dorsolateral temporal lobes were sensitive to the length of the non-words (in syllables). During active rehearsal of the non-words, we found additional significant activation in motor, premotor, and left inferior prefrontal cortex, which was sensitive to both the length of the non-words and to the consonant cluster complexities. This implies that motor fields are activated when the participants need to actively process or sub-articulate the speech stimuli. This is also consistent with the suggestion that verbal working memory phenomena are a consequence of interactions between speech perception and production systems (Jacquemot & Scott, 2006). The precise demands of verbal working memory rehearsal are seen in the recruitment of the motor cortices, cortical fields that are not significantly activated when participants listen passively to the same stimuli. The finding that only motor and premotor peaks were sensitive to the presence of consonant clusters in a way that auditory cortical fields were not is also consistent with the claim that phonemes may not exist as specific stages of processing in auditory cortex (Boucher, 1994) but may instead have a reality in motor representations.

A role for premotor and motor representations in verbal working memory phenomena and the representation of phonemes as units is also consistent with the many findings of a role for left premotor/prefrontal areas in speech processing tasks (Scott et al., 2009). The problem, of course, is that to identify a brain region as critical to syllable segmentation/phoneme detection/phoneme categorization is not synonymous with identifying a brain region that is critical to the perceptual processing of speech in a fashion that integrates with speech comprehension systems. Indeed, a study that directly contrasted speech comprehension mechanisms with a phoneme detection task found that transcranial magnetic stimulation (TMS) over the left IFC (inferior frontal cortex) and STS was detrimental to phoneme detection, but only TMS over the left STS was deleterious to speech comprehension (Krieger-Redwood, Gaskell, Lindsay, & Jefferies, 2013).

There are studies that have reported a sensitivity in motor and premotor areas to speech in a passive paradigm where no task was required. Using TMS, Watkins and colleagues (Watkins, Strafella, & Paus, 2003) showed a heightened orofacial electromyography (EMG) response to hearing speech and seeing moving lips. EMG is a method for quantifying activation in skeletal muscles, and the activation of facial musculature by speech without movement being necessary is an indication of motor responses during perception. This was a strong indication that there was a motor component to the perception of speech, in a passive task (with no overt task or working memory factors), as there was some sub-threshold activation of facial muscles. A similar response of motor actuation in passive listening was found in an fMRI study of speech perception and speech production (Wilson, Saygin, Sereno, & Iacoboni, 2004), which reported peaks of activation seen in both perception and production – peaks that were found in primary motor and premotor cortex.

These studies (Watkins et al., 2003; Wilson et al., 2004) were widely reported to show a role for motor representations in speech perception, and both did report evidence for motor responses to speech perception. The problem with both studies is the degree to which the identified motor responses were specific to speech. As is standard in functional imaging and TMS studies, both papers employed baseline stimuli as a contrast for the speech stimuli. In the TMS study, the baseline stimuli were environmental sounds (a control for the speech sounds) and eyes (a control for the moving lips). In the fMRI study, the baseline stimuli were environmental noises. These baseline stimuli are essential to understanding the meaning of the results. Within auditory cortex, "speech-specific" neural responses need to be identified with reference to a contrast against a baseline condition, in which the baseline condition controls for some aspects of the speech signal that are deemed important to exclude; for example, if one is interested in speech-specific responses, one likely needs to exclude neural responses that are seen to acoustic stimulation (Scott & Wise, 2004). Though both studies (Watkins et al., 2003; Wilson et al., 2004) use environmental sounds in the experiments as a control condition for the acoustically complex speech sounds, both studies found that the environmental sounds conditions activate the motor fields. In other words, the neural response to speech in the motor and premotor fields studied in both experiments did not show a specific response. In both studies, the environmental baseline conditions are not used to generate the contrasts of interest: in the TMS study, the audio and visual speech conditions are contrasted with the eyes condition, and in the fMRI study, the speech perception activation is contrasted with a scanner noise condition. The specificity of these motor responses to speech perception is therefore impossible to determine, and it remains possible that the motor responses reflect a more generic response to sound. This is not to suggest that such responses are meaningless but that there may be qualitative differences between the kinds of auditory processing seen in auditory and motor fields.

To address the specificity of auditory and motor responses to speech sounds and to other recognizable mouth sounds, we ran a study using spoken, isolated phonemes (e.g., /f/) and ingressive click sounds (e.g., "giddy up") (Agnew, McGettigan, & Scott, 2011). We chose these click sounds because they are acoustically similar to some English phonemes, but they are made in a distinctly different way and are not processed as speech by native English speakers (Best, McRoberts, & Sithole, 1988). The click sounds we chose – bilabial (kissing sounds), alveolar (tutting sounds), lateral (giddy up sounds) and palatal (a clopping sound) were used because they can be recognized and produced by English speakers (unlike many ingressive speech sounds). We used a signal-correlated noise (SCN) baseline condition (Schroeder, 1968).

We found that, relative to the baseline condition and relative to the click sounds, there was significant activation in the anterior dorsolateral temporal lobes to the isolated speech sounds, with greater activation in the left anterior STG. Both speech and click sounds, relative to the baseline SCN condition, led to activation in the right STG, consistent with descriptions of the role for voice processing in the right temporal lobe (Belin, Zatorre, & Ahad, 2002). Relative to speech and SCN stimuli, the click sounds led to significantly greater activation in the left posterior auditory cortex. In contrast, none of the auditory contrasts led to significant motor, premotor, or prefrontal activation at a whole brain level. Using a motor and a speech localiser to guide an ROI analysis, we contrasted activation to the speech relative to SCN sounds. Only the left STG showed a selective response to the speech sounds; there was no evidence for a motor response to speech or non-speech mouth sounds. A whole brain contrast of all the acoustic stimuli against rest showed a significant response in bilateral ventral sensorimotor cortex, but this was an acoustic response, not a speech selective response. This acoustic sensorimotor response was also considerably more ventral than the cortical responses to the supralaryngeal articulators that have been reported in other studies (e.g., Pulvermüller et al., 2006) and may implicate other elements of the motor control of speech in the kinds of motor responses seen – for example, respiratory control.

In conclusion, there is little strong evidence for a selectivity to speech sounds or indeed to any sounds in motor cortex during passive listening. In contrast, motor fields appear to be extremely sensitive to a wide range of sounds (Scott et al., 2009). In contrast, relatively specific responses to sounds can be seen within auditory cortex, varying from responses that are specific to speech sounds, specific for a wide class of mouth sounds, or responding only to the click sounds. In our study, no such patterns of specificity were seen in motor fields, except for a very general response to all the auditory stimuli in ventral sensorimotor cortex. This is in fact consistent with some of the earlier studies, which found that motor fields responded to speech but also to environmental noises (Watkins et al., 2003; Wilson et al., 2004).

Primary motor and premotor cortex are abundantly supplied with sensory inputs, with projections from somatosensory, auditory, and visual cortex (as well as vestibular and proprioceptive inputs) (e.g., Asanuma, 1981). While we might expect it to show a sensitivity to perceptual events, therefore, it is also at least feasible that motor processing of sound does not recapitulate the processing seen in auditory fields (and vice versa). The available data indeed suggest that for perceptual processing, auditory and motor cortices have distinctly different response profiles. This may have important implications for our understanding of the functional role of motor responses to speech and sound.

Motor responses to sound

A meta-analysis of the motor responses to speech and other categories of sound (Scott et al., 2009) showed that there are robust motor and premotor responses to a wide range of sounds. Indeed, the responses to speech are somewhat dwarfed in comparison to the responses to music and emotional vocalizations.

As it stands, it does not seem to be the case that responses to sound in motor cortex mirror those seen in auditory association fields. One intriguing possibility is that the kinds of motor and premotor responses to sounds are modulated by the behavioural consequences of the sounds – for example, highly behaviourally contagious sounds, such as yawning and laughing, are associated with robust orofacial mirror responses in sensorimotor cortex, a neural response that correlates with ratings of contagion (Arnott, Singhal, & Goodale, 2009; Warren et al., 2006). This association of motor responses to behavioural links would be consistent with more general claims that "mirror" responses are driven by associative links between perception and action (Brass & Heyes, 2005). For example, male and female ballet dancers show different motor responses to the perception of dance, which were selectively greater for the dance steps that men and women perform, respectively (Calvo-Merino, Grèzes, Glaser, Passingham, & Haggard, 2006). Thus, though the male and female dancers were familiar with all the dance movements that they watched, they showed greater motor responses only when perception was linked to a familiar action that they knew how to perform. Though we typically study speech perception in isolation from other factors, in the "wild" speech is primarily encountered as the dominant tool for social interactions, in which the interplay of production and perception is very tightly coordinated across talkers. To facilitate the tight temporal coordination of conversational speech, talkers in a conversation align many aspects of their speech, from the timing of their breathing to their pitch and rhythm. It has been claimed that motor fields are central to this behavioural alignment, in parallel with brain areas that are decoding the heard language and planning the content of responses (Scott et al., 2009).

Working with non-speech sounds, Bruno Repp (Repp, 2000, 2001) has shown that people who are tapping along to a rhythm can adjust the timing of their taps to cope with perturbations in the sequence: importantly, this is true for both perturbations that people are consciously aware of and for perturbations that are too small to be consciously reported. In other words, the conscious, perceptual processes involved in overtly reporting a temporal deviation have a higher threshold for detecting deviations than the sensorimotor processes involved in accurately tapping along to a regular sequence of tones. This may speak to a finer temporal sensitivity in sensorimotor processing of sound than is found in more ventral auditory streams. Rhythm and timing, as they affect motor control, may critically depend on the "how" pathway(s) and may be less dependent on the "what" pathways associated with perceptual recognition.

Moving beyond the motor theory and mirror neurons

There are anatomical and functional links between the speech perception and speech production fields, as well as several candidate roles for this association between perceptual and motoric components of speech and sound. In recent years, the explosive success of the mirror neurons literature has been widely linked with the motor theory of speech perception (Galantucci, Fowler, & Turvey, 2005) and with the idea that motor representations are critical to speech perception. As we have seen in this chapter, the specificity of this association has been harder to demonstrate empirically. However, there are two assumptions behind this hypothesized dependence of speech perception on speech production: the first is that the role of motor constraints on speech sounds must translate into access to motor output representations, and the second is that the direction of a link between speech perception and production must be in the direction of perception being dependent on production. Can both of these assumptions be addressed?

Production constraints in sound

Speech perception itself is complex and multistable, and listeners will exploit what cues are available to cope if the input is transformed or limited. The ways that speech is produced mean that certain combinations of phonetic features are impossible: one cannot produce a /p/ sound with the tongue forming a closure at the velum or at the same time as a glottal stop. These production constraints put limits on the way that acoustic information covaries in the speech signal, and listeners have been shown to be highly sensitive to such co-varying cues, even with novel non-speech sounds (Stilp et al., 2010). From this perspective, one would expect that speech perception utilizes information about the way that a sound is produced, as these naturally structure *all* the sounds we hear (McGettigan & Scott, 2012).

These kinds of motor constraints are not typically considered as part of the motor theory of speech perception, in which motor output representations and processes form the central critical aspects of the comprehension of speech. Similarly, auditory studies have not consistently addressed the issue of the ways that sounds are produced when addressing the acoustic processing of sound; instead, phonetic and syntactic constraints are more commonly addressed. This is an area where much further work will be necessary.

Speech production is essentially dependent on auditory processing

There is now abundant evidence that speech production is highly dependent on perceptual processes, from somatosensation to (perhaps to a different degree) proprioception and of course hearing.[1] In development, relatively moderate levels of hearing loss affect the acquisition of speech production skills, the implication being that a certain degree of hearing acuity is essential to the learning of the task of talking (Mogford, 1988). The opposite is not always true, and an absence of speech production skills does not necessarily limit speech perception abilities (Bishop, 1988). There are several cases in the literature of people born with cerebral palsy, who have been unable to speak but who were perfectly able to understand the spoken language they hear (e.g., the poet and novelist Christopher Nolan).

The directionality of these links make a great deal of sense if we consider speech production, like many other motor skills, to be heavily dependent on perceptual processing. From this perspective, it is incorrect to consider perception to be associated only with "input" processes and motor control with "output" processes: perception is centrally linked to both action and sensory registration processes. However, at a cortical level, this perceptual control of speech appears to be in distinctly different cortical fields from those perceptual areas that, for example, decode the sounds of spoken language. Thus, several functional imaging studies have shown a robust activation of posterior auditory cortex during speech production (Hickok et al., 2000), even if this production is silent mouthing (Agnew, McGettigan, Banks, & Scott, 2013; Wise et al., 2001). When the acoustic constraints on speech production are altered, for example by requiring talkers to produce highly rhythmic speech (Blank et al., 2002) or to talk under conditions of delayed concurrent auditory information (aka delayed auditory feedback), activity in these posterior auditory areas increases (Takaso, Eisner, Wise, & Scott, 2010). These same posterior fields are activated during phonological working memory tasks (McGettigan et al., 2011) and by ingressive click sounds more than by speech sounds in a perception task (Agnew et al., 2011). These posterior auditory regions, which have been expressly related to the relationship between the perception and production of sounds (Warren, Wise, & Warren, 2005), are anatomically separate from anterior and ventral fields in the rostral STG and STS, which respond to intelligibility in speech. Indeed, these anterior fields are actively suppressed during speech production – even silent mouthing (Agnew et al., 2013; Houde, Nagarajan, Sekihara, & Merzenich, 2002; Wise et al., 1999). Thus, within auditory perceptual areas, some distinctions can be drawn between anterior fields that are critical to the perception of sounds that are not self-generated and posterior fields that are processing sounds in a sensorimotor fashion and that are critical to the online guidance of sound production, for example speaking.

Conclusions

Speech production and speech perception are linked in many ways. In this chapter, I have argued against a primary role for motor output systems in speech perception mechanisms, a framework that has been implicated in these links (Pulvermüller & Fadiga, 2010). Instead, I have argued that perceptual systems are central to the control of speech production. Further studies, for example of individual differences in the acquisition of non-native contrasts, will be able to elaborate on how the different roles of posterior and anterior auditory fields contribute to this. I have also argued that perceptual processing within motor output systems – for example in motor and premotor cortex – may be absolutely key to the functional use of spoken language, playing a central role in entraining and aligning speech during conversation and in facilitating turn-taking within these conversations (Iacoboni, 2005; Scott et al., 2009). Perception for action may have fundamentally different goals from perception for comprehension and may be processed in parallel in distinct anatomical streams.

Note

1 Vision may also be important: children born blind often confuse the perception of /n/ and /m/ as these are primarily differentiated visually in perception.

References

Agnew ZK, McGettigan C, Banks B, Scott SK (2013) Articulatory movements modulate auditory responses to speech. *Neuroimage, 73*, 191–9.

Agnew Z, McGettigan C, Scott SK (2011) Discriminating between auditory and motor cortex responses to speech and non speech mouth sounds. *Journal of Cognitive Neuroscience, 23*, 4038–47.

Alcock KJ, Krawczyk K (2010) Individual differences in language development: relationship with motor skill at 21 months. *Developmental Science, 13*, 677–91. doi: 10.1111/j.1467-7687.2009.00924.x

Arnott SR, Singhal A, Goodale MA (2009) An investigation of auditory contagious yawning. *Cognitive, Affective, Behavioral Neuroscience, 9*, 335–42.

Asanuma H (1981) Functional role of sensory inputs to the motor cortex. *Progress in Neurobiology, 16*, 241–62.

Belin P, Zatorre RJ, Ahad P (2002) Human temporal-lobe response to vocal sounds. *Cognitive Brain Research, 13*, 17–26.

Best CT, McRoberts GW, Sithole NM (1988) Examination of perceptual reorganization for nonnative speech contrasts: Zulu click discrimination by English-speaking adults and infants. *Journal of Experimental Psychology: Human Perception and Performance, 14*, 345–60.

Bishop DVM (1988) Language development in children with abnormal structure or the speech apparatus. In *Language Development in Exceptional Circumstances* (eds Bishop DVM & Mogford K, pp. 220–38). New York: Churchill Livingstone.

Blank SC, Scott SK, Murphy K, Warburton E, Wise RJ (2002) Speech production: Wernicke, Broca and beyond. *Brain, 125*, 1829–38.

Bogen JE, Bogen GM (1976) Wernicke's region – where is it? *Annals of the New York Academy of Sciences, 280*, 834–43.

Boucher VJ (1994) Alphabet-related biases in psycholinguistic inquiries – considerations for direct theories of speech production and perception. *Journal of Phonetics, 22,* 1–18.

Brass M, Heyes C (2005) Imitation: is cognitive neuroscience solving the correspondence problem? *Trends in Cognitive Sciences, 9,* 489–95.

Broca P (1861) Nouvelle observation d'aphémie produite par une lésion de la moitié postérieure des deuxième et troisième circonvolution frontales gauches. *Bulletin de la Société Anatomique, 36,* 398–407.

Calvo-Merino B, Grèzes J, Glaser DE, Passingham RE, Haggard P (2006) Seeing or doing? Influence of visual and motor familiarity in action observation. *Current Biology, 16,* 1905–10.

Darainy M, Vahdat S, Ostry DJ (2013) Perceptual learning in sensorimotor adaptation. *Journal of Neurophysiology, 110,* 2152–62.

Dronkers, N. F. (1996). A new brain region for coordinating speech articulation. *Nature, 384,* 159–161.

Dum R P, Strick PL (1991) The origin of corticospinal projections from the premotor areas in the frontal lobe. *Journal of Neuroscience, 11,* 667–89.

Galantucci B, Fowler CA, Turvey MT (2005) The motor theory of speech perception reviewed. *Psychonomic Bulletin and Review, 13,* 361–77.

Hagoort P (2005) On Broca, brain, and binding: a new framework. *Trends in Cognitive Sciences, 9,* 416–23.

Hattori K, Iverson P (2009) English /r/-/l/ category assimilation by Japanese adults: individual differences and the link to identification accuracy. *Journal of the Acoustical Society of America, 12*(5), 469–79.

Hickok G, Erhard P, Kassubek J, Helms-Tillery AK, Naeve-Velguth S, Strupp JP, Strick PL, Ugurbil K (2000) A functional magnetic resonance imaging study of the role of left posterior superior temporal gyrus in speech production: implications for the explanation of conduction aphasia. *Neuroscience Letters, 287*(2), 156–60.

Houde JF, Nagarajan SS, Sekihara K, Merzenich MM (2002) Modulation of the auditory cortex during speech: an MEG study. *Journal of Cognitive Neuroscience, 14*(8), 1125–38.

Iacoboni M (2005) Understanding others: imitation, language, and empathy. In *Perspectives on Imitation: From Neuroscience to Social Science* (eds Hurley S & Chater N, pp. 77–100). Cambridge, MA: MIT Press.

Jacquemot C, Scott SK (2006) What is the relationship between phonological short-term memory and speech processing? *Trends in Cognitive Science, 10*(11), 480–6.

Kaas JH, Hackett TA (1999) 'What' and 'where' processing in auditory cortex. *Nature Neuroscience, 2*(12), 1045–7.

Krieger-Redwood K, Gaskell MG, Lindsay S, Jefferies E (2013) The selective role of premotor cortex in speech perception: a contribution to phoneme judgements but not speech comprehension. *Journal of Cognitive Neuroscience, 25*(12), 2179–88.

Kuhl PK, Conboy BT, Coffey-Corina S, Padden D, Rivera-Gaxiola M, Nelson T (2008) Phonetic learning as a pathway to language: new data and native language magnet theory expanded (NLM-e). *Philosophical Transactions of the Royal Society of London B: Biological Sciences, 363*(1493), 979–1000.

Liberman AM, Mattingly IG (1985) The motor theory of speech-perception revised. *Cognition, 21,* 1–36.

McGettigan C, Agnew ZK, Scott SK (2010) Are articulatory commands automatically and involuntarily activated during speech perception? *Proceedings of the National Academy of Sciences of the United States of America, 107*(12), E42; author reply E43.

McGettigan C, Scott SK (2012) Cortical asymmetries in speech perception: what's wrong, what's right and what's left? *Trends in Cognitive Science, 16*(5), 269–76.

McGettigan C, Warren JE, Eisner F, Marshall CR, Shanmugalingam P, Scott SK (2011) Neural correlates of sublexical processing in phonological working memory. *Journal of Cognitive Neuroscience, 23*(4), 961–77.

Mogford K (1988) Oral language acquisition in the prelinguistically deaf. In *Language Development in Exceptional Circumstances* (eds Bishop DVM & Mogford K, pp. 110–31). New York: Churchill Livingstone.

Mohr JP (1976) Broca's area and Broca's aphasia. (eds Whitaker H & Whitaker HA, pp. 201–35) *Studies in Neurolinguistics*, Vol. 1. New York: Academic Press.

Monsell S (1987) On the relation between lexical input and output pathways for speech. In *Language Perception and Production: Relationships between Listening, Reading, and Writing.* (eds Allport A, MacKay DG, Prinz W, Sheerer E, pp. 273–311), London: Academic Press.

Patterson K, Nestor PJ, Rogers TT (2007) Where do you know what you know? The representation of semantic knowledge in the human brain. *Nature Reviews Neuroscience, 8*(12), 976–87.

Penfield W, Welch K (1951) Supplementary motor area of the cerebral cortex. *Archives of Neurology & Psychiatry, 66*, 289–317.

Pulvermüller F, Fadiga L (2010) Active perception: sensorimotor circuits as a cortical basis for language. *Nature Reviews Neuroscience, 11*(5), 351–60.

Pulvermüller F, Huss M, Kherif F, Moscoso del Prado Martin F, Hauk O, Shtyrov Y (2006) Motor cortex maps articulatory features of speech sounds. *Proceedings of the National Academy of Sciences of the United States of America, 103*(20), 7865–70.

Rauschecker JP (2011) An expanded role for the dorsal auditory pathway in sensorimotor control and integration. *Hearing Research, 271*(1–2), 16–25.

Rauschecker JP, Scott SK (2009) Maps and streams in the auditory cortex: how work in non-human primates has contributed to our understanding of human speech processing. *Nature Neuroscience, 12*(6), 718–24.

Repp BH (2000) Compensation for subliminal timing perturbations in perceptual–motor synchronization. *Psychological Research, 63*, 106–28.

Repp BH (2001) Phase correction, phase resetting, and phase shifts after subliminal timing perturbations in sensorimotor synchronization. *Journal of Experimental Psychology: Human Perception & Performance, 27*, 600–21.

Schroeder MR (1968) Reference signal for signal quality studies. *Journal of the Acoustical Society of America, 44*, 1735–6.

Scott SK, Blank SC, Rosen S, Wise RJS (2000) Identification of a pathway for intelligible speech in the left temporal lobe. *Brain, 123*, 2400–6.

Scott SK, McGettigan C, Eisner F (2009) A little more conversation, a little less action: candidate roles for motor cortex in speech perception. *Nature Reviews Neuroscience, 10*(4), 295–302.

Scott SK, Wise RJ (2004) The functional neuroanatomy of prelexical processing in speech perception. *Cognition, 92*(1–2), 13–45.

Simonyan K, Horwitz B (2011) Laryngeal motor cortex and control of speech in humans. *Neuroscientist, 17*(2), 197–208.

Stilp CE, Rogers TT, Kluender KR (2010) Rapid efficient coding of correlated complex acoustic properties. *Proceedings of the National Academy of Sciences of the United States of America, 107*(50), 21914–9.

Takaso H, Eisner F, Wise RJ, Scott SK (2010) The effect of delayed auditory feedback on activity in the temporal lobe while speaking: a positron emission tomography study. *Journal of Speech, Language, and Hearing Research, 53*(2), 226–36.

Thompson-Schill SL, D'Esposito M, Aguirre GK, Farah MJ (1997) Role of left inferior prefrontal cortex in retrieval of semantic knowledge: a reevaluation. *Proceedings of the National Academy of Sciences of the United States of America, 94*(26), 14792–7.

Warren JE, Sauter DA, Eisner F, Wiland J, Dresner MA, Wise RJ, Rosen S, Scott SK (2006) Positive emotions preferentially engage an auditory-motor "mirror" system. *Journal of Neuroscience, 26*(50), 13067–75.

Warren JE, Wise RJ, Warren JD (2005) Sounds do-able: auditory-motor transformations and the posterior temporal plane. *Trends in Neurosciences*, *28*(12), 636–43.

Watkins KE, Strafella AP, Paus T (2003) Seeing and hearing speech excites the motor system involved in speech production. *Neuropsychologia*, *41*(8), 989–94.

Wernicke C. (1874) *Der aphasische Symptomencomplex: Eine psychologische Studie auf anatomischer Basis.* Breslau: Cohn & Weigert.

Wilson SM, Saygin AP, Sereno MI, Iacoboni M (2004) Listening to speech activates motor areas involved in speech production. *Nature Neuroscience*, *7*(7), 701–2.

Wise RJ (2003) Language systems in normal and aphasic human subjects: functional imaging studies and inferences from animal studies. *British Medical Bulletin*, *65*, 95–119.

Wise RJS, Greene J, Büchel C, Scott SK (1999) Brain systems for word perception and articulation. *The Lancet*, *353*(9158), 1057–61.

Wise RJS, Scott SK, Blank SC, Mummery CJ, Warburton E (2001) Identifying separate neural sub-systems within 'Wernicke's area'. *Brain*, *124*, 83–95.

Zwaan RA, Kaschak MP (2009) Language comprehension as a means of "re-situating" oneself. (eds Robbins P & Aydede M, pp. 368–81). *The Cambridge Handbook of Situated Cognition.* Cambridge, UK: Cambridge University Press.

3

CONSONANT BIAS IN THE USE OF PHONOLOGICAL INFORMATION DURING LEXICAL PROCESSING

A lifespan and cross-linguistic perspective

Thierry Nazzi and Silvana Poltrock

Thierry Nazzi is the corresponding author.
This study was supported by ANR-09-FRBR-015 and ANR-13-BSH2-0004 to TN, as well as by the Labex EFL (ANR-10-LABX-0083) to TN.

Introduction

Infants acquiring language have to learn about the phonology, the lexicon, and the syntax of their native language. The issue we are going to discuss in the present chapter relates to some of the mechanisms involved in learning a lexicon. A word corresponds to the specific pairing between the mental representation of a sound pattern of a word (a word form) and the abstract representation of an object or event in the world that constitutes the meaning associated to that word form (concept). The building of a lexicon then relies on the development of three sets of abilities: (1) to extract, represent with phonetic detail, and store word forms; (2) to build concepts for the objects and events in the world; and (3) to appropriately link word forms and concepts. Note that, although it was long thought that the acquisition of word forms and concepts precedes by several months the acquisition of the first words, recent studies show that all of these abilities emerge around 6 to 12 months of age: phonological acquisition (e.g., Best, McRoberts, & Sithole, 1988; Werker & Tees, 1984a, 1984b), segmentation of word forms (Jusczyk & Aslin, 1995), learning of concepts (Rakison & Oakes, 2003, for an overview), lexical acquisition (Tincoff & Jusczyk, 1999). This does not mean that these abilities are fully mature by 12 months, but it underlines the importance of studying these different abilities both separately and in their interaction.

More specifically, we focus on the ability to use phonological information in early lexically related acquisition and processing and in particular on the division-of-labor hypothesis, according to which infants give more weight to consonantal than vocalic information in these processes (Nespor, Peña, & Mehler, 2003). In the present chapter, we first briefly review what we know regarding early phonological acquisition. Second, we discuss the use of phonetic detail in lexical processing and present in detail the division-of-labor hypothesis and the evidence supporting this hypothesis coming in particular from studies on lexical processing by adults and toddlers/children. We then discuss the implications of these findings regarding the possible origin of the consonant bias in lexical processing and outline three hypotheses proposed to explain its origin. Lastly, we present the findings of ongoing research projects, adopting both a cross-linguistic and an early developmental perspective to evaluate these hypotheses.

Phonological and lexical acquisition during the first year of life

Infants are initially able to discriminate most native and non-native phoneme contrasts from the very first hours or days after birth (Jusczyk, 2000, for a review). The few contrasts that are not discriminated early in development appear to be acoustically less salient (Narayan, Werker, & Beddor, 2010) or not to correspond to language-general boundaries (Hoonhorst, Colin, Markessis, Radeau, Deltenre, & Serniclaes, 2009). It also appears that, as in adulthood, consonant discrimination is categorical (Eimas, 1974; Eimas, Siqueland, Jusczyk, & Vigorito, 1971), while vowel discrimination is rather continuous (Kuhl, Williams, Lacerda, Stevens, & Lindblom, 1992; Swoboda, Morse, & Leavitt, 1976). This suggests that young infants might already process consonants and vowels differently, possibly due to acoustic differences as vowels are usually longer, more periodic, and more steady (Ladefoged, 2001; Repp, 1984; see also Cutler & Mehler, 1993) than consonants.

It is also established that infants get attuned to the phonological characteristics of their ambient language during the first year of life (Jusczyk, 2000; Kuhl, 2004), a developmental phenomenon called phonetic attunement. These changes in phonetic discrimination ability appear to be language-specific in the sense that infants lose the ability to discriminate most, though not all, non-native contrasts (e.g., Best et al., 1988; Polka & Werker, 1994; Werker & Lalonde, 1988; Werker & Tees, 1984a, 1984b) while improvements in discrimination of native contrasts are observed (Hoonhorst et al., 2009; Kuhl, Stevens, Hayashi, Deguchi, Kiritani, & Iverson, 2006; Polka, Colantonio, & Sundara, 2001; Rivera-Gaxiola, Silva-Pereyra, & Kuhl, 2005; Sundara, Polka, & Genesee, 2006). Moreover, discrimination changes follow a different time course for vowels, with changes starting by 6 months (Kuhl et al., 1992; Polka & Werker, 1994), and consonants, with changes usually observed by 10–12 months (Werker & Lalonde, 1988; Werker & Tees, 1984a, 1984b; but see Hoonhorst et al., 2009, for changes by 8 months in French). Importantly, attunement begins before infants have acquired sizeable lexicons. Note, however, that attunement is not over at the end of the first year of life, as later changes are observed in childhood (e.g., Walley & Flege, 1999) and in relation to reading acquisition (e.g., Hoonhorst, Medina, Colin, Markessis, Radeau, Deltenre, & Serniclaes, 2011).

Several theories have been proposed to explain phonetic attunement. One influential proposal is the Perceptual Assimilation Model (PAM, Best, 1995; Best et al., 1988), which states that the observed changes result from the acquisition of the native phonological categories. Thus, if the phonemes to be discriminated are either native phonemes or non-native phonemes that assimilate to two different native categories, discrimination performance should increase with development (Rivera-Gaxiola et al., 2005). If they are non-native phonemes that assimilate to the same native category, performance should decrease over the same period (Werker & Tees, 1984a, 1984b), while if they are non-native phonemes that do not assimilate to any native category, performance should remain stable (Best et al., 1988). A complementary theory accounting for phonetic attunement, placing more emphasis on the neural bases of language acquisition, is the Native Language Neural Commitment (NLNC) hypothesis, proposing that during the first year of life, neural networks are formed that capture the acoustic properties/regularities of native sound categories (Kuhl, 2000, 2004). These changes in neural architecture will result in improved processing of native sound patterns and decreased non-native phonetic discrimination abilities and will support their use in learning higher levels of the native language.

While these studies outline the basic developmental trajectories for early phonological acquisition (though mostly for English), recent work has started focusing on the mechanisms that could drive this phonological acquisition. Several mechanisms have been proposed, which could contribute in parallel to the acquisition of native phonological categories. One such mechanism is distributional learning, according to which infants track the distribution of phonetic tokens in the acoustic space. Maye, Werker, and Gerken (2002) found evidence of such distributional learning in 6- and 8-month-old infants. However, it is unlikely that distributional learning alone can account for phonological acquisition, for example in cases in which there is a large overlap between the phonological categories in the acoustic space. Another proposed mechanism is acquired distinctiveness, the idea that when two sounds are presented in two different contexts (for example *ball* and *doll* with their respective referents), perceptual distance will be increased. The effects of perceptual distinctiveness on discrimination have recently been found in 9- to 10-month-old infants (e.g., Yeung & Nazzi, 2014; Yeung & Werker, 2009). Moreover, social interactions have an impact on phonetic attunement, performance at learning new categories being improved in a social context (live experimenter rather than video) at 9 months of age (Kuhl, Tsao, & Liu, 2003).

What about early lexical acquisition? While production studies point to an acquisition onset by 12 months, studies using experimental methods evaluating comprehension point to the earlier acquisition of some frequent words. While many such studies have established recognition of words thought to be familiar to infants (based on infant-directed speech corpora and parental reports) during the second year of life (e.g., Bailey & Plunkett, 2002; Swingley & Aslin, 2000, 2002), more recently, the onset of word comprehension (and thus acquisition) has been pushed down to around 6 months (Bergelson & Swingley, 2012; Tincoff & Jusczyk,

1999, 2012). At these ages, comprehension is restricted to a small set of highly familiar words such as *mommy*, *daddy*, *feet* and *hand*. Interestingly, it is possible that at this age, recognition is facilitated when the words are uttered by the infant's mother (Bergelson & Swingley, 2012), hence in a familiar voice, although recognition has also been found using an unfamiliar voice (Tincoff & Jusczyk, 1999, 2012).

Given their overlap in developmental time, it appears crucial to understand the link between early phonological and lexical acquisition. To do so, many studies have explored whether and under which circumstances infants recruit their early phonological-perceptual abilities in the process of early word learning and processing (for a review, see Hallé & Cristia, 2012), relying on perceptual/comprehension methods. Two lines of research have been particularly explored. The first one, investigating word recognition, evaluates the impact of mispronunciations on the recognition of *known* words. The second one focuses on *word learning*, testing infants' ability to simultaneously learn two phonetically similar words. In the following, we review some of the evidence on this issue and then turn to the question of whether all contrasts are equal, in the context of the proposal of a functional dissociation in the processing of consonants vs. vowels (Nespor et al., 2003).

Use of phonetic detail in word learning/recognition

Regarding the issue of the phonetic specificity of early lexical representations, some researchers, on the one hand, have proposed that early representations in a sparse lexicon do not need to be fully specified in order to be efficiently recognized (e.g., Hallé & de Boysson-Bardies, 1996; Jusczyk, 1993; Metsala, 1999; Storkel, 2002). According to these authors, early lexical representations would first be unspecified, and increases in the neighborhood density of a given word (Jusczyk, 1993) or in the number of times it was encountered (frequency of exposure, Metsala, 1999) would later lead to more specific representations. On the other hand, some researchers have proposed that early words are phonetically specified, and many studies have explored the effects of mispronunciation on the recognition of word forms or words or infants' ability to simultaneously learn words that differ only by one phoneme or phonological feature. The results of these studies suggest that early lexical representations are at least partially phonetically detailed.

Regarding tasks exploring these effects in the auditory modality only, several studies testing listening preferences at 11 months of age show that infants' recognition of frequent/known bisyllabic words (or word forms) is disrupted by a consonant change in the onset of an accented/stressed syllable (French: Halle & de Boysson-Bardies, 1996, and reanalyses in Vihman, Nakai, DePaolis, & Hallé, 2004; English: Vihman et al., 2004) and by an onset or a coda consonant change in monosyllabic (stressed) words (Dutch: Swingley, 2005). This suggests phonetic specificity in accented/stressed syllables. However, detection of phonetic mispronunciations appears more difficult in unaccented/unstressed syllables, with weaker and later emerging results (Vihman et al., 2004). Another study tested similar effects using word segmentation tasks and found that English-learning 7.5-month-olds correctly recognize at test monosyllabic words (e.g., *cup*) previously heard in sentences but do not do so when the first segment of these words is changed (e.g., *tup*). These findings suggest that at that age, the onset consonant of newly segmented (stressed) words is already phonetically specified (Jusczyk & Aslin, 1995).

Since these auditory-only studies cannot specify whether the locus of the mis-pronunciation effects is at the level of the word form or of the word itself, further studies looked at the impact of mispronunciations in word recognition, using audiovisual preferential looking tasks in which infants have to match an incoming auditory word with one of two objects (a target and a distractor) presented on a screen. These studies conducted on toddlers (14- to 24-month-olds) established phonetic specificity of early known words: infants looked less at the matching object upon hearing its incorrect pronunciation as compared to its correct pronunciation (e.g., *vaby* instead of *baby*; Bailey & Plunkett, 2002; Swingley & Aslin, 2000, 2002; see also Fennell & Werker, 2003). Importantly though, in most of these studies (except in some conditions in White & Morgan, 2008, using distractors with unfamiliar names), infants nevertheless look longer at the target than the distractor when hearing the mispronunciation, suggesting that while being sensitive to the phonetic change in one phoneme, they also notice the similarity between the target and its one-phoneme mispronunciation.

Finally, other studies have looked at the encoding of phonetic detail in *novel* words. Many of these studies have used a habituation technique (known as the switch task) in which infants are habituated with two novel word-object pairings and then tested on their ability to detect a switch in the pairings. Seventeen-, but not 14-month-olds, could simultaneously learn two phonetically similar words (*bih* and *dih*; Stager & Werker, 1997; Werker, Fennell, Corcoran, & Stager, 2002), initially suggesting that 14-month-olds could not recruit detailed phonetic information in word learning. However, 14-month-olds later succeeded in detecting mispronunciations of novel words when the testing procedure was changed, for example when the words were embedded in simple naming sentences (Fennell, 2006), when the objects were prefamiliarized (Fennell, 2004), when a training period with familiar objects was included (Fennell & Waxman, 2010), when a training phase was included in which the words were presented under variable phonetic contexts (Thiessen, 2007), or when presenting both objects during the test phase (Yoshida, Fennell, Swingley, & Werker, 2009). Taken together, these studies suggest that infants are able to integrate some phonetic detail in their lexical representations from the onset of the second year of life.

Hypothesis: Consonant-bias in lexical processing

Importantly, the studies reviewed so far mainly focused on consonants and did not systematically explore differences between vowels and consonants. There is, however, increasing evidence for an asymmetry in processing between consonants and vowels to the advantage of consonants. A first study by Nazzi (2005) found that in novel word learning, consonants are given more weight than vowels: while

French-learning 20-month-olds could simultaneously learn two words that differ by one of their consonants (e.g., /pize/ vs. /tize/), they failed to do so when the words differed only by one of their vowels (/pize/ vs. /pyze/). This was found using the name-based categorization task (hereafter NBC task), in which triads of unfamiliar objects are presented, two objects being labeled with the same name and the third object being labeled using a phonetically similar name. In the test phase, infants are asked to group together the objects with the same name. These findings provided the first developmental evidence for the proposal by Nespor and colleagues (2003) that consonants have a more important role than vowels in lexically related processes, while vowels have a more important role than consonants in marking prosodic and syntactic regularities. The idea behind this division-of-labor, or consonant-vowel, hypothesis is that these biases, if present early in development, would help young language learners to organize the rich speech input by assigning the two phonological categories to different learning mechanisms (consonants – acquisition of a lexicon; vowels – acquisition of prosody and syntax), resulting in facilitated language acquisition. In the following, we concentrate on the consonantal bias hypothesis in lexical processing (hereafter C-bias hypothesis).

Evidence in favor of the C-bias in lexical processing: Adult data

Adult studies provide strong evidence for this C-bias hypothesis. First, in word reconstruction tasks in which an auditory presented pseudo word has to be transformed into a real word by changing one phoneme, English, Dutch, and Spanish listeners prefer to preserve the consonantal structure over the vocalic one, so that *kebra* is changed into *cobra* rather than into *zebra*, suggesting that consonants constrain lexical access to a greater extent than vowels (Cutler, Sebastian-Galles, Soler-Vilageliu, & van Ooijen, 2000; Van Ooijen, 1996). Second, in a word learning study, Creel, Aslin, and Tanenhaus (2006) demonstrated with an artificial lexicon-learning paradigm that English-speaking adults confuse newly learned words more often when they share their consonants than when they share their vowels, an advantage independent of consonant/vowel ratio but modulated by segment position (weakened consonant advantage in coda position). A C-bias in an adult word-learning study was also found in French (Havy, Serres, & Nazzi, 2014), though in this study no difference was found between onset and coda processing. Third, lexical decision studies revealed a C-bias both in the written (French: New, Araujo, & Nazzi, 2008; New & Nazzi, 2014; Spanish: Carreiras, Dunabeitia, & Molinaro, 2009; Carreiras, Gillon-Dowens, Vergara, & Perea, 2009; English: Lee, Rayner, & Pollatsek, 2002; European Portuguese: Soares, Perea, & Comesaña, 2014) and in the oral (French and English: Delle Luche, Poltrock, Goslin, New, Floccia, & Nazzi, 2014) modalities. In these studies, adults were faster at deciding that a target (e.g., /diva/) was a word if it was primed by a pseudo word preserving its consonants (e.g., /duvo/) than a pseudo word preserving its vowels (e.g., /rifa/). Lastly, when discovering words in a continuous speech stream, French adults are successful when transitional probabilities highlight common consonants (e.g., /puragi/ /puregy/), but not when they highlight common vowels (e.g., /pOkima/ /pOtila/; Bonatti, Peña, Nespor, & Mehler, 2005; but see Newport & Aslin, 2004, for vowel effects in conditions allowing consecutive repetitions of the same word family). Complementarily, for the extraction of structural, grammar-like rules, the use of vocalic regularities seems privileged over the use of consonant regularities, even when the relative higher saliency of vowels over consonants is decreased (Toro, Nespor, Mehler, & Bonatti, 2008; Toro, Shukla, Nespor, & Endress, 2008).

Taken together, these psycholinguistic studies support the privileged lexical role of consonants in adults regardless of the language's phonological inventory, although some crucial languages (such as Danish, see the section on "Early cross-linguistic variation in the expression of a C-bias") have not been investigated yet. The origin of this bias and its trajectory in development are, however, less clear.

Consistent C-bias in early lexical processing in French

The hypothesis of the C-bias has been extensively studied in French-learning infants, toddlers, and children, and a C-bias has been found from 14 months of age onwards in different lexically related tasks. Word learning studies using the standard NBC task or variants of it show that 16-month-old infants learn pairs of new words if the words contrasted differ by one consonantal feature (place or voicing) but perform at chance if they differ by one vocalic feature (place or height; Havy & Nazzi, 2009). By 20 months of age, infants perform above chance even when learning words that differ by a continuous, non-plosive consonant (nasals, fricatives, liquids), therefore ruling out the possibility that the difference between vowels and consonants is due to phoneme continuity or sonority level (Nazzi & New, 2007), and both onset and coda consonants are well processed (Nazzi & Bertoncini, 2009). Together with the finding that 16-month-olds fail to use vowel contrasts even with vowel-initial words (Nazzi & Polka, in preparation), this shows that differences between vowels and consonants cannot be explained as a word/syllable onset positional effect. By 30 months of age, infants are now able to use vocalic information, but they still give more weight to consonantal information than to vocalic information in a conflict situation: when "matching" a target object (e.g., a /duk/) to one of two objects, they prefer choosing the object that differs by a vowel (e.g., a /dok/) rather than by a consonant (e.g., a /guk/; Nazzi, Floccia, Moquet, & Butler, 2009). Furthermore, the C-bias has been demonstrated in 3- to 5-year-old preschoolers and in adults in word-learning eye-tracking tasks that do not require an overt object choice (Havy et al., 2014; see also Havy, Bertoncini, & Nazzi, 2011). In preschoolers, both total looking time and shift latency measures indexed better performance for consonant than vowel contrasts (in adults, the C-bias was visible only in shift latency).

Moreover, other studies have extended these findings from new word learning to early lexical recognition. In a word recognition task with 14-month-olds, Zesiger and Jöhr (2011) demonstrated that recognition of familiar bisyllabic words is blocked by a consonant change in the second but not the first syllable, though not by a vowel change in either initial or final syllables, again suggesting that more weight is given to consonants than to vowels, importantly extending this bias (in French) to words already known by infants.

Origins of the C-bias

Proposed developmental scenarios

At least three different accounts for the C-bias have been considered. The *initial bias hypothesis* (Bonatti, Peña, Nespor, & Mehler, 2007; Nespor et al., 2003) states that infants start processing consonants and vowels as distinctive linguistic categories from the onset of language acquisition. According to this hypothesis, a C-bias in "lexically related" tasks should be observed from birth across languages, irrespective of the distributional/acoustic characteristics of the language.

Alternatively, this functional asymmetry could arise as a by-product of the properties of the input, and two factors are potentially implicated in the emergence of this asymmetry. The *acoustic/phonetic hypothesis* (Floccia, Nazzi, Delle Luche, Poltrock, & Goslin, 2014) proposes that the C-bias emerges during the first year of life. It would rely on the fact that there are intrinsic acoustic differences between consonants and vowels (because consonants are usually shorter, less periodic, and less stable, as they often correspond to articulation/sound transitions) that seem to result in a more categorical perception of consonants than of vowels (Ladefoged, 2001; Repp, 1984), even in very young infants (Eimas et al., 1971; Swoboda et al., 1976), possibly due to acoustically more distinct consonant categories (Bouchon, Floccia, Fux, Adda-Decker, & Nazzi, 2014). These acoustic differences would lead to the construction of the phonologically distinct categories of consonants and vowels in infants, as well as the acquisition of their different functional roles in language processing in the first year of life – that is, a C-bias in lexical processing (and a V-bias in prosodic/syntactic processing). The emergence of the C-bias could be observed before infants have acquired a sizeable lexicon, and the C-bias should be modulated over the course of development by the acoustic/distributional characteristics of the ambient language.

Lastly, the *lexical hypothesis* (Keidel, Jenison, Kluender, & Seidenberg, 2007) states that the C-bias reflects the linguistic experience of the learners at the lexical level, from which they learn that consonants are better, more informative cues to lexical identity than vowels once they have acquired a large enough lexicon. Therefore, biases in lexically related tasks would not appear before infants have acquired a sizeable lexicon, since it would require some analysis of the phonological structure (particularly in terms of phonological neighborhoods) of the lexicon and so are more likely after 12 months of age.

To evaluate these hypotheses, two different but complementary approaches have been used. The first, cross-linguistic approach, investigates whether the consonant bias in lexical processing found in French-learning toddlers and children extends to other languages. The second, developmental approach tests infants both before

12 months of age and at older ages in order to evaluate whether the C-bias is modulated by phonological and lexical acquisition. In the following, we review the (still patchy) results that have already been found, highlighting their implications for our understanding of the emergence of the consonant bias, and pointing out the necessity to continue such work in the future, combining both approaches.

Early cross-linguistic variation in the expression of a C-bias

As mentioned earlier, while the initial bias hypothesis predicts a general, cross-linguistic consonant bias, the two learning hypotheses (acoustic/phonetic and lexical) leave open the possibility for cross-linguistic variation based on the acoustic/phonetic or lexical properties of the language in acquisition. As with French, an early lexical C-bias has been found in Italian: 12-month-olds rely more on consonants than vowels when learning new word form-object pairings (Hochmann, Benavides-Varela, Nespor, & Mehler, 2011). However, that study used only a few consonant and vocalic changes, leaving it unclear whether the results would extend to more contrasts.

A different picture emerges for English. As already described, several studies using the switch task showed that English-learning infants are able to learn words differing only by one consonant feature as early as 14 months of age (e.g., Fennell & Waxman, 2010). However, for vowels, while infants sometimes succeed by 14–15 months when the words differ by several features (Curtin, Fennell, & Escudero, 2009; Mani & Plunkett, 2008, using a preferential looking task), there is no evidence so far that they succeed with one-feature contrasts before 18 months (Dietrich, Swingley, & Werker, 2007). While this suggests asymmetrical use of consonants and vowels during word learning, the C-bias has been more directly tested in studies using variants of the NBC task, revealing a C-bias at 30 months (Nazzi et al., 2009) but not in both 16- and 23-month-olds (Floccia et al., 2014). For known word recognition, Mani and Plunkett (2007, 2010) directly compared consonants and vowels using the preferential looking paradigm: English-learning infants were found to be as sensitive to one-feature consonant as to one-feature vowel mispronunciations in familiar words at 12, 18, and 24 months of age. The only exception is one experiment where 15-month-olds showed greater sensitivity to consonant than vowel changes (Mani & Plunkett, 2007). Overall however, this symmetry found in most English studies stands in contrast with the C-bias consistently found in French and suggests cross-linguistic English–French differences in the expression of the C-bias.

In German, one study tested toddlers' use of consonant and vowel information when learning new words: Using a simplified version of the NBC task, 20-month-olds were found to be able to choose the correct object when the two words to be learned differed minimally by one of their word-initial consonants but not when they differed by a vowel in a non-initial position. However, when the vocalic contrast appeared word-initially, infants learned successfully, whereas, when the minimal consonantal contrast occurred word-medially, infants performed at chance level (Schwytay & Höhle, 2012). These results suggest that the position of the contrasted phoneme in relation to lexical stress rather than the phoneme category itself determines whether one-phoneme contrasted words can be learnt. This again stands in contrast with French in which the C-bias was found to be position-independent (Nazzi & Bertoncini, 2009; Nazzi & Polka, in preparation).

Lastly, one study investigated Danish, a language that has more vowels than consonants (contrary to most other languages) and extensive consonant reduction, which increases the relative salience of vowels (Bleses, Basbøll, & Vach, 2011; Pharao, 2011). At 20 months, Danish-learning infants were found to rely more on vowels than consonants when learning words using the NBC task (Højen & Nazzi, 2016). This study is thus the first to reveal a *vocalic* rather than a consonant bias. In this context, it would be important to test whether Danish-speaking adults have a vocalic bias in lexical processing (as Danish-learning toddlers) or have a consonant bias in lexical processing, as found in all languages tested so far (e.g., Cutler et al., 2000; New et al., 2008), in which case one would need to understand the factors that would have given rise to such a developmental change.

Taken together, it appears that the expression of the C-bias, though possibly stable in adulthood, might not follow the same developmental path across languages, inasmuch as the preceding cross-linguistic data strongly suggest that the C-bias is modulated by the native language. How consistent are these findings with respect to the different hypotheses proposed to account for the C-bias? The innate bias hypothesis does not seem to be supported by the data just presented, since Danish toddlers show a V-bias (Højen & Nazzi, in revision) while German toddlers show no bias at 20 months (Schwytay & Höhle, 2012), and the C-bias seems to emerge rather later in development in English (Floccia et al., 2014; Nazzi et al., 2009). However, it is unclear at this point which among the acoustic/phonetic or lexical hypotheses best accounts for the results. Indeed, the V-bias found for Danish is compatible with both accounts. Danish may be exceptional from an acoustic/phonetic perspective, since extensive consonant reduction in that language could make consonants harder to categorize than in other languages. From a lexical perspective, the fact that Danish has more vowels than consonants might result in vowels being more informative at the level of the lexicon, contrary to what is found in languages like French, German, or English. Moreover, while the German and English data may not support the lexical hypothesis (both languages have relatively more consonants than vowels compared to French and yet show a weaker C-bias), there is no positive evidence supporting the acoustic/phonetic hypothesis either.

One limitation of this cross-linguistic approach is that it remains possible that the C-bias would be present at birth but that its expression in toddlerhood would be modulated across languages, following in some languages (English, German) a U-shape trajectory and even reversing in some other languages (Danish). In the following discussion, we present the results of recent studies that have investigated the expression of the consonant bias in lexical processing during the first year of life, in order to explore from a developmental perspective the origin of the C-bias and further weight the likelihood of the preceding three hypotheses.

Is the C-bias present at the onset of lexical acquisition?

Three recent studies have looked at the presence of a C-bias in French-acquiring infants in their first year of life, hence before a sizeable lexicon is acquired. French offers a good case to explore whether the C-bias is present from birth or, if not, when it emerges in development, given that studies on toddlers, children, and adults have so consistently found a consonant bias in lexical processing in that language. Two of these studies looked at the impact of mispronunciations on the recognition of known words, while the last study explored the impact of mispronunciations on the recognition of segmented word forms unknown prior to the lab visit.

The first study explored whether French-learning 11-month-olds already exhibit a consonant bias when recognizing familiar words (Poltrock & Nazzi, 2015). Since 11-month-olds have small vocabularies, a consonant bias is predicted by the acoustic/phonetic but not the lexical hypothesis. In a baseline experiment, infants preferred listening to familiar words over non-words, confirming a familiarity preference at this age. In a second experiment, infants preferred listening to one-feature vowel mispronunciations over one-feature consonant mispronunciations of the familiar words, demonstrating that consonantal alterations impact early word recognition to a greater extent than vowel alterations. This attests that the consonant bias is already in place at 11 months in French.

Can evidence of a consonant bias be found in younger infants? To test this, a second study explored 5-month-old infants' recognition of their own name (found in English at that age, Mandel, Jusczyk, & Pisoni, 1995) and how this recognition is impacted by mispronunciations (Bouchon et al., 2014). Infants were presented with repetitions of their well pronounced or mispronounced names. Name recognition was impaired by vowel but not consonant mispronunciations. Moreover, acoustic analyses revealed that contrasted vowels were more salient than contrasted consonants and that performance in the vowel condition was related to acoustic distance between the contrasted segments, suggesting the importance of acoustic factors in determining the pattern of performance observed. These findings suggest that infants start with a vocalic bias (possibly related to the higher salience of vowels), still in place at 5 months. This initial vocalic bias is compatible with some findings on newborns showing that they are more sensitive to the addition of a new syllable in a list of syllables when it has a different vowel than a different consonant than the original syllable set (Bertoncini, Bijeljac-Babic, Jusczyk, & Kennedy, 1988) and that they have better memory for vocalic than for consonantal information when hearing new word forms (Benavides-Varela, Hochmann, Macagno, Nespor, & Mehler, 2012).

A third study refines the age of emergence of the C-bias (Nishibayashi & Nazzi, in revision). Following evidence that both 6- and 8-month-old French-learning infants can segment monosyllabic words from fluent speech (Nishibayashi, Goyet, & Nazzi, 2015), infants were tested with consonant and vowel mispronunciations of the target words. At 8 months, infants were more sensitive to consonant than to vowel mispronunciations (e.g., accepting /pu/, but not /by/, as a possible instance of /py/). However, the opposite pattern was found at 6 months, infants being more sensitive to vowel mispronunciations. These results are compatible with those earlier, establishing that the C-bias in lexically related processing emerges between 6 and 8 months in French-learning infants. Importantly, in all of these studies, many different words and many different consonant and vowel contrasts were used, providing generality to the findings obtained.

In summary, all of these studies converge in suggesting that the C-bias in lexically related processing might not be present before 6 months of age and emerges around 7 to 8 months of age in both French and Italian. With respect to the origins of the consonant bias, the vocalic bias found in the younger infants goes against the initial bias hypothesis (Nespor et al., 2003). Moreover, the fact that the consonant bias is already present by 7 to 8 months of age, when infants still have very small vocabularies, goes against the predictions of the lexical hypothesis (Keidel et al., 2007). They are, however, compatible with the acoustic/phonetic hypothesis (Floccia et al., 2014), according to which this bias is related to early language-general processing of acoustic/ phonetic information and possibly to language-specific acquisition of the phonetic/phonological properties of the native language.

Concluding remarks and perspectives

In the present chapter, we have explored the early link between phonological and lexical development, evaluating in particular the hypothesis of a functional dissociation between the processing of consonants, proposed to be more important for lexical processing, and that of vowels, more central to prosodic and syntactic processing. We reviewed studies on French supporting the consonant bias in early lexical processing by 8 months onward. However, evidence was also found for two kinds of variation. First, cross-linguistic variation was found in toddlerhood, with a consistent consonant bias found for French and Italian, a later emerging bias in English, and a reversed vocalic bias in Danish. Second, developmental changes were found in French, younger infants exhibiting an acoustically based vocalic bias up to about 6 months, followed by the emergence of a consonant bias by 8 months. It thus appears that there is an early link between phonological and lexical developments, with linked changes around 6 to 8 months of age.

The pattern of findings so far has implications for our understanding of the origin of functional specialization, and we have argued that it favors the acoustic/ phonetic hypothesis rather than the initial bias and lexical hypotheses. This will have to be further explored in the future by extending this kind of research to more languages, in particular languages in which vowels bear crucial information for lexical identity (such as Danish or tone languages) and also by pursuing the work on the emergence of the bias, so far limited to French, in languages that have a different, less consistent C-bias pattern in toddlerhood. Within the framework of the acoustic/phonetic hypothesis, it will be crucial in the future to specify the acoustic and phonetic/phonological factors that lead to the emergence of these phonological biases in lexical processing.

Lastly, what are the implications of the emerging evidence that the C-bias is in fact acquired (rather than being an initial bias) regarding the original proposal that the functional division of labor between consonants and vowels (C-bias for lexical processing, V-bias for prosodic/syntactic processing) might help bootstrap language acquisition (Nespor et al., 2003)? Given the findings on newborns suggesting that they process vowels better than consonants (Benavides-Varela et al., 2012; Bertoncini et al., 1988) and those on 5- and 6-month-olds suggesting a vocalic bias even in lexically related processing (Bouchon et al., 2014; Nishibayashi & Nazzi, in preparation), it appears that infants might have a general bias towards vowels in the first months of life. Since prosodic information is carried mostly by vowels, this is consistent with findings, obtained within the framework of the prosodic bootstrapping theory (e.g., Gleitman & Wanner, 1982; Morgan & Demuth, 1996), that prosodic information plays a crucial role in early language processing and acquisition. Hence, the bases for the second part of the proposal of functional specialization (V-bias in prosodic/syntactic processing) might be grounded in this early focus on vowels and prosody, might be language-general, and might bootstrap early prosodic and (when prosodically marked) syntactic acquisition.

On the other hand, the C-bias for lexical processing appears to be dependent on language-specific properties and needs to be learned. While this potentially (but not necessarily) means that it might not guide the acquisition of the very first words (one's own name by 5 months of age), its acquisition by 8 to 11 months before infants know a sizeable vocabulary (Nishibayashi & Nazzi, in preparation; Poltrock & Nazzi, 2015) happens early enough for it to still be able to play a crucial role in early lexical acquisition and lexical access. Finally, because of its learned status and cross-linguistic variation, the C-bias (or V-bias, as found for Danish) might be more like other phonological biases that have been found to influence word acquisition, such as language-specific phonotactic constraints found to influence early word segmentation (Gonzalez Gomez & Nazzi, 2013; Mattys & Jusczyk, 2001) and word learning (Gonzalez Gomez, Poltrock, & Nazzi, 2013; Graf Estes, Edwards, & Saffran, 2011; MacKenzie, Curtin, & Graham, 2012). Whether or not the C-bias in lexical processing retains a special status in acquisition, as originally assumed by Nespor and colleagues (2003), will require future research comparing its scope and influence compared to that of other phonological biases.

References

Bailey, T.M., & Plunkett, K. (2002). Phonological specificity in early words. *Cognitive Development, 17*, 1265–1282.

Benavides-Varela, S., Hochmann, J.R., Macagno, F., Nespor, M., & Mehler, J. (2012). Newborn's brain activity signals the origin of word memories. *PNAS, 109*, 17908–17913.

Bergelson, E., & Swingley, D. (2012). At 6–9 months, human infants know the meanings of many common nouns. *PNAS, 109*, 3253–3258.

Bertoncini, J., Bijeljac-Babic, R., Jusczyk, P.W., & Kennedy, L.J. (1988). An investigation of young infants' perceptual representations of speech sounds. *Journal of Experimental Psychology: General, 117*(1), 21–33.

Best, C.T. (1995). A direct realist view of cross-language speech perception. In: Strange, W., (Ed.), *Speech perception and linguistic experience: Issues in cross-language research*. Timonium, MD: York Press. 171–204.

Best, C.T., McRoberts, G.W., & Sithole, N.M. (1988). Examination of perceptual reorganization for nonnative speech contrasts. *Journal of Experimental Psychology: Human Perception and Performance, 14*, 345–360.

Bleses, D., Basbøll, H., & Vach, W. (2011). Is Danish difficult to acquire? Evidence from Nordic past-tense studies. *Language and Cognitive Processes, 26*, 1193–231.

Bonatti, L.L., Peña, M., Nespor, M., & Mehler, J. (2005). Linguistic constraints on statistical computations: The role of consonants and vowels in continuous speech processing. *Psychological Science, 16*(6), 451–459.

Bonatti, L.L., Peña, M., Nespor, M., & Mehler, J. (2007). On consonants, vowels, chickens, and eggs. *Psychological Science, 18*, 924–925.

Bouchon, C., Floccia, C., Fux, T., Adda-Decker, M., & Nazzi, T. (2014). Call me Alix, not Elix: Vowels are more important than consonants in own name recognition at 5 months. *Developmental Science, 18*(4), 587–598. doi: 10.1111/desc.12242

Carreiras, M., Dunabeitia, J.A., & Molinaro, N. (2009). Consonants and vowels contribute differently to visual word recognition: ERPs of relative position priming. *Cerebral Cortex, 19*, 2659–2670.

Carreiras, M., Gillon-Dowens, M., Vergara, M., & Perea, M. (2009). Are vowels and consonants processed differently? *Journal of Cognitive Neuroscience, 21*, 275–288.

Creel, S.C., Aslin, R.N., & Tanenhaus, M.K. (2006). Acquiring an artificial lexicon: Segment type and order information in early lexical entries. *Journal of Memory and Language, 54*, 1–19.

Curtin, S., Fennell, C., & Escudero, P. (2009). Weighting of vowel cues explains patterns of word-object associative learning. *Developmental Science, 12*(5), 725–731.

Cutler, A., & Mehler, J. (1993). The periodicity bias. *Journal of Phonetics, 21*, 103–108.

Cutler, A., Sebastiàn-Gallès, N., Soler-Vilageliu, O., & van Ooijen, B. (2000). Constraints of vowels and consonants on lexical selection: Cross-linguistic comparisons. *Memory & Cognition, 28*, 746–755.

Delle Luche, C., Poltrock, S., Goslin, J., New, B., Floccia, C., & Nazzi, T. (2014). Differential processing of consonants and vowels in the auditory modality: A cross-linguistic study. *Journal of Memory and Language, 72*, 1–15.

Dietrich, C., Swingley, D., & Werker, J.F. (2007). Native language governs interpretation of salient speech sound differences at 18 months. *PNAS, 104*, 16027–16031.

Eimas, P. (1974). Auditory and linguistic processing of cues for place of articulation by infants. *Perception and Psychophysics, 16*(3), 513–521.

Eimas, P.D., Siqueland, E.R., Jusczyk, P., & Vigorito, J. (1971). Speech perception in infants. *Science, 171*, 303–306.

Fennell, C.T. (2004). Infant attention to phonetic detail in word forms: Knowledge and familiarity effects. Unpublished doctoral dissertation. The University of British Columbia, Vancouver.

Fennell, C.T. (2006). Infants of 14 months use phonetic detail in novel words embedded in naming phrases. In: *Proceedings of the 30th Annual Boston University Conference on Language Development*, Somerville, MA: Cascadilla Press. 178–189.

Fennell, C.T., & Waxman, S.R. (2010). What paradox? Referential cues allow for infant use of phonetic detail in word learning. *Child Development, 81*(5), 1376–1383.

Fennell, C.T., & Werker, J.F. (2003). Early word learners' ability to access phonetic detail in well-known words. *Language & Speech, 46*, 245–264.

Floccia, C., Nazzi, T., Delle Luche, C., Poltrock, S., & Goslin, J. (2014). English-learning one- to two-year-olds do not show a consonant bias in word learning. *Journal of Child Language, 41*(5), 1085–1114.

Gleitman, L.R., & Wanner, E. (1982). Language acquisition: The state of the state of the art. In: Wanner, E., & Gleitman, L.R. (Eds.), *Language acquisition: The state of the art.* Cambridge, MA: Cambridge University Press. 3–48.

Gonzalez Gomez, N., & Nazzi, T. (2013). Effects of prior phonotactic knowledge on infant word segmentation: The case of non-adjacent dependencies. *Journal of Speech, Language, and Hearing Research, 56*(3), 840–849.

Gonzalez Gomez, N., Poltrock, S., & Nazzi, T. (2013). A "bat" is easier to learn than a "tab": Effects of relative phonotactic frequency on infant word learning. *PlosOne, 8*(3), e59601.

Graf Estes, K., Edwards, J., & Saffran, J.R. (2011). Phonotactic constraints on infant word learning. *Infancy, 16,* 180–197.

Hallé, P., & Cristia, A. (2012). Global and detailed speech representations in early language acquisition. In: S. Fuchs, M. Weirich, D. Pape, & P. Perrier (Eds.), *Speech planning and dynamics.* Frankfurt am Main: Peter Lang. 11–38.

Hallé, P., & de Boysson-Bardies, B. (1996). The format of representation of recognized words in infants' early receptive lexicon. *Infant Behavior and Development, 19,* 463–481.

Havy, M., Bertoncini, J., & Nazzi, T. (2011). Word learning and phonetic processing in preschool age children. *Journal of Experimental Child Psychology, 108,* 25–43.

Havy, M., & Nazzi, T. (2009). Better processing of consonantal over vocalic information in word learning at 16 months of age. *Infancy, 14*(4), 439–456.

Havy, M., Serres, J., & Nazzi, T. (2014). A consonant/vowel asymmetry in word-form processing: Evidence in childhood and in adulthood. *Language and Speech, 57*(2), 254–281.

Hochmann, J.R., Benavides-Varela, S., Nespor, M., & Mehler, J. (2011). Consonants and vowels: Different roles in early language acquisition. *Developmental Science, 14,* 1445–1458.

Højen, A., & Nazzi, T. (2016). Vowel-bias in Danish-learning toddlers. *Developmental Science, 19*(1), 41–49.

Hoonhorst, I., Colin, C., Markessis, E., Radeau, M., Deltenre, P., & Serniclaes, W. (2009). French native speakers in the making: From language-general to language-specific voicing boundaries. *Journal of Experimental Child Psychology, 104,* 353–366.

Hoonhorst, I., Medina, V., Colin, C., Markessis, E., Radeau, M., Deltenre, P., & Serniclaes, W. (2011). The development of categorical perception: Comparisons between voicing, colors and facial expressions. *Speech Communication, 53,* 417–430.

Jusczyk, P.W. (1993). From general to language-specific capacities: The WRAPSA model of how speech perception develops. *Journal of Phonetics, 21,* 3–28.

Jusczyk, P.W. (2000). *The discovery of spoken language.* Cambridge, MA: MIT Press.

Jusczyk, P.W., & Aslin, R.N. (1995). Infants' detection of the sound patterns of words in fluent speech. *Cognitive Psychology, 29,* 1–23.

Keidel, J.L., Jenison, R.L., Kluender, K.R., & Seidenberg, M.S. (2007). Does grammar constrain statistical learning? Commentary on Bonatti, Pena, Nespor, and Mehler (2005). *Psychological Science, 18,* 922–923.

Kuhl, P.K. (2000). Language, mind, and brain: Experience alters perception. In: Gazzaniga, M.S. (Ed.), *The New Cognitive Neurosciences,* 2nd ed., Cambridge, MA: MIT Press, 99–115.

Kuhl, P.K. (2004). Early language acquisition: Cracking the speech code. *Nature Reviews Neuroscience, 5*(11), 831–843.

Kuhl, P.K., Stevens, E., Hayashi, A., Deguchi, T., Kiritani, S., & Iverson, P. (2006). Infants show facilitation for native language phonetic perception between 6 and 12 months. *Developmental Science, 9,* 13–21.

Kuhl, P.K., Tsao, F.M., & Liu, H.M. (2003). Foreign-language experience in infancy: Effects of short-term exposure and social interaction on phonetic learning. *Proceedings of the National Academy of Sciences, 100,* 9096–9101.

Kuhl, P.K., Williams, K.A., Lacerda, F., Stevens, K.N., & Lindblom, B. (1992). Linguistic experience alters phonetic perception in infants by 6 months of age. *Science, 255,* 606–608.

Ladefoged, P. (2001). *Vowels and consonants: An introduction to the sounds of language.* Oxford: Blackwell.

Lee, H.W., Rayner, K., & Pollatsek, A. (2002). The processing of consonants and vowels in reading: Evidence from the fast priming paradigm. *Psychonomic Bulletin & Review, 9,* 766–772.

MacKenzie, H., Curtin, S., & Graham, S.A. (2012). 12-month-olds' phonotactic knowledge guides their word–object mappings. *Child Development, 83,* 1129–1136.

Mandel, D.R., Jusczyk, P.W., & Pisoni, D.B. (1995). Infants' recognition of the sound patterns of their own names. *Psychological Science, 6,* 314–317.

Mani, N., & Plunkett, K. (2007). Phonological specificity of vowels and consonants in early lexical representations. *Journal of Memory and Language, 57,* 252–272.

Mani, N., & Plunkett, K. (2008). 14-month-olds pay attention to vowels in novel words. *Developmental Science, 11,* 53–59.

Mani, N., & Plunkett, K. (2010). 12-month-olds know their cups from their keps and tups. *Infancy, 15,* 445–470.

Mattys, S., & Jusczyk, P.W. (2001). Do infants segment words or recurring contiguous patterns? *Journal of Experimental Psychology: Human Perception and Performance, 27,* 644–655.

Maye, J., Werker, J.F., & Gerken, L.A. (2002). Infant sensitivity to distributional information can affect phonetic discrimination. *Cognition, 82*(3), B101–B111.

Metsala, J.L. (1999). Young children's phonological awareness and nonword repetition as a function of vocabulary development. *Journal of Educational Psychology, 91,* 3–19.

Morgan, J.L., & Demuth, K. (1996). *Signal to syntax.* Mahwah, NJ: Erlbaum.

Narayan, C.R., Werker, J.F., & Beddor, P.S. (2010). The interaction between acoustic salience and language experience in developmental speech perception: Evidence from nasal place discrimination. *Developmental Science, 13,* 407–420.

Nazzi, T. (2005). Use of phonetic specificity during the acquisition of new words: Differences between consonants and vowels. *Cognition, 98,* 13–30.

Nazzi, T., & Bertoncini, J. (2009). Phonetic specificity in early lexical acquisition: New evidence from consonants in coda positions. *Language and Speech, 52,* 463–480.

Nazzi, T., Floccia, C., Moquet, B., & Butler, J. (2009). Bias for consonantal over vocalic information in French- and English-learning 30-month-olds: Crosslinguistic evidence in early word learning. *Journal of Experimental Child Psychology, 102,* 522–537.

Nazzi, T., & New, B. (2007). Beyond stop consonants: Consonantal specificity in early lexical acquisition. *Cognitive Development, 22,* 271–279.

Nazzi, T., & Polka, L. (in preparation). Consonant bias in learning of new vowel-initial words.

Nespor, M., Peña, M., & Mehler, J. (2003). On the different roles of vowels and consonants in speech processing and language acquisition. *Lingue e Linguaggio, 2,* 221–247.

New, B., Araujo, V., & Nazzi, T. (2008). Differential processing of consonants and vowels in lexical access through reading. *Psychological Science, 19,* 1223–1227.

New, B., & Nazzi, T. (2014). The time course of consonant and vowel processing during word recognition. *Language, Cognition and Neuroscience, 29*(2), 147–157.

Newport, E.L., & Aslin, R.N. (2004). Learning at a distance. I. Statistical learning of non-adjacent dependencies. *Cognitive Psychology, 48,* 127–162.

Nishibayashi, L.L., Goyet, L., & Nazzi, T. (2015). Early speech segmentation in French-learning infants: Monosyllabic words versus embedded syllables. *Language and Speech, 58*(3), 334–350.

Nishibayashi, L.-L. & Nazzi, T. (in revision). Vowels then consonants: Emergence of a consonant bias in early word form segmentation.

Pharao, N. (2011). Plosive reduction at the group level and in the individual speaker. In: Lee, W.-S., & Zee, E. (Eds.), *Proceedings of the International Congress of Phonetic Science XVII 2011*. Hong Kong: City University of Hong Kong, Department of Chinese, Translation and Linguistics. 1590–1593.

Polka, L., Colantonio, C., & Sundara, M. (2001). Cross-language perception of /d–ð/: Evidence for a new developmental pattern. *Journal of the Acoustical Society of America, 109*(5), 2190–2200.

Polka, L., & Werker, J.F. (1994). Developmental changes in perception of nonnative vowel contrasts. *Journal of Experimental Psychology: Human Perception and Performance, 20*, 421–435.

Poltrock, S., & Nazzi, T. (2015). Consonant/vowel asymmetry in early word form recognition. *Journal of Experimental Child Psychology, 131*, 135–148.

Rakison, D.H., & Oakes, L.M. (Eds.), (2003). *Early category and concept development: Making sense of the blooming buzzing confusion*. New York: Oxford University Press.

Repp, B.H. (1984). Categorical perception: Issues, methods, findings. In: N.J. Lass (Ed.), *Speech and language: Advances in basic research and practice*, Vol. 10. New York: Academic Press. 243–335.

Rivera-Gaxiola, M., Silva-Pereyra, J., & Kuhl, P.K. (2005). Brain potentials to native and non-native speech contrasts in 7- and 11-month-old American infants. *Developmental Science, 8*(2), 162–172.

Schwytay, J., & Höhle, B. (2012). Vowels and consonants in early word learning: Evidence for positional asymmetries in German learning 20-month-olds. Talk given at the *18th Biennal Meeting of the International Society for Infant Studies*, Minneapolis, USA, 7–9 June.

Soares, A.P., Perea, M., & Comesaña, M. (2014). Tracking the emergence of the consonant bias in visual-word recognition: Evidence with developing readers. *PLoS ONE, 9*(2), e88580.

Stager, C.L., & Werker, J.F. (1997). Infants listen for more phonetic detail in speech perception than in word-learning tasks. *Nature, 388*, 381–382.

Storkel, H.L. (2002). Restructuring of similarity neighbourhoods in the developing mental lexicon. *Journal of Child Language, 29*, 251–274.

Sundara, M., Polka, L., & Genesee, F. (2006). Language-experience facilitates discrimination of /d–ð/ in monolingual and bilingual acquisition of English. *Cognition, 100*(2), 369–388.

Swingley, D. (2005). 11-month-olds' knowledge of how familiar words sound. *Developmental Science, 8*, 432–443.

Swingley, D., & Aslin, R.N. (2000). Spoken word recognition and lexical representation in very young children. *Cognition, 76*, 147–166.

Swingley, D., & Aslin, R.N. (2002). Lexical neighborhoods and the word-form representations of 14-month-olds. *Psychological Science, 13*, 480–484.

Swoboda, P.J., Morse, P.A., & Leavitt, L.A. (1976). Continuous vowel discrimination in normal and at risk infants. *Child Development, 47*(2), 459–465.

Thiessen, E.D. (2007). The effect of distributional information on children's use of phonemic contrasts. *Journal of Memory and Language, 56*, 16–34.

Tincoff, R., & Jusczyk, P.W. (1999). Some beginnings of word comprehension in 6-month-olds. *Psychological Science, 10*(2), 172–175.

Tincoff, R., & Jusczyk, P.W. (2012). Six-month-olds comprehend words that refer to parts of the body. *Infancy, 17*(4), 432–444.

Toro, J.M., Nespor, M., Mehler, J., & Bonatti, L. (2008). Finding words and rules in a speech stream: Functional differences between vowels and consonants. *Psychological Science, 19*, 137–144.

Toro, J.M., Shukla, M., Nespor, M., & Endress, A.D. (2008). The quest for generalizations over consonants: Asymmetries between consonants and vowels are not the by-product of acoustic differences. *Perception and Psychophysics, 70*(8), 1515–1525.

Van Ooijen, B. (1996). Vowel mutability and lexical selection in English: Evidence from a word reconstruction task. *Memory & Cognition*, *24*, 573–583.

Vihman, M., Nakai, S., De Paolis, R., & Hallé, P. (2004). The role of accentual pattern in early lexical representation. *Journal of Memory and Language*, *50*, 336–353.

Walley, A., & Flege, J. (1999). Effects of lexical status on children's and adults' perception of native and non-native vowels. *Journal of Phonetics*, *27*, 307–332.

Werker, J.F., Fennell, C.T., Corcoran, K.M., & Stager, C.L. (2002). Infants' ability to learn phonetically similar words: Effects of age and vocabulary. *Infancy*, *3*, 1–30.

Werker, J.F., & Lalonde, C.E. (1988). Cross-language speech perception: Initial capabilities and developmental change. *Developmental Psychology*, *24*, 672–683.

Werker, J.F., & Tees, R.C. (1984a). Cross-language speech perception: Evidence for perceptual reorganization during the first year of life. *Infant Behavior and Development*, *7*, 49–63.

Werker, J.F., & Tees, R.C. (1984b). Phonemic and phonetic factors in adult cross-language speech perception. *Journal of the Acoustical Society of America*, *75*, 1866–1878.

White, K.S.. & Morgan, J. (2008). Sub-segmental detail in early lexical representations. *Journal of Memory and Language*, *59*, 114–32.

Yeung, H.H., & Nazzi, T. (2014). Object labeling influences infant phonetic learning and generalization. *Cognition*, *132*(2), 151–163.

Yeung, H.H., & Werker, J.F. (2009). Learning words' sounds before learning how words sound: 9-month-old infants use distinct objects as cues to categorize speech information. *Cognition*, *113*(2), 234–243.

Yoshida, K.A., Fennell, C.T., Swingley, D., & Werker, J.F. (2009). Fourteen-month-old infants learn similar-sounding words. *Developmental Science*, *12*(3), 412–418.

Zesiger, P., & Jöhr, J. (2011). Les représentations phonologiques des mots chez le jeune enfant. *Enfance*, *3*, 293–309.

4

SPEECH SEGMENTATION

Sven L. Mattys and Heather Bortfeld

Introduction

Inspection of a speech waveform does not reveal clear correlates of what the listener perceives as word boundaries. Yet the absence of word boundary markers hardly poses a problem for listeners, as the subjective experience of speech is not of continuity but, rather, of discreteness – a sequence of individual words. This chapter is concerned with the perceptual and cognitive mechanisms underlying conversion of continuity into discreteness, namely speech segmentation.

Or so goes the story. Over the past 20 years, the concept of segmentation has been challenged on two fronts. First, how truly continuous is speech? Could the presence of clear boundary markers (e.g., pauses) be underestimated? This question is of particular importance for early stages of word learning, as infant-directed speech is known to have communication-oriented characteristics, some of which could guard against, or at least mitigate, continuity. Second, even if speech requires segmentation, to what extent does it need to be investigated separately from word recognition? Do we need to construe segmentation as a battery of cues and mechanisms, or is it an emergent property of lexical activation, an epiphenomenon of lexical competition?

These questions motivate the structure of this chapter. We argue that much depends on whether the language system has achieved a mature, steady state, is in a process of development, or is facing suboptimal listening conditions.

Segmentation in the mature system

For adult native speakers, segmentation consists of correctly mapping sound strings onto word representations, a process undermined by the temporal distribution of sounds and by lexical embeddedness (Cutler, 2012). The fact that the distribution of auditory information is time-bound and transient means that lexical activation must start before an entire word has been heard, resulting in multiple simultaneous activations. Embeddedness only exacerbates the problem. Some 84% of polysyllabic English words have at least one shorter word embedded in them ("captain" contains "cap"); indeed, most short words are embedded in longer ones (McQueen et al., 1995). Spurious words are also found across word boundaries ("belt" in "bell tower"). Corpus data in English reveal that more than a third of all word boundaries contain at least one embedded word (Roach et al., 1993).

Mechanisms underlying speech segmentation have been investigated from two standpoints: as an emergent property of lexical competition and contextual expectations (lexical and post-lexical phenomena) and as the product of a constellation of segmental and prosodic cues (non-lexical phenomena).

Segmentation as a lexical (and post-lexical) phenomenon

Word and world knowledge often constrain segmentation. For instance, "The goose trader needs a licence" might contain the spurious words "goo", "stray", "tray", "knee", "lie", "ice", in addition to the intended words, but only the intended words make the utterance lexically and semantically viable. Activation of the spurious words is therefore likely to be weak, especially in later parts of the sentence. Likewise, although cases of fully overlapping segmentation alternatives exist (e.g., "known ocean" vs, "no notion"), they are rare and usually get disambiguated by syntactic and/or semantic context. Segmentation is also constrained by whether or not the outcome *could be* a real word. In competition-based models, the possible-word constraint (Norris et al., 1997) reduces activation of word candidates that create phonologically impossible adjacent words. For instance, in "black bird", "lack" will be disfavoured not only because the preceding "b" portion is not an existing English word but also because it violates English morphological rules.

Modeling work demonstrates good segmentation performance through multiple lexical activation and competition (e.g., TRACE: McClelland & Elman, 1986; Shortlist: Norris, 1994). On this view, all words in running speech are temporarily activated, with relative activation levels fluctuating as a function of fit with the unfolding input. The activation of spurious words, possibly high at times (e.g., "goo" in "goose trader"), eventually is terminated through direct inhibition by better fitting competitors (TRACE) or dies down due to lack of sensory confirmation (Shortlist). A lexically guided process is effective for new words too. For instance, Dahan and Brent (1999) showed that listeners familiarized with five-syllable sequences (e.g., "dobuneripo") and three-syllable sequences embedded in the longer ones (e.g., "neripo"), subsequently better remembered a sequence corresponding with the remainder sequence (e.g., "dobu") than one that did not (e.g., "dobune"). Such segmentation-by-lexical-subtraction process likewise boosts first- and second-language learning (Bortfeld et al., 2005; White et al., 2010).

Semantic and syntactic expectations also provide constraints. Kim and colleagues (2012) showed that the segmentation of a stimulus ("along") was significantly determined by its sentential context ("along" in "try to get __" and "a long" in "it takes __ time"). Likewise, Mattys and associates (2007) found that segmentation of an ambiguous stimulus like "takespins" was influenced by whether the syntactic context suggested that the pivotal /s/ was a third-person inflection or the first phoneme of the object noun phrase.

Importantly, this knowledge-driven approach does not assign a specific computational status to segmentation, other than as the consequence of mechanisms associated with lexical competition and interactions with higher-order knowledge.

Segmentation as a non-lexical, cue-based, and probabilistic phenomenon

Although an effective mechanism in a majority of cases, lexical-driven segmentation fails in cases of multiple parses ("stray tissues"/"straight issues") and whenever new or unfamiliar words are encountered. Non-lexical cues fall within various categories. Some arise from distributional regularities within the lexicon (probabilistic phonotactics, lexical stress), and others operate independently (allophonic variations). Some are language-specific (generally those arising from regularities in the lexicon), and others are fairly constant across languages (some but not all rhythmic cues). Some align with actual word boundaries, and others contribute to word boundary detection only insofar as they align with phrase- or sentence-level boundaries (final lengthening). Because these categories are somewhat artificial and not mutually exclusive, we opt for a description based on whether non-lexical cues involve segmental, subsegmental, or suprasegmental regularities.

Segmental cues

Segmental cues refer to the probability that certain phonemes or sequences of phonemes align with word boundaries. For instance, the /j/ sound in English is more likely to be word-medial or word-final than word-initial. Similarly, sequences rarely found at the beginning of words (/mr/) are likely to be interpreted as straddling a word boundary (McQueen, 1998; Tagliapietra et al., 2009). These regularities are referred to as phonotactic cues. Since such regularities originate in the phonological structure of a language, sequences of phonemes perceived as legitimate word boundaries vary from language to language.

Rules about word-internal segmental harmony can also point to boundaries. In Finnish, for example, rules of harmony prevent certain categories of vowels from co-occurring within a word. Thus, assuming that vowel V_i cannot be found within the same word as vowel V_{ii}, a sequence like CV_iCV_{ii} could not constitute a single word; instead, it would have to include a word boundary somewhere between the two vowels (Suomi et al., 1997; Vroomen et al., 1998). Although they are weaker heuristics, segmental sandhis – a broad range of phonological changes that occur at morpheme or word boundaries – also cue segmentation. Liaison, for instance, is the addition of a segment between two words to avoid a non-permissible sequence of sounds. For example, while "petit frère" (younger brother) is produced as /pətifʀɐ/, "petit ami" (boyfriend) is produced as /pətit̪ami/, where /t/ is inserted between the two words to avoid a clash between /i/ and /a/. Since the most common liaising phonemes in French are /t/, /z/, and /n/, the occurrence of those sounds in continuous speech could be used as cues to word boundaries (Tremblay & Spinelli, 2014). Note that liaison-driven segmentation may partly be accounted for by acoustic differences between liaison phonemes and their non-liaison equivalents (Spinelli et al., 2003).

While lab-based findings show that segmentation is aided by listeners' sensitivity to phonotactic regularities, they represent an idealized view of how words are produced in everyday speech. Because conversational speech is plagued with phoneme deletions (Schuppler et al., 2011), insertions (Warner & Weber, 2001) and alterations, such as contextual variants (Janse et al., 2007) or phonological assimilation (Ohala, 1990), phonotactic statistics derived from lexical databases or transcribed corpora are only approximate. Indeed, we will argue that such expectations form a relatively minor influence on segmentation.

Subsegmental cues

The acoustic realization of a given phoneme (allophonic variant) can change from utterance to utterance. Some of this variation is reliably associated with word boundaries. We already mentioned that liaison phonemes in French are acoustically distinguishable from non-liaison phonemes, such that their acoustic signature could cue word junctures. Subsegmental cues allow listeners to distinguish phrase pairs ("dernier onion – dernier rognon" in French; "di amanti – diamanti" in Italian; "grey tanker – great anchor" in English) through a variety of phonetic processes such as word-onset glottalization (/ʔ/anchor), word-onset aspiration (/ʰ/tanker) and devoicing (in /r/ in "nitrate"). Position-specific durational contrasts (longer/pai/ in "high pay][per month . . .", where][is a phrase boundary, than in "paper") and changes in articulatory strength (phonemes are more weakly coarticulated across word boundaries than within words) provide additional cues.

The advantage of these subsegmental cues is that they supply information about word boundaries where lexical information cannot. Empirical evidence for listeners' sensitivity to these cues is abundant (e.g., Christophe et al., 2004; Davis et al., 2002; Shatzman & McQueen, 2006). However, in everyday listening conditions, lexically ambiguous phrases (e.g., "nitrate" vs. "night rate") are seldom heard outside of a disambiguating sentential context (e.g., "The soil contained a high concentration of nitrate."), which makes the actual contribution of subsegmental cues perhaps less substantial than laboratory speech research suggests. Furthermore, the reliability of subsegmental cues for segmentation is difficult to quantify. There are substantial individual variations in how systematically and fully speakers realize allophonic variations. Moreover, allophonic variations differ markedly in their acoustic salience, some showing clear qualitative contrasts (glottalization) and others showing small quantitative contrasts (lengthening). Finally, while some allophonic variations are chiefly language-general (final lengthening), most are language-specific (aspiration, glottalization). Thus, languages differ considerably in the number, type, and effectiveness of the sub-lexical cues they provide. As with segmental cues, subsegmental cues act as supplementary heuristics rather than deterministic boundary markers.

Suprasegmental cues

Suprasegmental cues are variations in duration, fundamental frequency, and amplitude that coincide with word boundaries either proximally or distally. Lengthening is found within the word, phrase, and sentence domains (Wightman et al., 1992). A significant challenge for a speech recognizer, however, is that lengthening has been documented at both the initial and the final edges of domains. However, lengthening within a syllable may be interpretable as a word onset as opposed to a word offset by taking the distribution of the durational effect into account (Monaghan et al., 2013; White, 2014).

Fundamental frequency ($F0$), the acoustic source of perceived pitch, shows a high degree of correlation with major syntactic boundaries (Vaissière, 1983) and hence with the boundaries of words at the edge of syntactic constituents. Pitch movements that specifically align with word boundaries, independent of syntactic boundaries, are more elusive and are often constrained by other factors. For instance, Welby (2007) showed that the early rise in $F0$ typically found at the left edge of French content words cues the beginning of a new word, but this effect is modulated by other suprasegmental cues (phoneme duration) and lexical frequency. The locus of pitch movements relative to word boundaries is disputed, even within a single language. Using an artificial language learning paradigm (Saffran et al., 1996a), Tyler and Cutler (2009) showed that French listeners used right-edge rather than left-edge pitch movements as word boundary cues. English listeners showed the opposite pattern, and Dutch listeners used both left- and right-edge pitch movements. Although discrepancies may be partly due to differences in materials, tasks, and methods of pitch manipulation, it is clear that $F0$ alone provides limited support for the detection of word boundaries (see Toro et al., 2009, for additional evidence).

The combination of suprasegmental cues provides a stronger heuristic, such as is the case for lexical stress, the accentuation of syllables within words. Languages differ in the suprasegmental features ($F0$, duration, intensity) contributing to stress and the position of typically stressed syllables. Within a language, however, stress can be a highly reliable cue for word boundaries. In so-called fixed-stress languages, where stress always falls in a particular position (fixed word–final stress in Hungarian), inference based on stress should lead to high word boundary detection. In free-stress languages (English, Dutch, Italian), where stress placement varies, predominant stress positions can be used as a probabilistic cue. For instance, the predominance of stress-initial words is exploited in English (Cutler & Norris, 1988) and in Dutch (Vroomen et al., 1996). Languages for which stress is not a contrastive feature might provide rhythmic cues tied to their own phonology (syllables for French, Banel & Bacri, 1997; morae for Japanese, Otake et al., 1993). Cutler (2012) provides an extensive review of how listeners use rhythm in general and lexical stress in particular to infer word boundaries.

While these suprasegmental cues can be characterized as proximal prosody, distal prosody leads to grouping and segmentation of speech materials several syllables after the prosodic cues themselves. Inspired by research on auditory grouping, Dilley and McAuley (2008) created auditory sequences beginning with two stress-initial words and ending with four syllables that could form words in more than one way. They then manipulated the duration and/or the $F0$ of both of the first five syllables in order to create a rhythmic pattern to induce either a weak-strong-weak (WSW) or strong-weak-strong (SWS) grouping in the final un-manipulated syllables. When participants were asked to report the last word of the sequence, they produced more monosyllabic words in the SWS-inducing condition and more disyllabic words in the WSW-inducing condition. The manipulation of either duration, or $F0$, worked, and the combination of both cues yielded an even larger effect. These results and others (Brown et al., 2011) are groundbreaking because they reveal anticipatory segmentation mechanisms that generate place holders for words not yet heard. It is precisely those types of mechanisms that could disambiguate sentence-final phrases like "night rate" and "nitrate", alongside the sentential context and the acoustic realisation of the test words themselves.

Segmentation as a multi-cue integration phenomenon

The investigation of cues in isolation highlights sources of information that the perceptual system can use. How they are used – if at all – is another matter. Likewise, computational models offer suggestions about how segmentation can be achieved parsimoniously, not necessarily how segmentation actually happens. For instance, Cairns and colleagues (1997) devised a neural network that correctly detected a third of the word boundaries in the London-Lund corpus of conversational English relying solely on phonotactic regularities. In contrast, TRACE assumes a pre-existing lexicon, entirely eschewing the involvement of non-lexical cues by making segmentation a by-product of lexical competition and selection (Frauenfelder & Peeters, 1990). Perhaps as a compromise, Shortlist (Norris, 1994) relies on lexically driven segmentation (per TRACE) but further fine-tunes it via statistical regularities (lexical stress, phonotactics) and corpus allophones (Shortlist B, Norris & McQueen, 2008). When between-word transitional probabilities are taken into account, the performance of computational models increases even further (Goldwater et al., 2009).

Although cues are likely to converge rather than diverge, pitting cues against one another has revealed much about their relative weights. Drawing on a battery of perceptual experiments, Mattys and colleagues (2005, 2007) demonstrated that listeners rely on lexical, syntactic, and contextual information whenever listening conditions permit (intelligible speech and meaningful sentences) in both read and conversational speech (White et al., 2012). Segmentation then simply "falls out" of word recognition, as implemented in TRACE. Sub-lexical cues intervene only when lexical and contextual information is absent or incomplete – common in laboratory experiments but unusual in real life. And stress is used only as a last-resort, when intelligibility is too compromised to provide sufficient lexical, segmental, and subsegmental evidence.

With respect to ranking the weight of non-lexical cues, Newman and colleagues (2011) have argued that subsegmental cues (word-onset vowel glottalization) are as powerful as Norris and associates' (1997) Possible Word Constraint but that segmental probabilities (permissible syllable-final vowels) rank lower. In contrast, the robustness of distal prosody has been observed in the face of conflicting intensity, duration, $F0$ cues (Heffner et al., 2013), and even semantic information (Dilley et al., 2010), although there is evidence that these cues trade off as a function of their internal magnitude (Heffner et al., 2013).

Segmentation in the developing language system

The emergence of a mental lexicon is fundamental to how the speech signal is processed. Several decades of research have converged on the view that infants gradually integrate a range of cues in the service of segmentation. In isolation, these cues would be insufficient; together, they allow the child to segment in progressively greater detail. Several questions are relevant to understanding this process. First, to what extent is each cue reliably present in the infant's input? Second, can infants perceive and profitably use these cues? Finally, how do the cues interact? These questions are now addressed.

Cue presence

For a language user, the most elementary juncture marker is a silent pause. Silent pauses are usually found at boundaries between utterances, clauses, and phrases (Goldman-Eisler, 1972). Their contribution is particularly notable in infant-directed speech because utterances in that form are particularly short (Fernald et al., 1989; Snow, 1972). Likewise, corpus research has shown that words in isolation (e.g., "Milk!") constitute approximately 10% of the utterances that parents address to their infant (Brent & Siskind, 2001).

The features of infant-directed speech further increase its overall salience, providing a scaffold for infants to learn words by highlighting particular forms in the auditory stream. Infants' changing sensitivity reflects the emergence of a lexicon as well, with the development of stable word-form representations providing the necessary first step towards robust segmentation. For example, 6-month-old infants prefer the repetitive structure of infant-directed speech, whereas their earlier preference is for its prosodic elements (McRoberts et al., 2009). This shift in focus from prosodic to repetitive elements may be an indication of when infants transition from processing the general characteristics of speech to recognizing its components (i.e., words). This is consistent with findings showing that infants discriminate among words relatively early in life (Bergelson & Swingley, 2012; Tincoff & Jusczyk,

1999). Factors that add to the nascent lexicon are highly familiar items in the input (Bortfeld et al., 2005; Mandel et al., 1995), inclusion of word-like units in varying sentence frames (Gomez, 2002), and consistent production of the infant-directed rhythmic form (Ma et al., 2011).

Cue use

A pioneering demonstration of infant speech segmentation at 7.5 months (Jusczyk & Aslin, 1995) focused on the importance of emergent word knowledge well before those words are associated with meaning. In this study, infants were familiarized with a pair of novel words, such as "cup" and "feet", and then tested on their recognition of the words in passages. Results showed that infants listened longer to passages containing familiarized words compared with those containing novel words, demonstrating quite early segmentation ability. Subsequent studies using modifications of this paradigm have revealed limitations on infants' performance when words change in emotion, talker gender, or fundamental frequency (Bortfeld & Morgan, 2010; Houston & Jusczyk, 2000; Singh et al., 2004, 2008).

Other limitations include the finding that infants are able to segment only words that conform to the predominant stress pattern of their language (Jusczyk, 1999). For example, Weber and colleagues (2004) compared 4- and 5-month-old German-exposed infants with German-speaking adults specifically focusing on participants' mismatch negativity (MMN) responses to consonant-vowel-consonant-vowel sequences produced with either trochaic stress (stress placed on the initial syllable, which is predominant in German) or iambic stress (stress placed on the second syllable, which is atypical in German). Half of the participants experienced the trochaically stressed words as "standards" and the iambically stressed words as the MMN-dependent "deviants". The reverse was true for the other half of the participants. For the adults, an MMN response occurred whether the deviant was a trochaic or iambic sequence, suggesting that adults were sensitive to both stress patterns. However, for 5-month-olds, an MMN response was observed for deviant trochaic stimuli only, while neither stress type provoked a significant MMN response in the 4-month-olds. This suggests that by five months, infants are sensitive to the most common stress patterns of their exposure language, though they have yet to reach adult-like discrimination abilities for unfamiliar stress patterns (see also Hohle et al., 2009).

Cue interaction

Infants are sensitive to statistical regularities in their environment, using them as a guide to structure (e.g., Saffran et al., 1996b). However, statistical cues fail when variation in word length is introduced (Johnson & Tyler, 2010) or when they clash with subsegmental or stress cues (Johnson & Jusczyk, 2001). There are many other such interactions. For example, Mersad and Nazzi (2012) created an artificial language made of words that were varied (rather than fixed) in length. Consistent with

Johnson and Tyler's (2010) finding, 8-month-olds were hindered in their ability to segment words of varying lengths when presented with no other cues. However, they could segment them when the words were preceded with a familiar word (e.g., "maman"). In other words, infants were able to use the familiar item as a top-down guide for parsing the more complex signal.

With respect to the structure of cues used in the mature system, the developmental trajectory appears to follow a weighting system roughly opposite to that followed in adult processing (Figure 4.1). Stress and distributional regularities provide an early, albeit coarse first pass at the signal (Jusczyk et al., 1999; Saffran et al., 1996b). Although it is unclear whether sensitivity to stress spawns sensitivity to distributional regularities (Jusczyk, 1999) or vice versa (Thiessen & Saffran, 2003), these basic segmentation mechanisms appear to be progressively phased out by more subtle segmental and acoustic-phonetic cues by around 9 months of age (Morgan &

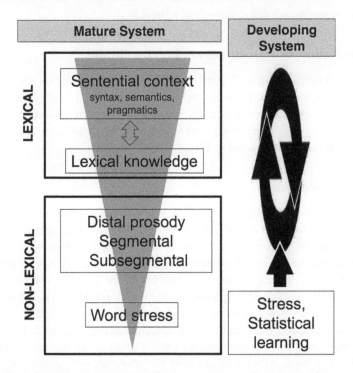

FIGURE 4.1 Schematic representation of primary segmentation cues in the mature and developing language systems. The relative weights of the cues in the mature speech system are symbolized by the width of the grey triangle (wider = greater weight). The developmental trajectory of the cues is illustrated by the black arrows. Reliance on stress and statistical learning cues is initially predominant. These, along with other non-lexical cues, promote the acquisition of a small vocabulary, which, in return, leads to the discovery of additional sub-lexical cues. Over time, reliance on non-lexical cues is downplayed in favour of lexical and contextual information (figure revised from Mattys et al. [2005]).

Saffran, 1995; Mattys et al., 1999). As these promote development of a lexicon, they become secondary to lexically driven segmentation, reflecting a move toward an increasingly adult-like weighting system.

These findings reveal both impressive capability and serious limitations on early word recognition. The second half of the first year of life clearly represents an important period of transition for language learning, as the ability to track spoken words in running speech and to detect repetitions of those words in different contexts is likely to be a prerequisite to later mapping of those words onto meaning. Indeed, longitudinal evidence for a link between early segmentation ability, on the one hand, and vocabulary growth at 2 years and higher-order language measures at 4 to 6 years on the other hand, confirms the constraining role of speech segmentation for successful language development (Newman et al., 2006). Important questions remain regarding the specific mechanisms linking the two and, perhaps more critically, how limitations in early segmentation might (negatively) impact the subsequent emergence and expansion of a vocabulary.

Segmentation in adverse (everyday) conditions

Not surprisingly, a majority of segmentation studies have focused on unrealistically ideal listening conditions. Comparatively few have examined how mechanisms are modulated by everyday conditions (noise, divided attention). Next we examine such modulations following Mattys and colleagues' (2012) typology of adverse conditions. A summary is depicted in Figure 4.2.

Source degradation

Perhaps the most detailed analysis of the link between source (speaker) degradation and speech segmentation comes from the work by Liss and colleagues on dysarthric speech perception. Dysarthrias are motor speech disorders subsequent to central or peripheral nervous system abnormalities such as Parkinson's disease or Huntington's chorea (for detailed nomenclature, see Darley et al., 1969), characterized by segmental, subsegmental, and suprasegmental disturbances. Liss et al. (1998) showed that healthy participants listening to English dysarthric speech made substantial use of the alternation between perceived weak and strong syllables to hypothesize word boundaries: perceived boundaries were inserted before strong syllables and deleted before weak syllables, in line with the dominant stress pattern of English (see also Cutler & Butterfield, 1992). However, Liss and associates (2000) found that stress-based segmentation was far more effective in dysarthrias that preserved rhythmic contrasts (hypokinetic) than dysarthrias that exhibited equal-and-even stress (ataxic). In a subsequent resynthesis study of non-dysarthric speech, Spitzer and colleagues (2007) demonstrated that neutralizing $F0$ (a suprasegmental cue) and blurring vowel identity (a segmental cue) had the most detrimental impact on listeners' adherence to stress-based segmentation. Equalizing vowel duration (a subsegmental and suprasegmental cue) had almost no effect. These analyses specify

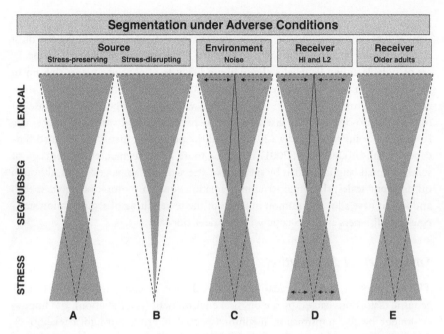

FIGURE 4.2 Schematic modulations of Figure 4.1 as a function of adverse listening conditions. As in Figure 4.1, the relative weights of the cues (lexical knowledge, segmental/subsegmental cues, stress) are symbolized by the width of the grey triangle (wider = greater weight). For comparison, the dark dashed outline illustrates optimal listening conditions, as shown in Figure 4.1. (A) Degradation at the source preserving the prosodic features necessary to perceive and use stress contrasts for segmentation, e.g., hypokinetic dysarthria or accented speech originating from the same rhythmic class as the target. (B) Degradation at the source disrupting or neutralizing stress contrast, e.g., ataxic dysarthria or accented speech originating from a different rhythmic class than the target. (C) Environmental degradation due to background noise. While reliance on stress is generally increased under noise, the contribution of lexical knowledge can be compromised in very low signal-to-noise ratios. (D) Receiver limitations due to hearing impairment (HI) or non-native (L2) knowledge of the target language. Reliance on lexical knowledge and stress in those cases is variable and primarily determined by the hearing impairment etiology and severity, the type of hearing device, the degree of overlap between L1 and the target language, and the level of L2 proficiency. (E) Older adults' generally increased reliance on lexical (and contextual) knowledge and stress contrast. For all depicted cases, note a reduction in reliance on segmental/subsegmental cues compared to segmentation in optimal conditions.

how naturally occurring speech degradations can turn lower-tier segmentation cues (Mattys et al., 2005) into powerful tools in the face of reduced intelligibility.

Accented speech constitutes another type of source degradation in that it departs from native or regional expectations on subsets (or all) of the non-lexical segmentation cues reviewed earlier – leaving aside the issue of lexical and syntactic deviations. The cost of processing a non-native/unfamiliar accent compared to a native/familiar accent has been documented comprehensively (Munro & Derwing, 1995). Alongside phoneme miscategorization (Cutler et al., 2005), the most challenging cross-accent mismatch is likely to be prosodic. For instance, as speakers of syllable-timed languages (French) are likely to apply their native rhythm to the production of a non-native stress-timed language (English), word-initial stress cues normally used by native English listeners will no longer be available. Cases of misleading prosody can likewise be found between regional variations of a single language. For instance, Cutler (2012) raised the possibility that syllable-timed Singapore English (Deterding, 2001) might be more easily segmented by speakers of syllable-timed languages than by speakers of stress-timed languages. Thus, although on different scales, rhythmic structure violations due to motor-disordered speech and accent have a lot in common in terms of the reweighting of segmentation strategies that listeners apply to cope with the deviations.

Environmental degradation

This category includes degradations of speech due to competing signals (noise), acoustic distortions caused by the physical environment (reverberation), and impoverishment by the transmission medium (spectral filtering through a telephone). Segmentation research has focused mainly on broadband noise. Mattys and associates (2005) found that the effectiveness of lexical-semantic knowledge drops steadily as a function of noise level, probably reflecting the increasingly diffuse lexical activity that results from inaccurately encoded sensory information. The greater reliance on non-lexical cues resulting from lexical-access failure depends on the regions of the frequency spectrum where signal and noise overlap. Generally speaking, non-lexical cues consisting of broad variations over relatively long stretches of the signal fare best. For example, suprasegmental cues such as stress and $F0$ movements are resilient to 5- to 10-dB signal-to-noise ratios (Mattys, 2004; Smith et al., 1989; Welby, 2007). In contrast, coarticulatory cues and transitional probabilities show greater vulnerability (Mattys et al., 2005), with the former more fragile than the latter (Fernandes et al., 2007).

The generalizability of these results is unclear, however. Disruption caused by even the loudest broadband steady-state noise is negligible if it coincides with energy dips or highly redundant portions of the signal. Conversely, a brief burst of energy in a critical frequency range could have consequences cascading from misheard allophones to sentence misinterpretation. Thus, unlike cue re-ranking in the face of dysarthric speech, cue re-ranking under noise is highly dependent on complex interactions between the spectro-temporal structure of the noise and the phonetic, lexical, and semantic composition of the signal (Bronkhorst, 2000).

It should be noted that correctly perceiving speech in the presence of noise should be particularly challenging for infants and young children. And indeed, 66% of parents report talking to their infants while other family members are talking at the same time (Barker & Newman, 2004). Not surprisingly, signal-to-noise ratio (SNR) is an important factor to consider. Children presumably cannot rely on top-down information to the same extent as adults (Newman, 2006; Nittrouer & Boothroyd, 1990), which means that they should weigh other cues in the signal more heavily (Fallon et al., 2000). This, in turn, means that they may be affected by noise much more or at least differently than adults. As evidence of this, Newman (2004) found that 5-month-old infants failed to recognize their own names in a multi-talker stream unless the masking signal was at least 10 dB below the target signal. Moreover, with a 0 dB SNR, she found that infants performed at chance and continued to do so until at least the end of the first year. But this changes quickly as children begin to acquire the lexicon. For example, children's word learning between 2.5 and 3 years was equally likely whether the learning took place in quiet, +5, or 0 dB SNR (Dombroski & Newman, 2014). Although these latter findings bode well for language development in spite of the varied environments in which children find themselves, the input they receive is a critical factor in the rate and success of this development.

Receiver limitations

In this section, we review findings from hearing-impaired, non-native, and older listeners, groups with contrasting, though not fully orthogonal segmentation challenges.

Segmentation in hearing-impaired listeners

Relatively little is known about the segmentation limitations faced by hearing aid and cochlear implant (CI) users. Research suggests that hearing device users rely on higher-order knowledge to fill gaps in the impoverished signal. For instance, using noise-vocoded speech (i.e., substitution of frequency bands with amplitude-modulated noise, Shannon et al., 1995) as a simulation of CI input, Davis and colleagues (2005) showed that low-level interpretation of the distorted signal was better when it contained known and meaningful words than when it contained non-words. Thus, to the extent that contextual information is available from the distorted signal, it is likely that lexically driven segmentation mechanisms are primary.

Because hearing devices alter spectral rather than temporal aspects of the signal, segmental, allophonic, and $F0$ cues to word boundaries are more affected than durational cues. Given the contribution of $F0$ to the perception of stress contrast in English (Spitzer et al., 2007), stress-based segmentation could potentially be seriously compromised by CI. Indeed, Spitzer et al. (2009) showed that the detrimental effect of flattening $F0$ on stress-based segmentation was more pronounced for normal-hearing and hearing-impaired individuals with residual low-frequency hearing than for CI users. The authors interpreted this result as showing that $F0$ representation in the CI group was poor to start with, and hence flattening $F0$ had little effect. This conclusion, however, must be restricted to languages in which stress is realised mainly through $F0$. Stress-based segmentation of languages where stress correlates with syllable lengthening rather than $F0$ is likely to remain comparatively robust.

To a large extent, the segmentation problems that CI users face are comparable, albeit on a more dramatic scale, to those faced by people listening to accented speech: The distortions affect some sounds more than others, and they do so systematically. The predictable nature of such distortions makes correction through perceptual learning possible, unlike conditions in which the signal is masked by random noise. Thus, the study of speech segmentation through hearing devices is more likely to make headway if it is investigated in the context of progressive cue recalibration than if it is seen solely from the perspective of signal impoverishment.

Segmentation in non-native (L2) listeners

Although comparable to the problems faced by infant learners, the segmentation challenge faced by L2 listeners involves substantial differences. On the one hand, L2 listeners know a lot more about language (in general) than infants do, and they are likely to be literate. On the other hand, the segmentation cues of a native language (L1) can be at odds with those of L2, thus making the mastery of L2 a matter of both learning the segmentation cues of L2 and suppressing those of L1.

Not unlike infants, non-native speakers use their growing L2 lexicon to discover new words. For instance, White and associates (2010) showed that adult L1 Hungarian speakers learning English used known English words to segment adjacent sound sequences. Importantly, this segmentation-by-lexical-subtraction process applied even when stress cues were inconsistent with it. Given that Hungarian is a fixed-stress language (initial stress in all content words), this provides clear evidence for the primacy of lexically driven (over non-lexical) cues.

The success of L2 segmentation in the absence of lexical information depends on the respective hierarchies of non-lexical cues in L1 and L2. In general, languages with similar junctural regularities (comparable phonotactic rules or stress placement) will facilitate the transfer of segmentation strategies, whereas those with divergent regularities may create interference. The cost of persevering with L2-inappropriate cues has been shown for phonotactic regularities (Weber & Cutler, 2006), acoustic-phonetic cues (Tremblay & Spinelli, 2014) and stress (Sanders et al., 2002a; Tremblay et al., 2012). Thus, the process of becoming a proficient L2 listener involves not only vocabulary growth and syntactic learning (Sanders et al., 2002a, 2003) but also increased control over potentially contradictory sets of non-lexical segmentation strategies.

Segmentation in older listeners

There are two theoretical reasons to be interested in segmentation in older listeners. First, aging is accompanied with a steady decline in auditory abilities, particularly high-frequency perception, temporal processing, and sound stream segregation (CHABA, 1988). Second, vocabulary shows comparatively little decline (Singer et al., 2003). This combination of decline and stability suggests that segmentation is likely to become increasingly lexically driven in later years, with segmental and subsegmental cues becoming less impactful. Interestingly, the perception of suprasegmental patterns such as stress is relatively well preserved (Baum, 2003; Wingfield et al., 2000), thus making segmentation in older adults possibly a lexico-prosodic matter.

Finally, the large literature on perceptual and cognitive decline in older adults indicates a heightened sensitivity to noise and cognitive load (Burke & Shafto, 2008). Therefore, segmentation challenges are likely to be amplified under conditions of environmental degradation, especially when these tax working memory (Rönnberg et al., 2010), another declining faculty in older adults (McDaniel et al., 2008). Recent research by Weiss and colleagues (2010) suggests that resolving conflicts between segmentation cues might require increased processing resources. Given age-related decline in cognitive capacity (Craik & Byrd, 1982), cue conflict is likely to be particularly challenging for older adults.

Conclusion

Speech segmentation is an elusive construct insofar as it is often little more than a by-product of word recognition. In that sense, segmentation is implicitly built into models of speech recognition. However, segmentation arises as a concrete challenge whenever the interface between signal and lexical representations fails. In a narrow sense, the goal of this chapter was to review the factors at the root of such failures. These included lexical embeddedness, a developing lexicon or language system (L1 or L2), input degradation, and auditory limitations. Our contention is that the extent to which segmental, subsegmental, and suprasegmental cues influence segmentation can be predicted based on the specific characteristics of each of these factors, as well as the statistical structure of the language. Modelling speech segmentation remains an ambitious enterprise, however, because the relative weights of lexical and non-lexical information are likely to change on a moment-by-moment basis during the unfolding of speech. Online experimental measures of segmentation such as eye movements (e.g., Tremblay, 2011) and electrophysiological brain responses (e.g., Cunillera et al., 2009; Sanders et al., 2002b) are providing finer analyses of such temporal fluctuations. Likewise, significant advances in understanding the segmentation process can be made through a better appreciation of the dynamic flow of information between layers of the language system. Recent studies relying on causality analyses of magnetoencephalographic (MEG) and electroencephalographic (EEG) data during speech perception tasks (Gow et al., 2008, 2009) are providing a useful hypothetical functional architecture in which segmentation can be further analysed.

References

Banel, M. H., & Bacri, N. (1997). Reconnaissance de la parole et indices de segmentation métriques et phonotactiques. *L'Année psychologique, 97*, 77–112.
Barker, B. A., & Newman, R. S. (2004). Listen to your mother! The role of talker familiarity in infant streaming. *Cognition, 94*, B45–53.

Baum, S. R. (2003). Age differences in the influence of metrical structure on phonetic identification. *Speech Communication, 39*, 231–242.

Bergelson, E., & Swingley, D. (2012). At 6–9 months, human infants know the meanings of many common nouns. *Proceedings of the National Academy of Sciences, 109*, 3253–3258.

Bortfeld, H., & Morgan, J. (2010). Is early word-form processing stress-full? How natural variability supports recognition. *Cognitive Psychology, 60*, 241–266.

Bortfeld, H., Morgan, J. L., Golinkoff, R., & Rathbun, K. (2005). Mommy and me: Familiar names help launch babies into speech-stream segmentation. *Psychological Science, 16*, 298–304.

Brent, M. R., & Siskind, J. M. (2001). The role of exposure to isolated words in early vocabulary development. *Cognition, 81*, B33–B44.

Bronkhorst, A. W. (2000). The cocktail party phenomenon: A review of research on speech intelligibility in multiple-talker conditions. *Acta Acustica, 86*, 117–128.

Brown, M., Salverda, A. P., Dilley, L. C., & Tanenhaus, M. K. (2011). Expectations from preceding prosody influence segmentation in online sentence processing. *Psychonomic Bulletin & Review, 18*, 1189–1196.

Burke, D. M., & Shafto, M. A. (2008). Language and aging. In F. I. M. Craik & T. A. Salthouse (Eds.), *The handbook of aging and cognition* (3rd ed., pp. 373–443). New York: Psychology Press.

Cairns, P., Shillcock, R., Chater, N., & Levy, J. (1997). Bootstrapping word boundaries: A bottom-up corpus-based approach to speech segmentation. *Cognitive Psychology, 33*, 111–153.

Christophe, A., Peperkamp, S., Pallier, C., Block, E., & Mehler, J. (2004). Phonological phrase boundaries constrain lexical access I. Adult data. *Journal of Memory and Language, 51*, 523–547.

Committee on Hearing and Bioacoustics and Biomechanics (CHABA). (1988). Speech understanding and aging. *Journal of the Acoustical Society of America, 83*, 859–895.

Craik, F. I. M., & Byrd, M. (1982). Aging and cognitive deficits: The role of attentional resources. In F. I. M. Craik & S. Trehub (Eds.), *Aging and cognitive processes* (pp. 191–211). New York: Plenum Press.

Cunillera, T., Càmara, E., Toro, J. M., Marco-Pallares, J., Sebastián-Galles, N., Ortiz, H., Pujol, J., & Rodríguez-Fornells, A. (2009). Time course and functional neuroanatomy of speech segmentation in adults. *Neuroimage, 48*, 541–553.

Cutler, A. (2012). *Native listening: Language experience and the recognition of spoken words*. Cambridge, MA: MIT Press.

Cutler, A., & Butterfield, S. (1992). Rhythmic cues to speech segmentation: Evidence from juncture misperception. *Journal of Memory and Language, 31*, 218–236.

Cutler, A., & Norris, D. (1988). The role of strong syllables in segmentation for lexical access. *Journal of Experimental Psychology: Human Perception and Performance, 14*, 113–121.

Cutler, A., Smits, R., & Cooper, N. (2005). Vowel perception: Effects of non-native language vs. non-native dialect. *Speech communication, 47*, 32–42.

Dahan, D., & Brent, M. R. (1999). On the discovery of novel wordlike units from utterances: An artificial-language study with implications for native-language acquisition. *Journal of Experimental Psychology: General, 128*, 165–185.

Darley, F. L., Aronson, A. E., & Brown, J. R. (1969). Differential diagnostic patterns of dysarthria. *Journal of Speech, Language, and Hearing Research, 12*, 246–269.

Davis, M. H., Johnsrude, I. S., Hervais-Adelman, A., Taylor, K., & McGettigan, C. (2005). Lexical information drives perceptual learning of distorted speech: Evidence from the comprehension of noise-vocoded sentences. *Journal of Experimental Psychology: General, 134*, 222.

Davis, M. H., Marslen-Wilson, W. D., & Gaskell, M. G. (2002). Leading up the lexical garden path: Segmentation and ambiguity in spoken word recognition. *Journal of Experimental Psychology: Human Perception and Performance, 28,* 218–244.

Deterding, D. (2001). The measurement of rhythm: A comparison of Singapore and British English. *Journal of Phonetics, 29,* 217–230.

Dilley, L. C., Mattys, S. L., & Vinke, L. (2010). Potent prosody: Comparing the effects of distal prosody, proximal prosody, and semantic context on word segmentation. *Journal of Memory and Language, 63*(3), 274–294.

Dilley, L. C., & McAuley, J. D. (2008). Distal prosodic context affects word segmentation and lexical processing. *Journal of Memory and Language, 59,* 294–311.

Dombroski, J., & Newman, R. (2014). Toddlers' ability to map the meaning of new words in multi-talker environments. *Journal of the Acoustical Society of America, 136,* 2807–2815.

Fallon, M., Trehub, S. E., & Schneider, B. A. (2000). Children's perception of speech in multitalker babble. *Journal of the Acoustical Society of America, 108,* 3023–3029.

Fernald, A., Taeschner, T., Dunn, J., Papousek, M., Boysson-Bardies, B., & Fukui, I. (1989). A cross-language study of prosodic modifications in mothers' and fathers' speech to preverbal infants. *Journal of Child Language, 16,* 477–501.

Fernandes, T., Ventura, P., & Kolinsky, R. (2007). Statistical information and coarticulation as cues to word boundaries: A matter of signal quality. *Perception & Psychophysics, 69,* 856–864.

Frauenfelder, U. H., & Peeters, G. (1990). Lexical segmentation in TRACE: An exercise in simulation. In G. Altmann (Ed.), *Cognitive models of speech processing: Psycholinguistic and computational perspectives* (pp. 50–86). Cambridge, MA: MIT Press.

Goldman-Eisler, F. (1972). Pauses, clauses, sentences. *Language and Speech, 15,* 103–113.

Goldwater, S., Griffiths, T. L., & Johnson, M. (2009). A Bayesian framework for word segmentation: Exploring the effects of context. *Cognition, 112,* 21–54.

Gomez, R. (2002). Variability and detection of invariant structure. *Psychological Science, 13,* 431–436.

Gow Jr, D. W., Keller, C. J., Eskandar, E., Meng, N., & Cash, S. S. (2009). Parallel versus serial processing dependencies in the perisylvian speech network: A Granger analysis of intracranial EEG data. *Brain and Language, 110,* 43–48.

Gow Jr, D. W., Segawa, J. A., Ahlfors, S. P., & Lin, F. H. (2008). Lexical influences on speech perception: A Granger causality analysis of MEG and EEG source estimates. *Neuroimage, 43,* 614–623.

Heffner, C. C., Dilley, L. C., McAuley, J. D., & Pitt, M. A. (2013). When cues combine: How distal and proximal acoustic cues are integrated in word segmentation. *Language and Cognitive Processes, 28,* 1275–1302.

Hohle, B., Bijeljac-Babic, R., Herold, B., Weissenborn, J., & Nazzi, T. (2009). Language specific prosodic preferences during the first half year of life: Evidence from German and French infants. *Infant Behavior and Development, 32,* 262–274.

Houston, D. M., & Jusczyk, P. W. (2000). The role of talker specific information in word segmentation by infants. *Journal of Experimental Psychology: Human Perception and Performance, 26,* 1570–1582.

Janse, E., Nooteboom, S. G., & Quené, H. (2007). Coping with gradient forms of /t/-deletion and lexical ambiguity in spoken word recognition. *Language and Cognitive Processes, 22,* 161–200.

Johnson, E. K., & Jusczyk, P. W. (2001). Word segmentation by 8-month-olds: When speech cues count more than statistics. *Journal of Memory and Language, 44,* 548–567.

Johnson, E. K., & Tyler, M. D. (2010). Testing the limits of statistical learning for word segmentation. *Developmental Science, 13,* 339–345.

Jusczyk, P. W. (1999). How infants begin to extract words from speech. *Trends in Cognitive Sciences, 3*, 323–328.

Jusczyk, P. W., & Aslin, R. N. (1995). Infants' detection of the sound patterns of words in fluent speech. *Cognitive Psychology, 29*, 1–23.

Jusczyk, P. W., Houston, D. M., & Newsome, M. (1999). The beginnings of word segmentation in English-learning infants. *Cognitive Psychology, 39*, 159–207.

Kim, D., Stephens, J. D., & Pitt, M. A. (2012). How does context play a part in splitting words apart? Production and perception of word boundaries in casual speech. *Journal of Memory and Language, 66*, 509–529.

Liss, J. M., Spitzer, S., Caviness, J. N., Adler, C., & Edwards, B. (1998). Syllabic strength and lexical boundary decisions in the perception of hypokinetic dysarthric speech. *The Journal of the Acoustical Society of America, 104*, 2457–2466.

Liss, J. M., Spitzer, S. M., Caviness, J. N., Adler, C., & Edwards, B. W. (2000). Lexical boundary error analysis in hypokinetic and ataxic dysarthria. *The Journal of the Acoustical Society of America, 107*, 3415–3424.

Ma, W., Golinkoff, R., Houston, D. M., & Hirsh-Pasek, K. (2011). Word learning in infant- and adult-directed speech. *Language Learning and Development, 7*, 185–201.

Mandel, D. R., Jusczyk, P. W., & Pisoni, D. B. (1995). Infants' recognition of the sound patterns of their own names. *Psychological Science, 6*, 314–317.

Mattys, S. L. (2004). Stress versus coarticulation: Towards an integrated approach to explicit speech segmentation. *Journal of Experimental Psychology: Human Perception and Performance, 30*, 397–408.

Mattys, S. L., Davis, M. H., Bradlow, A. R., & Scott, S. K. (2012). Speech recognition in adverse conditions: A review. *Language and Cognitive Processes, 27*, 953–978.

Mattys, S. L., Jusczyk, P. W., Luce, P. A., & Morgan, J. L. (1999). Phonotactic and prosodic effects on word segmentation in infants. *Cognitive Psychology, 38*, 465–494.

Mattys, S. L., Melhorn, J. F., & White, L. (2007). Effects of syntactic expectations on speech segmentation. *Journal of Experimental Psychology: Human Perception and Performance, 33*, 960–977.

Mattys, S. L., White, L., & Melhorn, J. F. (2005). Integration of multiple segmentation cues: A hierarchical framework. *Journal of Experimental Psychology: General, 134*, 477–500.

McClelland, J. L., & Elman, J. L. (1986). The TRACE model of speech perception. *Cognitive Psychology, 18*, 1–86.

McDaniel, M., Einstein, G., & Jacoby, L. (2008). New considerations in aging and memory: The glass may be half full. In F. I. M. Craik & T. A. Salthouse (Eds.), *The handbook of aging and cognition* (3rd ed., pp. 251–310). New York: Psychology Press.

McQueen, J. M. (1998). Segmentation of continuous speech using phonotactics. *Journal of Memory and Language, 39*, 21–46.

McQueen, J. M., Cutler, A., Briscoe, T., & Norris, D. (1995). Models of continuous speech recognition and the contents of the vocabulary. *Language and Cognitive Processes, 10*, 309–331.

McRoberts, G. W., McDonough, C., & Lakusta, L. (2009). The role of verbal repetition in the development of infant speech preferences from 4 to 14 months of age. *Infancy, 14*, 162–194.

Mersad, K., & Nazzi, T. (2012). When mommy comes to the rescue of statistics: Infants combine top-down and bottom-up cues to segment speech. *Language Learning and Development, 8*, 303–315.

Monaghan, P., White, L., & Merkx, M. M. (2013). Disambiguating durational cues for speech segmentation. *Journal of the Acoustical Society of America, 134*, EL45–EL51.

Morgan, J. L., & Saffran, J. R. (1995). Emerging integration of sequential and suprasegmental information in preverbal speech segmentation. *Child Development, 66*, 911–936.

Munro, M. J., & Derwing, T. M. (1995). Processing time, accent, and comprehensibility in the perception of native and foreign-accented speech. *Language and Speech, 38*, 289–306.

Newman, R. S. (2004). Perceptual restoration in children versus adults. *Applied Psycholinguistics, 25*, 481–493.

Newman, R. S. (2006). Perceptual restoration in toddlers. *Perception & Psychophysics, 68*, 625–642.

Newman, R. S., Ratner, N. B., Jusczyk, A. M., Jusczyk, P. W., & Dow, K. A. (2006). Infants' early ability to segment the conversational speech signal predicts later language development: A retrospective analysis. *Developmental Psychology, 42*, 643–655.

Newman, R. S., Sawusch, J. R., & Wunnenberg, T. (2011). Cues and cue interactions in segmenting words in fluent speech. *Journal of Memory and Language, 64*, 460–476.

Nittrouer, S., & Boothroyd, A. (1990). Context effects in phoneme and word recognition by young children and older adults. *Journal of the Acoustical Society of America, 87*, 2705–2715.

Norris, D. (1994). Shortlist: A connectionist model of continuous speech recognition. *Cognition, 52*, 189–234.

Norris, D., & McQueen, J. M. (2008). Shortlist B: A Bayesian model of continuous speech recognition. *Psychological Review, 115*, 357–395.

Norris, D., McQueen, J. M., Cutler, A., & Butterfield, S. (1997). The possible-word constraint in the segmentation of continuous speech. *Cognitive Psychology, 34*, 191–243.

Ohala, J. J. (1990). The phonetics and phonology of aspects of assimilation. *Papers in Laboratory Phonology, 1*, 258–275.

Otake, T., Hatano, G., Cutler, A., & Mehler, J. (1993). Mora or syllable? Speech segmentation in Japanese. *Journal of Memory and Language, 32*, 258–278.

Roach, P., Knowles, G., Varadi, T., & Arnfield, S. (1993). Marsec: A machine-readable spoken English corpus. *Journal of the International Phonetic Association, 23*, 47–54.

Rönnberg, J., Rudner, M., Lunner, T., & Zekveld, A. A. (2010). When cognition kicks in: Working memory and speech understanding in noise. *Noise and Health, 12*, 263–269.

Saffran, J. R., Aslin, R. N., & Newport, E. L. (1996b). Statistical learning by 8-month-old infants. *Science, 274*, 1926–1928.

Saffran, J. R., Newport, E. L., & Aslin, R. N. (1996a). Word segmentation: The role of distributional cues. *Journal of Memory and Language, 35*, 606–621.

Sanders, L. D., & Neville, H. J. (2003). An ERP study of continuous speech processing: II. Segmentation, semantics, and syntax in non-native speakers. *Cognitive Brain Research, 15*, 214–227.

Sanders, L. D., Neville, H. J., & Woldorff, M. G. (2002a). Speech segmentation of native and nonnative speakers: The use of lexical, syntactic and stress pattern cues. *Journal of Speech, Language and Hearing Research, 45*, 519–530.

Sanders, L. D., Newport, E. L., & Neville, H. J. (2002b). Segmenting nonsense: An event-related potential index of perceived onsets in continuous speech. *Nature Neuroscience, 5*, 700–703.

Schuppler, B., Ernestus, M., Scharenborg, O., & Boves, L. (2011). Acoustic reduction in conversational Dutch: A quantitative analysis based on automatically generated segmental transcriptions. *Journal of Phonetics, 39*, 96–109.

Shannon, R. V., Zeng, F. G., Kamath, V., Wygonski, J., & Ekelid, M. (1995). Speech recognition with primarily temporal cues. *Science, 270*, 303–304.

Shatzman, K. B., & McQueen, J. M. (2006). Segment duration as a cue to word boundaries in spoken-word recognition. *Perception & Psychophysics, 68*, 1–16.

Singer, T., Verhaeghen, P., Ghisletta, P., Lindenberger, U., & Baltes, P. B. (2003). The fate of cognition in very old age: Six-year longitudinal findings in the Berlin Aging Study (BASE). *Psychology and Aging, 18*, 318–331.

Singh, L., Morgan, J. L., & White, K. S. (2004). Preference and processing: The role of speech affect in early spoken word recognition. *Journal of Memory and Language, 51*, 173–189.

Singh, L., Nestor, S. S., & Bortfeld, H. (2008). Overcoming effects of variation on infant word recognition: Influences on word familiarity. *Infancy, 13*, 57–74.

Smith, M. R., Cutler, A., Butterfield, S., & Nimmo-Smith, I. (1989). The perception of rhythm and word boundaries in noise-masked speech. *Journal of Speech, Language, and Hearing Research, 32*, 912–920.

Snow, C. E. (1972). Mothers' speech to children learning language. *Child Development, 43*, 549–565.

Spinelli, E., McQueen, J. M., & Cutler, A. (2003). Processing resyllabified words in French. *Journal of Memory and Language, 48*, 233–254.

Spitzer, S. M., Liss, J. M., & Mattys, S. L. (2007). Acoustic cues to lexical segmentation: A study of resynthesized speech. *Journal of the Acoustical Society of America, 122*, 3678–3687.

Spitzer, S., Liss, J., Spahr, T., Dorman, M., & Lansford, K. (2009). The use of fundamental frequency for lexical segmentation in listeners with cochlear implants. *The Journal of the Acoustical Society of America, 125*, EL236–EL241.

Suomi, K., McQueen, J. M., & Cutler, A. (1997). Vowel harmony and speech segmentation in Finnish. *Journal of Memory and Language, 36*, 422–444.

Tagliapietra, L., Fanari, R., De Candia, C., & Tabossi, P. (2009). Phonotactic regularities in the segmentation of spoken Italian. *The Quarterly Journal of Experimental Psychology, 62*, 392–415.

Thiessen, E. D., & Saffran, J. R. (2003). When cues collide: Use of stress and statistical cues to word boundaries by 7- to 9-month-old infants. *Developmental Psychology, 39*, 706–716.

Tincoff, R., & Jusczyk, P. W. (1999). Some beginnings of word comprehension in 6-month-olds. *Psychological Science, 10*, 172–175.

Toro, J. M., Sebastián-Gallés, N., & Mattys, S. L. (2009). The role of perceptual salience during the segmentation of connected speech. *European Journal of Cognitive Psychology, 21*, 786–800.

Tremblay, A. (2011). Learning to parse liaison-initial words: An eye-tracking study. *Bilingualism: Language and Cognition, 14*, 257–279.

Tremblay, A., Coughlin, C. E., Bahler, C., & Gaillard, S. (2012). Differential contribution of prosodic cues in the native and non-native segmentation of French speech. *Laboratory Phonology, 3*, 385–423.

Tremblay, A., & Spinelli, E. (2014). English listeners' use of distributional and acoustic-phonetic cues to liaison in French: Evidence from eye movements. *Language and Speech, 57*, 310–337.

Tyler, M. D., & Cutler, A. (2009). Cross-language differences in cue use for speech segmentation. *The Journal of the Acoustical Society of America, 126*, 367–376.

Vaissière, J. (1983). Language-independent prosodic features. In A. Cutler & D. L. Ladd (Eds.), *Prosody: Models and measurements* (pp. 53–66). Berlin/Heidelberg: Springer.

Vroomen, J., Tuomainen, J., & de Gelder, B. (1998). The roles of word stress and vowel harmony in speech segmentation. *Journal of Memory and Language, 38*, 133–149.

Vroomen, J., Van Zon, M., & de Gelder, B. (1996). Cues to speech segmentation: Evidence from juncture misperceptions and word spotting. *Memory & Cognition, 24*, 744–755.

Warner, N., & Weber, A. (2001). Perception of epenthetic stops. *Journal of Phonetics, 29*, 53–87.

Weber, A., & Cutler, A. (2006). First-language phonotactics in second-language listening. *The Journal of the Acoustical Society of America, 119*, 597–607.

Weber, C., Hahne, A., Friedrich, M., & Friederici, A. D. (2004). Discrimination of word stress in early infant perception: Electrophysiological evidence. *Cognitive Brain Research, 18*, 149–161.

Weiss, D. J., Gerfen, C., & Mitchel, A. D. (2010). Colliding cues in word segmentation: The role of cue strength and general cognitive processes. *Language and Cognitive Processes, 25*, 402–422.

Welby, P. (2007). The role of early fundamental frequency rises and elbows in French word segmentation. *Speech Communication, 49,* 28–48.

White, L. (2014). Communicative function and prosodic form in speech timing. *Speech Communication, 63,* 38–54.

White, L., Mattys, S. L., & Wiget, L. (2012). Segmentation cues in conversational speech: Robust semantics and fragile phonotactics. *Frontiers, 3,* 1–9.

White, L., Melhorn, J. F., & Mattys, S. L. (2010). Segmentation by lexical subtraction in Hungarian L2 speakers of English. *Quarterly Journal of Experimental Psychology, 63,* 544–554.

Wightman, C. W., Shattuck-Hufnagel, S., Ostendorf, M., & Price, P. J. (1992). Segmental durations in the vicinity of prosodic phrase boundaries. *The Journal of the Acoustical Society of America, 91,* 1707–1717.

Wingfield, A., Lindfield, K. C., & Goodglass, H. (2000). Effects of age and hearing sensitivity on the use of prosodic information in spoken word recognition. *Journal of Speech, Language, and Hearing Research, 43,* 915–925.

5

MAPPING SPOKEN WORDS TO MEANING

James S. Magnuson

Introduction

The ultimate goal of language is to communicate *meaning*. As Marslen-Wilson (1987) put it, "to understand spoken language is to relate sound to meaning." As the acoustic events that make up a spoken word occur, listeners must map phonological forms to intended words in memory. Most research on spoken word processing focuses on form recognition – determining what words are activated in memory as a spoken word is heard, whether and how much they compete, and what factors promote or inhibit recognition. But models that end with abstract, phonological word forms ignore the primary function of words: accessing meaning and generating compositional meaning (based upon word combinations and syntactic structure). For many years, many psycholinguists assumed spoken word processing proceeded in modular stages, with exhaustive activation of words matching a phonological form, followed shortly by access to meaning and integration with syntax (e.g., Marslen-Wilson, 1987; Swinney, 1979; Tanenhaus, Leiman, & Seidenberg, 1979). Over the course of this chapter, we shall see that the notion of modular stages must be discarded; how quickly semantic access can be detected depends on the strength of expectations (based on semantic features or context), although human spoken language processing appears to conform to the principles of *bottom-up priority* and *delayed commitment* (Luce & Cluff, 1998; Marr, 1982): top-down expectations are not sufficient to drive full access or recognition without bottom-up support. I will begin by reviewing the nature of conceptual knowledge, then turn to the semantic details associated with individual words and how they are accessed in word recognition, discuss the very few computational models of spoken word processing that incorporate semantics, and conclude with a review of how word-level semantics interact in sentence and discourse contexts. Space is short, and each section is necessarily brief and selective.

Nature of conceptual representations

Before we can address what semantic representations are associated with words, we must consider theories of semantic representations. Important concerns regarding distinctions between semantic knowledge and memory (world knowledge) vs. lexical knowledge are beyond the scope of this chapter; we will dive straight into proposals for representations of lexical knowledge.

Classical accounts based on necessary and sufficient features were rejected in the latter half of the twentieth century since many if not most concepts cannot be defined in such a way (cf. Wittgenstein's [1953] example of GAME). Collins and Quillian (1969) proposed that semantic knowledge might be organized as taxonomic networks embodying positive aspects of classical accounts while providing a compact basis for generalizations. For example, a node for ANIMAL would branch into subordinate nodes such as BIRDS, MAMMALS, REPTILES, etc. Any features associated with ANIMAL (HAS-SKIN, BREATHES) would be inherited by all subordinate nodes, just as subordinates of BIRD (RAPTOR, SONGBIRD) would inherit all properties associated with BIRD. However, core predictions of the taxonomic approach were quickly falsified (e.g., time needed to evaluate "a pig is a mammal" should be proportional to nodes that must be traversed, but participants confirm "a pig is an animal" [two nodes] faster than "a pig is a mammal" [one node]).

Collins and Loftus (1975) abandoned hierarchy for a network model where associated concepts were linked with strengths proportional to *association*. Association strengths can be quantified by asking many subjects to list words brought to mind by a target word (Nelson, McEvoy, & Schreiber, 2004). Association norms provide reliable predictions of priming and other behavior, and there is a rich tradition in psycholinguistics of exploiting associations to explore lexical access. For example, in *cross-modal semantic priming*, a series of spoken words are presented. Occasionally, a letter string is displayed, and participants make a lexical decision. Priming from auditory to printed words is used to infer what words the auditory word activated. While spoken words prime themselves and associates (i.e., a target word is processed faster when preceded by itself or an associate vs. an unrelated word), more subtle chains of priming can be observed. For example, hearing DOCK can prime CAT, indicating that as DOCK is heard, phonologically similar words are activated (e.g., DOG) and in turn spread activation to their associates (Marslen-Wilson, 1987). However, the bases of associations are unclear (McRae, de Sa, & Seidenberg, 1997), as they include items related by category/feature overlap (BANANA-APPLE), synonymy (COUCH-SOFA), antonymy (NIGHT-DAY), function (LOCK-KEY), co-occurrence (BREAD-BUTTER), events (BRIDE-WEDDING), idiomatic expressions (KICK-BUCKET), or combinations (CAT and DOG overlap in features, children [or adults under time pressure] are likely to call them opposites, one is a likely chaser of the other in a CHASE event and occur in idiomatic expressions such as "fighting like/raining cats and dogs"). The Collins and Loftus approach was eventually rejected as too limited and circular; networks constructed from empirically observed association strengths can do little beyond redescribing those associations.

Rosch and colleagues proposed a radically different approach based on featural similarity (e.g., Rosch & Mervis, 1975). On their "prototype" view, the basis for a concept is a set of prototypical features abstracted from the members of a category – a frequency-weighted composite of experienced features (e.g., the BIRD prototype would be a combination of body size, body part sizes, color, singing/calling, and feeding preferences [etc.] that do not occur in any single subtype or instance of BIRD). This view motivated many experimental paradigms that greatly expanded the known phenomena related to concepts and categories. For example: when participants list features of a concept, they first list highly typical features, whether or not they are distinctive (e.g., "has fur" might be elicited for virtually any mammal); processing time in many tasks depends on how close the target concept is to its prototype; there is graded membership within a category and fuzzy boundaries between categories, such that WHALE is rated both a poor MAMMAL *and* a poor FISH; there is a "sweet spot"–level of specification based on expertise – the "entry" or "basic level" – that most observers default to, e.g., for nonexperts, GUITAR rather than INSTRUMENT or TELECASTER. However, prototype theory fails to account for within-category structure (covariation among properties) that human subjects are sensitive to (for example, that smaller-bodied birds are more likely to sing and larger-bodied birds are more likely to eat fish). Such findings motivated *exemplar theory* (e.g., Medin & Schaeffer, 1978; Smith & Medin, 1981), which proposes that a system in which each exemplar of a category is stored in memory would account for everything prototype theory did, while preserving a basis for sensitivity to within-category structure.

Tremendous progress has been made in feature-based approaches thanks to work eliciting features for concepts from human subjects (e.g., McRae et al., 1997; Vigliocco, Vinson, Lewis, & Garrett, 2004). Elicited features can provide a basis for quantifying semantic distance between concepts in the form of *semantic feature vectors*. Such vectors have one element for every feature that was elicited for any concept. The representation for a concept is a vector with a 1 for any feature that was elicited for that concept and a 0 for any feature that was never elicited for that concept. Semantic distance can then be operationalized as Euclidean or cosine distance between vectors. Such similarity spaces provide accurate predictions of semantic similarity, priming, and other aspects of behavior associated with word-level semantics, despite not explicitly encoding category structure or causal relations (some experiments are described in more detail later in the chapter).

But some phenomena are difficult to accommodate within feature-based approaches, most notably, ad hoc and goal-directed categories (Barsalou, 1983), such as "good vehicles for crossing the desert" or "good activities for kids when you've missed a connecting flight". Even when such goals are first encountered, people propose instances and features with the same robust and gradient structure around prototypical tendencies observed for established categories (Barsalou, 1985). A prototype or exemplar approach cannot readily accommodate these phenomena; both theories require experience with exemplars for a structured category to form. Motivated by such results, Murphy and Medin (1985) argued that similarity-based theories of categorization failed to provide an account of *conceptual coherence* – what makes "some groupings . . . informative, useful and efficient" – and also lacked a truly explanatory account of "intra- and inter-concept relations". They argued that concepts are based on *theories* – "mental 'explanations'" – of *why* a category exists (what links members with their purposes and functions). For example, people know that an airplane made of whipped cream could not fly, while one made of plexiglass *might* be able to, and even young children agree that while a blender could be reconfigured into a toaster, a skunk cannot be reconfigured into a cat (Keil, 1989). But this "theory-theory" replaces prototype abstraction or exemplar clustering with something mysterious; what would be the nature of "mental explanations" underlying categories on this view? What kind of general mechanism might generate them based on experience with exemplars? (For a review, see Murphy, 2002.)

Another possibility is that conceptual coherence could emerge from simple learning mechanisms that encode appropriate relations. McClelland and Rogers (2003) developed a simple feedforward network that maps *Items* (concepts) and a small set of core *Relations* (IS, CAN, HAS) to *Attributes* (features) via layers of hidden nodes. After training, the model exhibits human-like clustering in its learned representations as well as generalization (e.g., given a subset of features for a new concept, it "infers" [partially activates] features that have not yet been experienced based on "coherent covariation" of feature relations it has learned). In contrast to theory-theory, the model becomes sensitive to causal structure within categories without any understanding or theory-like propositional representations. While the model does not provide a full account of conceptual coherence, it is a promissory note for an approach that might be extended to do so.

Other crucial approaches include *embodied* or *grounded* theories of cognition, which stem from the *symbol grounding problem* (the idea that words cannot be "ungrounded" symbols that are defined by other words but must to be linked to semantics outside a linguistic system; Harnad, 1990) and from empirical findings. On this view, representations are not amodal abstractions; instead modal (sensory, motoric) brain areas provide an important component of representations (Barsalou, 2008). The neural representation of REACH, for example, would include activation of areas involved in perceiving and/or performing reaching. Many studies have demonstrated that performance on linguistic tasks can be facilitated or inhibited depending on the compatibility of a linguistic stimulus with the motor action required to respond (Glenberg & Kaschak, 2003), suggesting that linguistic forms trigger modal activations that engage perception–action systems. Barsalou (1999) proposes that hearing or thinking about a concept induces a "perceptual simulation" via appropriate modal activations (see also Paivio, 1986). A growing body of neuroimaging studies are consistent with this view. In an elegant, comprehensive theoretical and empirical review, Meteyard, Cuadrado, Bahrami, and Vigliocco (2012) conclude that behavioral and neural data point towards Damasio's (1989) proposal for *convergence zones* – neural regions that respond to and activate a variety of modal and amodal semantic details. Delving more deeply into neural representations is beyond the scope of this chapter, but Gow (2012) provides a recent review that also introduces a novel theory of phonetic and semantic neural representation.

Finally, a crucial consideration is the distinction between concrete and abstract concepts. It may seem that neither feature-based nor grounded approaches would provide a basis for representing abstract concepts. While one can get surprisingly far with intuitive features for many abstract concepts (see, e.g., Plaut & Shallice, 1993), simple features for many concepts may be difficult to derive, and features for many abstract concepts may be context- or situation-specific, much like ad hoc and goal-derived categories. While Barsalou and Weimer-Hastings (2005) have proposed that even abstract concepts could rely on situation-specific perceptual simulations, Crutch and Warrington (2005) proposed that concrete and abstract concepts depend upon "qualitatively different representations". Specifically, they proposed that concrete concepts are represented via semantic features, while meanings of abstract concepts are based on associations with other concepts. Andrews, Vigliocco, and Vinson (2009) also propose a qualitative distinction, arguing that concrete concepts are based primarily on experiential learning (based on co-occurrence of language and physical objects and events), while abstract concepts are learned distributionally (i.e., based on co-occurrence statistics derivable from linguistic sources [speech or print], as in the Hyperspace Analog to Language [HAL, Lund & Burgess, 1996] or Latent Semantic Analysis [LSA, Landauer & Dumais, 1997]), although they propose that the two sources are intercorrelated (their Bayesian model exhibits benefits from having both sources that are not a simple effect of having more data but that follow from having two qualitatively distinct types of data). We will review results that bear on this issue later in the chapter. With these preliminaries in hand, let us turn to empirical results in the processing of spoken words.

Aspects of meaning activated by single spoken words

Experiments on semantic access from single spoken words[1] can be divided into two primary types that sometimes appear to provide conflicting data. *Pairwise approaches* examine effects for specific word pairs (e.g., Does DOG prime CAT?) or in a paradigm where multiple images are presented (Do participants look to CAT when they are told to select DOG?). *Lexical dimension approaches* examine processing for *sets* of words as a function of lexical variables, such as frequency of occurrence, phonological neighborhood size, or semantic variables such as how imageable a word is, how many semantic features it has, and so on. We shall see that while convergent results are often found using these approaches, they can reveal different aspects of lexical access.[2]

Pairwise approaches

A foundational *pairwise approach* was reported by Moss, Ostrin, Tyler, and Marslen-Wilson (1995), who examined multiple types of semantic relation effects in spoken word recognition. They used "category coordinate" pairs belonging to the same category that were also associated or non-associated and were natural or artifacts (e.g., associated natural category coordinates: DOG-CAT; non-associated artifact category coordinates: SPADE-RAKE). "Functionally related" pairs were also associated or not and were related by "script" or instrumental relations (associated, instrument: HAMMER-NAIL; non-associated, script: RESTAURANT-WINE). There were also many pairs of unrelated filler words. Word-word or word–non-word pairs were presented and participants made lexical decisions on the second item. For spoken presentation, reliable effects of relatedness were found for all item classes, along with significant boosts for association and an interaction of relatedness and association (greater priming for associated than nonassociated pairs). Concerns about strategic effects that could arise from word pairs motivated a second experiment with lexical decisions for each item. The results replicated, though priming for nonassociates was greatly reduced. A third experiment used visual word presentation, and the results were markedly different. Functionally related pairs primed whether they were associated or not, category coordinate pairs primed only if they were associated, and script-related pairs did not prime whether they were associated or not. One possibility is that only the third study measured automatic priming and that surviving effects indicate automatically activated dimensions. However, as Moss and colleagues argued, differences may have followed from variation in prime-target intervals (200 ms for the first experiment, 1000 ms for the second, variable for the third). Another possibility is that differences in the way spoken words and written words are experienced (segment by segment vs. all at once) could have influenced the outcomes. What is clear is that not all semantic relationships are equivalent, and some may be activated more strongly and/or quickly, with complex differences in visual and spoken modalities.

The advent of the *visual world paradigm* (Tanenhaus, Spivey-Knowlton, Eberhard, & Sedivy, 1995), or VWP, opened up new ways of looking at pairwise relations as well as lexical dimensions. Allopenna, Magnuson, and Tanenhaus (1998) used it to examine phonological competition (see also Spivey-Knowlton, 1996) and introduced the use of fixation proportions over time to provide estimates of word activations. Yee and Sedivy (2001, 2006) conducted the first pairwise explorations of semantic features using the VWP. In one study, they displayed pictures of semantically related items (primarily category coordinates, such as CAR-BIKE or PIANO-TRUMPET, but also some functionally related items like LOCK-KEY or HAMMER-NAIL) along with unrelated distractors. Given an instruction to touch a target item, participants were significantly more likely to look at functionally related than unrelated items. Follow-up analyses confirmed that results were robust when restricted to item sets where the visual similarity (shape) of targets and semantic relatives was matched to target-unrelated similarity or to non-associated target-relative pairs. A second experiment sought to eliminate any possibility of the results being driven by strategy or visual properties of displayed pictures by replacing targets with phonological cohorts (e.g., CARDS replaced CAR, LOGS replaced LOCK). The logic was that Allopenna and colleagues and Spivey-Knowlton had demonstrated robust coactivation of onset competitors, and robustly activated items should spread activation to semantic relatives. Indeed, LOGS activated KEY (for example) significantly, though not as much as LOCK had.

In a similar study, Huettig and Altmann (2005) examined fixations over time as participants heard sentences mentioning a critical item as they viewed a display with pictures of the target (e.g., PIANO) and either (a) three unrelated distractors, (b) a category coordinate of the target (e.g., TRUMPET) and three unrelated distractors, or (c) both the target and the category competitor and two unrelated distractors. Participants were more likely to fixate targets and competitors than unrelated items, with earlier and higher peak fixation proportions for targets than competitors. Huettig and Altmann argued that fixations in the VWP reflect a variety of bottom-up (spoken word forms and pictures) and top-down activations (e.g., activation of TRUMPET from a MUSICAL INSTRUMENT feature activated by PIANO or spreading activation among category members).

It seems implausible that visual displays would not impact processing in the VWP, despite the shape-similarity control analysis of Yee and Sedivy (2006). Indeed, Dahan and Tanenhaus (2005) found that items with shape similarity but no semantic relation to a target word (e.g., SNAKE-ROPE, CATERPILLAR-TRAIN) were fixated reliably more than unrelated items. Dahan and Tanenhaus argued that the VWP does not involve implicit naming of displayed objects; their interpretation was that if participants activated phonological forms of displayed pictures prior to the spoken target, one would not expect fixations to visual (shape) competitors. Fixations to those competitors suggest that visual features were activated by hearing the target word.

Huettig and Altmann (2007) came to a very different conclusion. Their key experiment involved shape-similar pairs like SNAKE-CABLE, with two display types (three unrelated pictures displayed either with a target [SNAKE] or a shape competitor of the target [CABLE]), and two sentence types: neutral (e.g., "In the beginning, the man watched closely, but then he looked at the snake and realized that it was harmless".) or biasing (e.g., with "man" replaced with "zookeeper"). Competitor displays were paired only with biasing sentences. Participants were more likely to fixate competitors than unrelated items. They found a very small but reliable "anticipation" effect in the biasing condition: subjects were reliably more likely to be fixating targets by word onset. Contra Dahan and Tanenhaus, they concluded that fixations in the VWP are not a pure reflection of spoken words activating visual features that then guide saccades; rather, they argued that item names are activated when items are viewed, and spoken words reactivate or boost those picture-based activations – otherwise, there should have also been anticipatory looks to the shape-similar competitor.

However, there are several reasons that further experimentation would be needed to confirm this. First, they used exceptionally long preview times; pictures preceded sentences by 1 second, and target word onsets were approximately 5 seconds after picture presentation. Long previews allow substantial time for strategic exploration or subvocal naming of pictures. Second, key biasing context words (e.g., zookeeper) would not activate targets specifically, but rather a target's category (e.g., although a zoo animal would be expected, the cloze probability for SNAKE specifically would be extremely low). One could not expect the category to activate perceptual features of all category members (e.g., ANIMAL would not be expected to activate shape features for SNAKE, such as LONG and CYLINDRICAL). Finally, substantial time between key context words and target words (~2 seconds) would allow fixations to each object, allowing one to guess that, for example, the one animal would likely be the target. Very high fixation probabilities for shape competitors, *despite* participants having so much time to examine the display, reinforces the Dahan and Tanenhaus conclusion that hearing a word strongly activates perceptual features of its referent; if subjects *knew* what the pictures were and had activated their names, why else should hearing SNAKE activate its visual features sufficiently to drive fixations to the shape competitor?

Yee and colleagues have conducted several additional studies on semantic activation using the VWP. Yee, Overton, and Thompson-Schill (2009) compared activations for associated word pairs that were weakly vs. strongly semantically related. They found robust competition for strongly semantically similar pairs but not for weakly similar pairs, suggesting that in the VWP, words activate distributed semantic features rather than simply spreading activation among associated words.

Yee, Huffstetler, and Thompson-Schill (2011) compared competition between pairs related by shape (FRISBEE-PIZZA) or function (TAPE-GLUE). An elegant aspect of their design was that shape competitors were similar to targets in their *prototypical* shape (round, for FRISBEE-PIZZA), but shape competitors were displayed with non-canonical shape (e.g., a pizza *slice* was displayed). With a 1000-ms preview, robust, sustained fixations to shape competitors emerged early, while fixations to function competitors were weak and late (but still significantly greater than for unrelated items). With a 2000-ms preview, the pattern flipped. Yee and associates suggested that increasing preview duration allowed them to tap the system later and that, therefore, shape features must be activated early and function features must be activated late. This makes sense only if we assume that each displayed item is processed in some way during the preview and not that the longer preview affords time for strategies to emerge – for example, for subjects to notice relations among items. However, even if there was a strategic element in play, the complete flip of shape vs. function dominance with preview time is consistent with the idea that function features are less readily activated.

Yee, Chrysikou, Hoffman, and Thompson-Schill (2013) asked participants to make concreteness judgments for spoken words while performing either a concurrent manual task or a mental rotation task with a foot-based response. Manual tasks interfered specifically with items with which participants have more experience touching (e.g., pencils vs. tigers), while the mental rotation task interfered with both. The growing body of research on grounded/embodied cognition demonstrating sensory-motor interactions with language processing challenges any notion of abstract, amodal lexical symbols in the brain. While such interactions are often taken as *prima facie* evidence that neural bases for action and perception are integral to concept representations, caution is warranted. One might argue that all we can be confident of is that interaction is evidence of interaction and that alternative explanations, such as a "simple" spread of activation, must be ruled out. On the other hand, two other theoretical principles are relevant. First, sensory-motor interactions satisfy criteria for Garner (1974) interference, where irrelevant variation in one dimension (e.g., type of motor response) disrupts processing of another (e.g., words), which is a long-standing test for integrality of representational dimensions. Second, on radical distributed perspectives (e.g., Elman, 2009; Spivey, 2007), there is no mental lexicon or discrete representations of words; instead, the representation of a word is distributed neural activity over the entire brain as the word is processed (and so changes dynamically over time). That said, as Hickock (2014) reminds us, "neurons compute." Once a concept is represented neurally, to a first approximation, it does not matter where those neurons are or what other concepts, percepts, or actions they may also help represent. A neural code in the absence of its referent is still a representation, no matter how closely it resembles codes active for perception or action. On the other hand, the specific neurons and circuits involved in conceptual memory and their proximity to or identity with those active in perception and action may afford important functional advantages in terms of speed of processing and preparation for action.

Finally, let's reconsider the possible differences in representations of abstract and concrete concepts. For obvious reasons, VWP studies focus on concrete objects. But there have been at least two attempts to use the VWP to address whether abstract and concrete objects depend on fundamentally different mental representations. As mentioned in the previous section, Crutch and Warrington (2005) proposed the *qualitatively different representations* (QDR) hypothesis, motivated by patient studies finding interference for associated abstract words (WAR-PEACE) but not for associated concrete words (NAIL-HAMMER) and interference for semantically related concrete words (NAIL-SCREW) but not for semantically related abstract words (WAR-CONFLICT). Crutch and Warrington argue that this dissociation suggests that concrete words are organized by category relations, while abstract words are organized by association (though it is not clear how associations provide a sufficient basis for understanding abstract concepts). Crutch and Warrington dismiss prior computational work, arguing that differences between abstract and concrete words follow from relative sparsity of available features (Plaut & Shallice, 1993), since features for those simulations were intuited rather than empirically derived. Duñabeitia, Avilés, Afonso, Scheepers, and Carreiras (2009) posited that it follows from QDR that hearing/seeing abstract words should activate primarily associated concepts, while hearing/seeing concrete words should primarily activate semantically similar concepts, and, crucially, abstract words should activate associates more rapidly than concrete words should, given the primacy of association for abstract words. In critical trials in a VWP study, Duñabeitia and colleagues asked participants to click on pictures that "best corresponded" to spoken words. "Best correspondents" were concrete associates of abstract (SMELL) or concrete (CRIB) spoken words (associates for these examples were NOSE and BABY). Indeed, associates of abstract words were fixated earlier and more than associates of concrete words. Duñabeitia associates concluded that the QDR hypothesis was strongly supported.

Brozdowski, Gordils, and Magnuson (in preparation) and Brozdowski, Gordils, and Magnuson (2013) revisited this result, given concerns about Duñabeitia and colleagues' metalinguistic task (clicking on "best correspondents", which could motivate various strategies) and materials (many "abstract" words had relatively low imageability but were still concrete, such as PASSENGER). In order to use only concrete spoken targets in the VWP, we used the phonologically mediated paradigm of Yee and Sedivy (2006). In critical displays, an instruction might be "click on the fist". Distractors included one unrelated item, and two phonologically linked associates: CLOTHING (related to FIST's abstract phonological cohort, FIT) and OCEAN (related to FIST's concrete phonological cohort, FISH). Contra Duñabeitia and colleagues, associates of concrete phonological cohorts were fixated slightly but reliably more than those of abstract cohorts or unrelated items (which did not differ reliably from each other). In a follow-up experiment, pictures were replaced with printed words, allowing us to use both concrete and abstract items, and the primary results replicated. Either there is not a privileged route for abstract associations, or differences between highly abstract and highly concrete objects are quantitative rather than qualitative.

Lexical dimensions approaches

In a foundational study of *lexical dimensions* in the auditory domain, Tyler, Voice, and Moss (2000) examined interactions of imageability and phonological density. In lexical decision and naming tasks, high-imageability words were processed faster than low-imageability words. In naming, there was an interaction with phonological cohort size (two words are cohorts [in the same recognition *cohort* according to the Cohort model; Marslen-Wilson, 1989] if they overlap in at least the first two segments): there was a reliable effect of imageability (faster responses for high imageability) for large but not small cohorts. Following arguments from Plaut and Shallice (1993), Tyler and colleagues suggested that imageability speeds processing because high-imageability words tend to have more semantic features, which in Plaut and Shallice's computational model promotes stronger basins of attraction. The interaction with cohort size is consistent with many prior results in which the effect of one variable is more pronounced at weaker levels of a second variable. For example, orthographic regularity interacts with word frequency, such that regularity effects are much more pronounced for low-frequency words than high-frequency words (e.g., Andrews, 1982), presumably because high-frequency words approach a ceiling level of processing facility based on how often they are experienced. Because of activation of phonological competitors, words with large cohorts are expected to be more difficult to process than those with small cohorts, providing an opportunity for imageability effects to manifest. Tyler and associates argued that the interaction of imageability with cohort size indicated continuous, cascaded integration of semantic and phonological activations.

Another important consideration is what happens when a spoken or written word form is lexically ambiguous because it maps onto multiple unrelated meanings (homophony, as in BARK) or multiple related meanings (polysemy, as in TWIST). Rodd, Gaskell, and Marslen-Wilson (2002) pointed out that previous claims of an ambiguity advantage had not controlled for ambiguity due to homophony vs. polysemy. In visual and auditory lexical decision studies, they found inhibitory effects of homophony but facilitatory effects of polysemy. Mirman, Strauss, Dixon, and Magnuson (2010) followed up this work with lexical decision and VWP studies, comparing nouns with noun homophones (e.g., DECK [cards], DECK [boat]), verb homophones (e.g., SWALLOW [bird], to SWALLOW), and unambiguous nouns equated on numerous lexical dimensions (frequency, neighborhood density, cohort density, uniqueness point, number of syllables, length, and recorded duration). In lexical decisions, responses to nouns with noun homophones were reliably slower than responses to nouns with verb homophones, while responses to unambiguous nouns were reliably faster than responses to both types of homophone. In the VWP, targets were presented among three unrelated distractors. Response time patterns converged with lexical decision results, and participants fixated pictures of unambiguous nouns more quickly than noun-verb homophones, which they fixated more quickly than noun-noun homophones (mean fixation proportions showed the same pattern). In the context of Rodd and colleagues' (2002) finding of facilitation for polysemy, we interpreted our results as indicating a U-shaped function: high similarity with overlapping representations (polysemy) facilitates processing, but when overlap is low or absent (as for homophones with distinct meanings), lower representational distance (our noun-noun case) leads to greater competition, with decreasing competition for less overlap (noun-verb homophones) and even less for unambiguous items. We shall see later in the chapter that this supposition may be difficult to reconcile with other effects of semantic distance.

Sajin and Connine (2014) extended findings from visual word recognition (Pexman, Holyk, & Monfils, 2003) that semantic richness, as indexed by *number of features* (NOF), speeds processing. NOF was operationalized using feature norms collected by McRae and colleagues (McRae, Cree, Seidenberg, & McNorgan, 2005; McRae et al., 1997). In lexical decision and VWP studies, words with relatively high NOF were processed more quickly than words with lower NOF for clear speech, and words with high NOF were less affected by the addition of background "babble".

Mirman and Magnuson (2008) used the same semantic features to investigate semantic *neighborhood*, in analogy to phonological neighborhood (using visual presentation and lexical decision or animacy judgment). As mentioned earlier, using McRae and associates' norms, concepts can be represented as vectors of 1s and 0s indicating which features participants listed for each concept. Distance between vectors can be captured with vector cosine. Having relatively many (2 or more) near neighbors (cosine > 0.5) predicted relatively slower processing, while having relatively many (200 or more) distant neighbors (0 < cosine < 0.25) predicted faster processing. We interpreted this in terms of attractor dynamics; having many distant neighbors can be conceptualized as a creating a region of many attractors that collectively create a large basin of attraction that speeds initial trajectories toward a general "region" of state space, while having many near neighbors slows trajectories due to multiple strong nearby attractors creating strong competition within a (densely packed) region.

Reconciling pairwise and lexical dimensions approaches

Mirman and Magnuson (2009) followed up the Mirman and Magnuson (2008) study with an auditory VWP study employing a pairwise approach. On critical trials, a target (e.g., FALCON) and near semantic neighbor (e.g., PARTRIDGE) or distant semantic neighbor (e.g., OSTRICH) were displayed with two unrelated items. Fixation proportions were reliably higher for near than distant neighbors and for distant neighbors than unrelated items. Notably, competition for distant neighbors was not detected in previous studies using priming paradigms, pointing to (a) the sensitivity of the VWP and (b) the power of the McRae et al. (1997, 2005) feature-based approach to semantic similarity. While apparent *competition* with distant neighbors in a pairwise study like this one may seem incompatible with facilitation in a lexical dimensions approach (i.e., Mirman & Magnuson, 2008), Mirman and Magnuson used the same attractor network (Cree, McRae, & McNorgan, 1999) to simulate both sets of results. Mirman and Magnuson (2008) found that the model predicted increases in indices of competition as near neighbors increased and decreases as the number of distant neighbors increased. Mirman and Magnuson (2009) found that the same model predicted graded decreases in priming as neighbor distance increases. This raises a crucial question: how can we differentiate simple coactivation from competition in the VWP?

A study combining pairwise and lexical dimension approaches is instructive on this point. Apfelbaum, Blumstein, and McMurray (2011) used the VWP to examine activation of semantic associates (a mixture of different relationship types) as a function of frequency-weighted (phonological) neighborhood (FWN) size. Words were chosen from relatively high or low FWNs and were displayed with a semantic relative and two unrelated items. They predicted that because words in low FWNs are subject to less phonological competition, they would activate more quickly and thus be more likely to robustly activate semantic associates than words in high FWNs (the same logic behind the Tyler and colleagues [2000] study previously reviewed: the effect of one variable should be most pronounced at a "difficult" level of another variable). Although they did find greater fixations for semantic relatives in the low-density condition, there was an unanalyzed but strong trend for faster and greater fixation proportions for *high-FWN* targets than for low-FWN. This would seem to contradict the explanation that semantic relatives were more strongly activated in the low-FWN condition (because low-density targets should activate more quickly than high-FWN targets). However, even classes of items that tend to facilitate one another *must* compete when they are simultaneously displayed in the VWP, minimally at the level of decision processes guiding gaze selection and mouse or button presses since only one item can be selected at any instant for gaze or other behavioral action. So if a low-FWN target spreads greater activation to a displayed semantic relative and fixation proportions are proportional to activation, then that semantic relative will attract more fixations. Since the participant can fixate only one item at a time, this will necessarily reduce fixations to the low-FWN target. Isolating the FWN effect would require displaying targets varying in FWN among unrelated items, as Magnuson, Dixon, Tanenhaus, and Aslin (2007) did for word frequency and phonological density (and found robust effects of frequency, neighborhood density, and cohort density).

The same principles hold for *any* pairwise experimental paradigm; detecting coactivation of a pair of items that tend to facilitate one another implies competition at the decision level: as more items are activated, decisions should be slowed. Detecting facilitation requires that the overall facilitative influences outweigh competitive influences. Thus, facilitative pairwise relations (for items simultaneously displayed) must manifest as competition effects in the VWP, but appropriately designed lexical dimension studies can detect both inhibition and facilitation. So while the VWP provides essential time course information, both pairwise and lexical dimension VWP designs may and must be employed to obtain full understanding of cooperative and competitive influences. Computational models are also essential and are considered next.

Computational models

The Cree and associates (1999) model used by Mirman and Magnuson (2008, 2009) is not a model of spoken word recognition; abstract form units are presented simultaneously and feed forward directly to feature units. Attractor dynamics follow from the settling process for recurrent connections among feature units. But the essential difference between visual and spoken word recognition is that spoken inputs are necessarily serial and have temporal extent. Very few models incorporate both the temporal extent of spoken words and representations of meaning; most SWR models are simply form recognition models (see Magnuson, Mirman, & Harris, 2012 and Mirman, Chapter 6 in this volume, for reviews), although there are three notable exceptions.

First, Gaskell and Marslen-Wilson (1997, 1999) introduced their *Distributed Cohort Model* (DCM), which is a simple recurrent network (SRN; Elman, 1990) mapping phonetic features (one time step per phoneme) to distributed phonological forms and to "semantics" – 50-element vectors with 50% of nodes set randomly to 1 and the rest to 0 (random sparse vectors are often used as convenience representations for semantics [Plaut, 1997], on the rationale that form-meaning mappings are nearly always arbitrary). Initial papers used lexicons of 36 to 276 words, establishing that the DCM accounts for basic aspects of word recognition (Gaskell & Marslen-Wilson, 1997), and focused on the notion of *blending* in distributed models vs. inhibition-based competition in localist models. The idea is that when an input strongly supports two words (e.g., upon hearing /kæpt/, which could result in CAPTAIN or CAPTIVE), an output representation of distributed semantic features does not allow concept representations to compete as they do in localist representations with a separate node for each concept with inhibitory connections. Instead, the state of the network will blend the two semantic feature vectors (assuming for the sake of example that no other words are strongly activated by the input /kæpt/).

Gaskell and Marslen-Wilson (2002) tested predictions of the DCM using ambiguous word onsets expected to result in semantic blending (e.g., /kæpt/) and unambiguous onsets (e.g., /garm/, consistent with one word, GARMENT). Ambiguous word fragments did not prime semantic relatives of consistent words (e.g., COMMANDER), but unambiguous fragments did. They provide a nuanced discussion of how such results follow naturally from distributed representations but might not follow as easily from models using "direct competition" (dedicated inhibitory connections between localist nodes). Indeed, a localist model *could* simulate the same results. Without any modification, TRACE (McClelland & Elman, 1986) provides a basis for the prediction: an ambiguous fragment will activate multiple words, and competition among them will depress any consistent word's activation compared to the level of activation that would follow from a fragment consistent with only one word. We can predict from that difference that priming should be weaker in the former case. If we modified the model and added semantic representations (e.g., with phonemic nodes mapping to semantic features that in turn map to lemma nodes; cf. Magnuson et al., 2012), the priming effects could be modeled. Nonetheless, the DCM stands out as the most promising approach to both time course and meaning for modeling spoken words to date, although it has not been extended since 1999.

The second exception is an interactive activation and competition model developed by Chen and Mirman (2012). The model is conceived as having three layers: input forms (abstract letters or phonemes) connect reciprocally to word nodes, which connect reciprocally to semantic features, although only form-word or word-semantic layers were used for any single simulation. As with the DCM, semantic features were abstract (as were their letter and phoneme representations). Simulations used very few input forms (0 or 7), word nodes (1–11), and semantic features (0, 10, 12, or 70), and simulations were designed to isolate essential principles of competition. Form-word simulations demonstrated how the simultaneous presentation of input elements (as in print) vs. sequential input (as in speech) change competition dynamics (specifically, form neighbors facilitate in the former case but inhibit in the latter case; cf. Magnuson & Mirman, 2007). Word-semantic simulations demonstrated how distant semantic neighbors can speed processing while near neighbors inhibit processing (though it is not clear how the approach could account for the U-shaped facilitation/competition function proposed by Mirman et al. [2010] previously reviewed). The simplicity of Chen and Mirman (2012) is a double-edged sword. It affords elegant demonstrations of disparate competition dynamics, but demonstration proofs of "micro-models" can be considered only promissory notes until they are shown to scale to, for example, realistic phoneme and word inventories (Magnuson, 2015).

The third exception is Plaut and Kello's (1999) ambitious attractor network model of the co-development of speech and word perception and production. The model learned to map over-time analogs of acoustic inputs to phonological forms and semantic features (again, arbitrary vectors), as well as to map from semantics back through phonology to an articulatory system. Unfortunately, this model has not been extended beyond some initial demonstration proofs, but it is the most promising approach to date for advancing understanding not just of how sound is mapped to meaning but of how that mapping emerges over development.

Perhaps the two greatest challenges for models of spoken word recognition are greater input realism (ideally working with real speech rather than with the abstractions all current models assume for convenience) and connection not just to word meaning but to the syntactic and semantic complexities of sentence contexts. Next, let's consider how aspects of word meaning change dynamically in sentences and other contexts.

Sentence and other context effects

Swinney (1979) and Tanenhaus and colleagues (1979) reported classic results that motivated a modular view of form and meaning processing that dominated psycholinguistics for nearly 15 years. In a neutral context, ambiguous homophones prime all consistent meanings (e.g., BUG primes both *insect* and *spy*). A context biased towards one meaning eventually primes the context-appropriate meaning much more strongly than other meanings, but both Swinney and Tanenhaus and associates found that such effects appeared to take a few hundred milliseconds to emerge. Such results suggested two stages of processing: exhaustive bottom-up form access followed by semantic-based selection. Shillcock and Bard (1993) demonstrated that immediate effects *can* be observed with very strong expectations established by syntactic and semantic constraints. For example, given a context such as, "John said he didn't want to do the job, but his brother would", no cross-modal priming was found for TIMBER (a semantic relative of WOOD) from WOULD even when the probe was displayed *during* the critical word. Using the VWP, Dahan and Tanenhaus (2004) found that sentence contexts predicting a specific lexical item seemed to eliminate phonological competition from context-inappropriate competitors. Similarly, Magnuson, Tanenhaus, and Aslin (2008) found that syntactic and pragmatic constraints (whether an adjective or noun was expected next, given VWP display contents) immediately restricted competition; no phonological competition was observed from nouns when adjectives were expected and vice versa. Chambers, Tanenhaus, and Magnuson (2004) found that object affordances and implications of a verb and/or instrument constrained competition. For example, given an instruction to "pour the egg . . ." when there were a liquid egg and an egg still in its shell, fixation proportions to the egg-in-shell were no greater than to unrelated objects. Given a hook to manipulate objects in a workspace and two whistles (only one of which was hookable, via a string attached to it), fixations to the unhookable whistle did not differ from fixation proportions to unrelated objects.

Such results demonstrate *preemption*: the absence of competition expected from the bottom-up input, which is weak evidence for *anticipation*. Strong evidence for anticipation comes primarily from two sorts of studies: event-related potential experiments where large N400 responses indicate specific word expectations (e.g., at "an" in "The day was breezy, so the boy went outside to fly *an* airplane", given the very strong expectation for the final noun phrase to be "a kite"; DeLong, Urbach, & Kutas, 2005) and VWP studies where expected items are fixated before they are named. For example, given a display with a boy, a piece of cake, and some toys, fixations were equivalent for inanimate objects when subjects heard, "The boy will move the . . .", but fixations were directed toward the cake anticipatorily given, "The boy will eat the . . ." (Altmann & Kamide, 1999). Kamide, Altmann, and Haywood (2003) reported more complex interactions of scenes and word meaning. Given two possible riders (GIRL, MAN) and two rideable objects (CAROUSEL, MOTORBIKE), fixation proportions favored expected relationships (greater fixations to CAROUSEL than to MOTORBIKE given, "The girl will ride the . . .", and vice versa for, "The man will ride the . . ."), although expectations appear to be probabilistic (e.g., although most fixations were directed to CAROUSEL given, "The girl will ride the . . .", fixations to MOTORBIKE were greater than to non-ridable items).

Ferretti, McRae, and Hatherell (2001) found additional support for strong impact of sentence context. After establishing that verbs prime typical agents, patients, instruments, and even specific features of patients (MANIPULATING primes NAÏVE), though not typical locations, they presented auditory sentence fragments such as, "She arrested the . . ." (agent role filled, should only prime patient) or "She was arrested by the . . ." (patient role filled, should only prime agent) and then presented a visual target word appropriate for an agent or patient role (e.g., COP/CROOK), which participants had to name. Naming was facilitated only for expected roles. However, given that the VWP has proved more sensitive than a variety of cross-modal paradigms (e.g., Allopenna et al., 1998), Kukona, Fang, Aicher, Chen, and Magnuson (2011) explored similar sentence constraints using the VWP. In one experiment, every sentence was about something that "Toby" was doing (e.g., "Toby arrests the crook"). In critical displays, excellent agents and patients of the verb were displayed (e.g., CROOK and POLICEMAN). Despite the fact that the agent role was *always* filled by Toby (always pictured in the center of the display), equivalent "anticipatory" fixations were observed to both good patients and good agents (which would not be expected if participants make optimal use of context); fixations reliably favored patients only after the onset of the word naming the patient. A second experiment demonstrated reliable anticipatory preference with additional syntactic cues and time for constraints to have impact; all sentences were about things that happened to Toby (e.g., "Toby was arrested by the . . ."), and, while initial fixations to the good patient and agent were equivalent as the verb was heard, a reliable anticipatory preference to fixate the agent emerged during the preposition. It seems that naming in the Ferretti and colleagues (2001) study measured the late dominance of the context-appropriate role and was not sufficiently sensitive to pick up the weaker early coactivation of both roles.

Finally, meaning ascribed to objects in the world also includes something like discourse tags or situation models. Chambers and San Juan (2008) used the VWP and had participants follow a series of instructions with displayed items (e.g., "Move the chair to area 2; now move the chair to area 5; now return the chair to area 2"). An instruction beginning "now return" led to anticipatory eye movements to previously "visited" areas. Thus, recognition of spoken words entails accessing long-term knowledge of semantic features but also situation-specific mappings among words, the environment, and discourse history.

Conclusions

The implications for the mapping from spoken words to meaning is that exactly what dimensions of lexical representations are activated can vary tremendously with context. Normally, bottom-up details have substantial priority, and lexical activation involves complex interactions between bottom-up and top-down constraints and context. Under extreme constraints (that is, unusually strong expectations), preemption, preactivation, and anticipation can be observed for specific semantic classes (e.g., Altmann & Kamide, 1999) or for lexical items (DeLong et al., 2005, Kukona et al., 2011), but such expectations do not override bottom-up input (which would lead to hallucination). Indeed, even under strong constraint, we activate semantic and syntactic classes that are incompatible with context given strong bottom-up cues (Kukona et al., 2011), which only unusually strong constraints appear to circumvent (Shillcock & Bard, 1993). Developing theories of the complex dynamics of how over-time speech input interacts with the phonological and semantic features of words and linguistic and nonlinguistic contexts – as well as how those interactions develop throughout the lifespan – will require the development of more comprehensive computational models, building on the foundational work of Chen and Mirman (2012), Cree and associates (1999), Elman (2009), Gaskell and Marslen-Wilson (1999), and Plaut and Kello (1999).

Notes

1 Note that the literature on semantic dimensions is vastly larger for written than spoken words. However, we cannot be certain that effects from studies with visual words will generalize to spoken words, given differences in how words are experienced in the two modalities (all at once for visual but serially over time for spoken).
2 A crucial preliminary issue is that whether one is able to detect semantic effects in an experiment depends on the type of task used. For example, subtle semantic effects are difficult to find using a lexical decision task (Press "YES" if what you hear is a word, press "NO" if it is not a word.). Among the problems with this task is that it is possible for responses to be generated based on familiarity rather than recognition, and some have argued that it may reflect post-perceptual processing (e.g., Balota & Chumbley, 1984). Tasks that explicitly tap semantic dimensions are, unsurprisingly, much more sensitive to semantic dimensions (e.g., artifact judgments [Press "ARTIFICIAL" or "NATURAL".] or imageability/concreteness judgments [Can you visualize this object? Or can you touch this object?]).

References

Allopenna, P. D., Magnuson, J. S., & Tanenhaus, M. K. (1998). Tracking the time course of spoken word recognition using eye movements: Evidence for continuous mapping models. *Journal of Memory and Language, 38*, 419–439.

Altmann, G. T. M., & Kamide, Y. (1999). Incremental interpretation at verbs: Restricting the domain of subsequent reference. *Cognition, 73*, 247–264.

Andrews, M., Vigliocco, G., & Vinson, D. P. (2009). Integrating experiential and distributional data to learn semantic representations. *Psychological Review, 116*(3), 463–498.

Andrews, S. (1982). Phonological recoding: Is the regularity effect consistent? *Memory & Cognition, 10,* 565–575.

Apfelbaum, K., Blumstein, S. E., & McMurray, B. (2011). Semantic priming is affected by real-time phonological competition: Evidence for continuous cascading systems. *Psychonomic Bulletin & Review, 18,* 141–149.

Balota, D. A., & Chumbley, J. I. (1984). Are lexical decisions a good measure of lexical access? The role of word frequency in the neglected decision stage. *Journal of Experimental Psychology: Human Perception and Performance, 10,* 340–357.

Barsalou, L. W. (1983). Ad hoc categories. *Memory & Cognition, 11,* 211–227.

Barsalou, L. W. (1985). Ideals, central tendency, and frequency of instantiation as determinants of graded structure in categories. *Journal of Experimental Psychology: Learning, Memory, and Cognition, 11,* 629–654.

Barsalou, L. W. (1999). Perceptual symbol systems. *Behavioral and Brain Sciences, 22,* 577–609.

Barsalou, L. W. (2008). Grounded cognition. *Annual Review of Psychology, 59,* 617–645.

Barsalou, L. W., & Wiemer-Hastings, K. (2005). Situating abstract concepts. In D. Pecher & R. Zwaan (Eds.), *Grounding cognition: The role of perception and action in memory, language, and thought* (pp. 129–163). New York: Cambridge University Press.

Brozdowski, C. R., Gordils, J., & Magnuson, J. S. (2013, November). *Contra the Qualitatively Different Representation Hypothesis (QDRH), concrete concepts activate associates faster than abstract concepts.* Talk presented at the Psychonomic Society, Toronto.

Brozdowski, C. R., Gordils, J., & Magnuson J. S. (in preparation). A concreteness advantage for concrete and abstract associations.

Chambers, C., & San Juan, V. (2008). Perception and presupposition in real-time language comprehension: Insights from anticipatory processing. *Cognition, 108,* 26–50.

Chambers, C. G., Tanenhaus, M. K., & Magnuson, J. S. (2004). Actions and affordances in syntactic ambiguity resolution. *Journal of Experimental Psychology: Learning, Memory, & Cognition, 30,* 687–696.

Chen, Q., & Mirman, D. (2012). Competition and cooperation among similar representations: Toward a unified account of facilitative and inhibitory effects of lexical neighbors. *Psychological Review, 119*(2), 417–430.

Collins, A. M., & Loftus, E. F. (1975). A spreading-activation theory of semantic processing. *Psychological Review, 82*(6), 407–428.

Collins, A. M., & Quillian, M. R. (1969). Retrieval time from semantic memory. *Journal of Learning and Verbal Behavior, 8,* 240–247.

Cree, G. S., McRae, K., & McNorgan, C. (1999). An attractor model of lexical conceptual processing: Simulating semantic priming. *Cognitive Science, 23,* 371–414.

Crutch, S. J., & Warrington, E. K. (2005). Abstract and concrete concepts have structurally different representational frameworks. *Brain, 128,* 615–627.

Dahan, D., & Tanenhaus, M. K. (2004). Continuous mapping from sound to meaning in spoken-language comprehension: Immediate effects of verb-based thematic constraints. *Journal of Experimental Psychology: Learning, Memory, and Cognition, 30,* 498–513.

Dahan, D., & Tanenhaus, M. K. (2005). Looking at the rope when looking for the snake: Conceptually mediated eye movements during spoken-word recognition. *Psychonomic Bulletin & Review, 12,* 453–459.

Damasio, A. R. (1989). The brain binds entities and events by multiregional activation from convergence zones. *Neural Computation, 1,* 123–132.

Delong, K., Urbach, T., & Kutas, M. (2005). Probabilistic word pre-activation during language comprehension inferred from electrical brain activity. *Nature Neuroscience, 8,* 1117–1121.

Duñabeitia, J. A., Avilés, A., Afonso, O., Scheepers, C., & Carreiras, M. (2009). Qualitative differences in the representation of abstract versus concrete words: Evidence from the visual-world paradigm. *Cognition, 110*, 284–292.

Elman, J. L. (1990). Finding structure in time. *Cognitive Science, 14*, 179–211.

Elman, J. L. (2009). On the meaning of words and dinosaur bones: Lexical knowledge without a lexicon. *Cognitive Science, 33*, 1–36.

Ferretti, T., McRae, K., & Hatherell, A. (2001). Integrating verbs, situation schemas, and thematic role concepts. *Journal of Memory and Language, 44*, 516–547.

Garner, W. R. (1974). *The processing of information and structure.* New York: Wiley.

Gaskell, M. G., & Marslen-Wilson, W. D. (1997). Integrating form and meaning: A distributed model of speech perception. *Language and Cognitive Processes, 12*, 613–656.

Gaskell, M. G., & Marslen-Wilson, W. D. (1999). Ambiguity, competition, and blending in spoken word recognition. *Cognitive Science, 23*, 439–462.

Gaskell, M. G., & Marslen-Wilson, W. D. (2002). Representation and competition in the perception of spoken words. *Cognitive Psychology, 45*, 220–266.

Glenberg, A. M., & Kaschak M. P. (2003). The body's contribution to language. In B. H. Ross (Ed.), *The psychology of learning and motivation* (pp. 93–126). San Diego, CA: Academic Press.

Gow, D. W. (2012). The cortical organization of lexical knowledge: A dual lexicon model of spoken language processing. *Brain & Language, 121*, 273–288.

Harnad, S. (1990). The symbol grounding problem. *Physica D, 42*, 335–346.

Hickock, G. (2014). *The myth of mirror neurons: The real neuroscience of communication and cognition.* New York: Norton.

Huettig, F., & Altmann, G. T. M. (2005). Word meaning and the control of eye fixation: Semantic competitor effects and the visual world paradigm. *Cognition, 96*(1), 23–32.

Huettig, F., & Altmann, G. T. M. (2007). Visual-shape competition and the control of eye fixation during the processing of unambiguous and ambiguous words. *Visual Cognition, 15*(8), 985–1018.

Kamide, Y., Altmann, G. T. M., & Haywood, S. (2003). The time-course of prediction in incremental sentence processing: Evidence from anticipatory eye movements. *Journal of Memory and Language, 49*, 133–156.

Keil, F. (1989). *Concepts, kinds, and cognitive development.* Cambridge, MA: MIT Press.

Kukona, A., Fang, S., Aicher, K. A., Chen, H., & Magnuson, J. S. (2011). The time course of anticipatory constraint integration. *Cognition, 119*, 23–42.

Landauer, T. K., & Dumais, S. T. (1997). A solution to Plato's problem: The latent semantic analysis theory of acquisition, induction, and representation of knowledge. *Psychological Review, 104*(2), 211–240.

Luce, P. A., & Cluff, M. S. (1998). Delayed commitment in spoken word recognition: Evidence from cross-modal priming. *Perception & Psychophysics, 60*, 484–490.

Lund, K., & Burgess, C. (1996). Producing high-dimensional semantic spaces from lexical co-occurrence. *Behavior Research Methods, Instruments, & Computers, 28*(2), 203–208.

Magnuson, J. S. (2015), Phoneme restoration and empirical coverage of interactive activation and adaptive resonance models of human speech processing. *Journal of the Acoustical Society of America, 137*(3), 1481–1492.

Magnuson, J. S., Dixon, J., Tanenhaus, M. K., & Aslin, R. N. (2007). The dynamics of lexical competition during spoken word recognition. *Cognitive Science, 31*, 133–156.

Magnuson, J. S., & Mirman, D. (2007). *Neighborhood effects in word recognition: It's not where you live, it's how you get home.* Paper presented at the 48th Annual Meeting of the Psychonomic Society, Long Beach, California.

Magnuson, J. S., Mirman, D., & Harris, H. D. (2012). Computational models of spoken word recognition. In M. Spivey, K. McRae, & M. Joanisse (Eds.), *The Cambridge handbook of psycholinguistics* (pp. 76–103). New York: Cambridge University Press.

Magnuson, J. S., Tanenhaus, M. K., & Aslin, R. N. (2008). Immediate effects of form-class constraints on spoken word recognition. *Cognition, 108,* 866–873.

Marr, D. (1982). *Vision.* San Francisco: W. H. Freeman.

Marslen-Wilson, W. D. (1987). Functional parallelism in spoken word recognition. *Cognition, 25,* 71–102.

McClelland, J. L., & Elman, J. L. (1986). The TRACE model of speech perception. *Cognitive Psychology, 18,* 1–86.

McClelland, J. L., & Rogers, T. T. (2003). The parallel distributed processing approach to semantic cognition. *Nature Reviews Neuroscience, 4,* 310–322.

McRae, K., Cree, G. S., Seidenberg, M. S., & McNorgan, C. (2005). Semantic feature production norms for a large set of living and nonliving things. *Behavior Research Methods, 37,* 547–559.

McRae, K., de Sa, V. R., & Seidenberg, M. S. (1997). On the nature and scope of featural representations of word meaning. *Journal of Experimental Psychology: General, 126*(2), 99–130.

Medin, D. L., & Schaeffer, M. M. (1978). Context theory of classification learning. *Psychological Review, 85,* 207–238.

Meteyard, L., Cuadrado, S. R., Bahrami, B., & Vigliocco, G. (2012). Coming of age: A review of embodiment and the neuroscience of semantics. *Cortex, 48,* 788–804.

Mirman, D., & Magnuson, J. S. (2008). Attractor dynamics and semantic neighborhood density: Processing is slowed by near neighbors and speeded by distant neighbors. *Journal of Experimental Psychology: Learning, Memory & Cognition, 34,* 65–79.

Mirman, D., & Magnuson, J. S. (2009). Dynamics of activation of semantically similar concepts during spoken word recognition. *Memory & Cognition, 37,* 1026–1039.

Mirman, D., Strauss, T. J., Dixon, J. A., & Magnuson, J. S. (2010). Effect of representational distance between meanings on recognition of ambiguous spoken words. *Cognitive Science, 34,* 161–173.

Moss, H. E., Ostrin, R. K., Tyler, L. K., & Marslen-Wilson, W. D. (1995). Accessing different types of lexical semantic information: Evidence from priming. *Journal of Experimental Psychology: Learning, Memory & Cognition, 21,* 863–883.

Murphy, G. L. (2002). *The big book of concepts.* Cambridge, MA: MIT Press.

Murphy, G. L., & Medin, D. L. (1985). The role of theories in conceptual coherence. *Psychological Review, 92,* 289–316.

Nelson, D. L., McEvoy, C. L., & Schreiber, T. A. (2004). The University of South Florida free association, rhyme, and word fragment norms. *Behavior Research Methods, Instruments, & Computers, 36*(3), 402–407.

Paivio, A. (1986). *Mental representations: A dual-coding approach.* New York: Oxford University Press.

Pexman, P. M., Holyk, G. G., & Monfils, M.-H. (2003). Number of features effects and semantic processing. *Memory & Cognition, 31,* 842–855.

Plaut, D. C. (1997). Structure and function in the lexical system: Insights from distributed models of word reading and lexical decision. *Language and Cognitive Processes, 12,* 765–805.

Plaut, D. C., & Kello, C. T. (1999). The emergence of phonology from the interplay of speech comprehension and production: A distributed connectionist approach. In B. MacWhinney (Ed.), *The emergence of language* (pp. 381–415). Mahwah, NJ: Erlbaum.

Plaut, D. C., & Shallice, T. (1993). Deep dyslexia: A case study of connectionist neuropsychology. *Cognitive Neuropsychology, 10,* 377–500.

Rodd, J. M., Gaskell, M. G., & Marslen-Wilson, W. D. (2002). Making sense out of ambiguity: Semantic competition in lexical access. *Journal of Memory and Language, 46*(2), 245–266.

Rosch, E., & Mervis, C. B. (1975). Family resemblances: Studies in the internal structure of categories. *Cognitive Psychology, 7,* 573–605.

Sajin, S. M., & Connine, C. M. (2014). Semantic richness: The role of semantic features in processing spoken words. *Journal of Memory & Language, 70,* 13–35.

Shillcock, R., & Bard, E. G. (1993). Modularity and the processing of closed-class words. In G. T. M. Altmann & R. Shillcock (Eds.), *Cognitive models of speech processing: The second Sperlonga meeting* (pp. 163–185). Mahwah, NJ: Erlbaum.

Smith, E. E., & Medin, D. L. (1981). *Categories and concepts.* Cambridge, MA: Harvard University Press.

Spivey-Knowlton, M. J. (1996): *Integration of visual and linguistic information: Human data and model simulations.* PhD dissertation. University of Rochester, Rochester, New York.

Spivey, M. J. (2007). *The continuity of mind.* New York: Oxford University Press.

Swinney, D. (1979). Lexical access during sentence comprehension: (Re)consideration of context effects. *Journal of Verbal Learning and Verbal Behavior, 18,* 645–659.

Tanenhaus, M. K., Leiman, J., & Seidenberg, M. (1979). Evidence for multiple stages in the processing of ambiguous words in syntactic contexts. *Journal of Verbal Learning and Verbal Behavior, 18,* 427–440.

Tanenhaus, M. K., Spivey-Knowlton, M. J., Eberhard, K. M., & Sedivy, J. C. (1995). Integration of visual and linguistic information in spoken language comprehension. *Science, 268,* 1632–1634.

Tyler, L. K., Voice, J. K., & Moss, H. E. (2000). The interaction of meaning and sound in spoken word recognition. *Psychonomic Bulletin & Review, 7,* 320–326.

Vigliocco, G., Vinson, D. P., Lewis, W., & Garrett, M. F. (2004). Representing the meanings of object and action words: The featural and unitary semantic space hypothesis. *Cognitive Psychology, 48*(4), 422–488.

Wittgenstein, L. (1953). *Philosophical investigations.* New York: MacMillan.

Yee, E., Chrysikou, E., Hoffman, E., & Thompson-Schill, S. L. (2013). Manual experience shapes object representation. *Psychological Science, 24*(6), 909–919.

Yee, E., Huffstetler, S., & Thompson-Schill, S. L. (2011). Function follows form: Activation of shape and function features during object identification. *Journal of Experimental Psychology: General, 140*(3), 348–363.

Yee, E., Overton, E., & Thompson-Schill, S. L. (2009). Looking for meaning: Eye movements are sensitive to overlapping semantic features, not association. *Psychonomic Bulletin and Review, 16*(5), 869–874.

Yee, E., & Sedivy, J. (2001). *Using eye movements to track the spread of semantic activation during spoken word recognition.* Paper presented to the 13th Annual CUNY Sentence Processing Conference, Philadelphia.

Yee, E., & Sedivy, J. C. (2006). Eye movements to pictures reveal transient semantic activation during spoken word recognition. *Journal of Experimental Psychology: Learning, Memory, and Cognition, 32,* 1–14.

6

ZONES OF PROXIMAL DEVELOPMENT FOR MODELS OF SPOKEN WORD RECOGNITION

Daniel Mirman

Preparation of this chapter was supported by grant R01DC010805 to D. M. from the National Institutes of Health.

Computational accounts of spoken word recognition have largely relied on the TRACE model (McClelland & Elman, 1986) and simple recurrent networks (SRNs) (Elman, 1990). It is a testament to their explanatory power that, 25 years later, these models remain the dominant computational frameworks for spoken word recognition. These models have been so successful that they have largely defined the agenda for models of spoken word recognition, but there are now well-documented, important phenomena that are relevant to spoken word recognition and yet are (largely) not addressed by models of spoken word recognition. The goal of this chapter is to look forward from these models. Detailed reviews of spoken word recognition (e.g., Magnuson, Mirman, & Myers, 2013) and comprehensive historical reviews of models of spoken word recognition (e.g., Magnuson, Mirman, & Harris, 2012; Weber & Scharenborg, 2012) are available elsewhere; I will provide only a basic introduction to the computational problem of spoken word recognition and the architectures of the TRACE model and SRNs, then focus on a few important behavioral phenomena that these models have addressed and a few challenges for these models. The challenges take the form of neighboring domains that are important for understanding spoken word recognition and where a substantial behavioral literature has accrued but where computational accounts are still lacking. Other models offer more focused accounts of phenomena either within spoken word recognition or in related domains, but none offer a substantive account of spoken word recognition that also addresses the challenges discussed in this chapter. I will conclude with some suggestions for expanding the scope of models of spoken word recognition through the integration of computational accounts of spoken word recognition and other domains.

Spoken word recognition

The computational problem of spoken word recognition is typically defined as mapping a string of speech sounds to a lexical representation (e.g., Magnuson et al., 2013). The speech sounds are often represented abstractly, as distinct phonemes, which may be defined by articulatory features (voicing, place of articulation, etc.) in order to allow the model to capture the effects of feature similarity between phonemes (e.g., that /b/ is more similar to /p/ than to /s/). The lexical representation is a critical intermediate step in the arbitrary mapping from the auditory (phonological) input to word meaning (semantics). That is, the lexical representations pull apart similar auditory/phonological representations in order to facilitate their mapping to very different semantic representations (for example, "bat" and "pat" sound similar but have very different meanings). Whether these non-semantic lexical representations are a theoretical claim or just a convenient simplification, "lexical access" is typically taken to mean activation of a representation of a unique word-form without necessarily activating its semantic, syntactic, or pragmatic relations.

Even within this narrow definition, spoken word recognition is a very challenging computational problem. The speech signal is transient, and its rate is not controlled by the listener, and, unlike printed words and letters, individual speech sounds are blended together due to coarticulation, lacking invariant cues to boundaries between speech sounds or spoken words. The word segmentation and recognition problem is further complicated by the fact that many longer words have shorter words embedded within them (e.g., "window" includes "win", "wind", "in", and "dough"/"doe"). Many of these issues are discussed in more detail in other chapters of this volume.

The computational difficulty of this problem is belied by the fact that typical adults seem to recognize spoken words effortlessly. There is broad agreement about the core aspects of how spoken word recognition is carried out:

- *Incremental activation*: Activation of lexical candidates begins as soon as the initial sound is heard.
- *Parallel activation*: Multiple lexical candidates are activated simultaneously, with activation strength proportional to their similarity to the input and their prior probability (frequency and fit with context).
- *Competition*: Lexical candidates compete for recognition.
- *Interactivity*: Activation of lexical candidates feeds back to influence speech perception and is influenced by top-down signals from semantic, syntactic, and pragmatic context.

The TRACE model and simple recurrent networks

The TRACE model (McClelland & Elman, 1986) and SRNs (Elman, 1990) have been the two most influential models of speech perception and spoken word recognition. At the time of their introduction, these models already captured many of the important behavioral phenomena, and they have continued to be remarkably successful at making novel predictions and explaining new phenomena. Detailed descriptions of these models and their relations to other models of spoken word recognition are provided in the original articles and other recent reviews (Magnuson et al., 2012; Weber & Scharenborg, 2012).

The TRACE model (Figure 6.1, left panel) is an implementation of interactive activation and competition principles in the domain of speech perception and spoken word recognition. It consists of a feature layer, a phoneme layer, and a lexical layer, with each layer consisting of a set of simple processing units. Activation of each unit corresponds to the combined evidence that the corresponding linguistic unit occurred at a particular time within the spoken input. When input is presented at the feature layer, it is propagated in a cascading manner to the phoneme layer, then to the lexical layer through hand-coded excitatory connections between mutually consistent units. As phoneme and lexical units become active, mutually exclusive units within layers compete through inhibitory connections and send excitation back, so the excitatory process is bidirectional ("interactive") with both bottom-up (features to phonemes to words) and top-down (words to phonemes to features) signals. Processing proceeds incrementally with between-layer excitation and within-layer competitive inhibition. The units follow the standard interactive activation function: negative net input drives the unit towards its minimum activation level, positive net input drives the unit towards its maximum activation level, and activation decays toward a baseline rest activation level. A fully documented Java implementation of TRACE is available at http://maglab.psy.uconn.edu/jtrace/ (Strauss, Harris, & Magnuson, 2007).

Unlike the TRACE model, which is a specific implementation of certain computational principles, simple recurrent networks constitute a diverse class of models that share certain implementational and computational features. A standard SRN

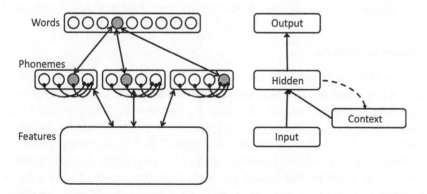

FIGURE 6.1 Left: Schematic diagram of the TRACE model of speech perception and spoken word recognition. Arrows represent hand-coded weights (only a subset is shown). Right: Schematic diagram of simple recurrent network. Solid arrows represent trainable weights; dashed arrow represents copy weights.

(Elman, 1990) consists of simple processing units organized into four layers: input, hidden, output, and context (Figure 6.1, right panel). There are feedforward connections from input to hidden units and from hidden to output units, as in a standard feedforward network. The context units contain an exact copy of the hidden units at the previous time step and are fully connected to the hidden units. These recurrent connections provide the network with the potential for graded memory of previous time steps. Except for the fixed "copy" hidden-to-context connections, all connections in the network are trained through backpropagation of error (Rumelhart, Hinton, & Williams, 1986), which is a generalization of the "delta rule" gradient-descent learning algorithm in which the observed network output is compared to a target pattern and connection weights are adjusted to reduce this error.

A typical approach to modeling spoken word recognition with SRNs is to present a sequence of input vectors corresponding to segments of auditory/phonological input (e.g., features, phonemes, or syllables) and set the desired output to be the next input segment or the current word. This is an important innovation over other supervised learning algorithms because it does not require an external teaching signal; the input signal itself provides the target activation information. The model is trained to predict the input, which forces it to learn the structure of the input (for a more detailed discussion of the importance of prediction in the related domain of sentence processing, see Altmann & Mirković, 2009). Depending on the nature of the training corpus and the size of the network, SRNs can develop sensitivity to fairly long stretches of context. For the purposes of modeling spoken word recognition, an effective strategy (e.g., Magnuson, Tanenhaus, Aslin, & Dahan, 2003) is to use a feature-based representation of phonemes as input and localist lexical representations as output (like the TRACE model); however, one can use distributed output representations (e.g., Gaskell & Marslen-Wilson, 1997) or have multiple output layers for simulating simultaneous performance in different tasks (e.g., Gaskell & Marslen-Wilson, 1997; Mirman, Graf Estes, & Magnuson, 2010).

Model successes

The TRACE model and SRNs can account for dozens of behavioral phenomena in speech perception and spoken word recognition; this section highlights several sets of behavioral phenomena selected because (1) they critically involve lexical representations, (2) they continue to be the subject of active behavioral research in spoken word recognition, and (3) they were demonstrated (largely) *after* the introduction of these models so the models were not designed to account for these phenomena. This last point is important because one of the primary strengths of computational models – that they make concrete testable predictions – typically leads them to be revised or even completely rejected. The fact that the TRACE model and SRNs have accounted for so many *new* phenomena represents their most impressive successes and is largely responsible for their continued relevance in current research on spoken word recognition.

Time course of activation and competition

Allopenna, Magnuson, and Tanenhaus (1998) tracked participants' eye movements while they performed a spoken word-to-picture matching task and found that, as the input signal unfolds, fixation probabilities rise equivalently for words matching the input ("cohorts", such as "penny" and "pencil") until disambiguating information becomes available. Later in the time course, words that rhyme with the target (e.g., "carrot" and "parrot") are also fixated more than baseline unrelated words, though this effect is smaller than the cohort effect. Figure 6.2 (left panel) shows an example of data from such an experiment. Simulations of the TRACE model (Figure 6.2, middle panel) reveal the same pattern: strong initial activation of cohort competitors followed by later and (much) weaker activation of rhyme competitors. The rhyme activation is lower than cohort activation because it is being suppressed by the already active target and cohorts. Together, these behavioral and simulation results demonstrate that the incremental and parallel activation principles must operate as a "continuous mapping" process with incoming input providing bottom-up support for all lexical representations that are consistent with it (for more discussion of different types of incrementality and continuous mapping, see Allopenna et al., 1998).

In a subsequent study, Magnuson et al. (2003) demonstrated that the same effect is produced by an SRN (Figure 6.2, right panel). Their SRN was trained to predict the current word based on sequential input of articulatory/auditory features. The cohort competition effect is straightforward: the model was trying to guess the incoming word, so given /bi/, it would partially activate all words in its lexicon that started with /bi/ – "beaker", "beetle", etc. Similarly, later information (e.g., /-ik^r/) would provide partial bottom-up support for words sharing that offset (e.g., "beaker", "speaker", etc.). The SRN did not have inhibitory weights between lexical units, so the magnitude of the rhyme effect was based entirely on

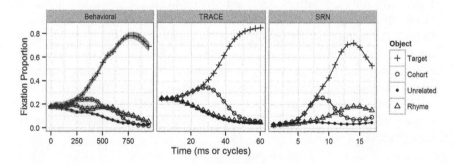

FIGURE 6.2 Cohort and rhyme competition effects. Left: Example of behavioral (eye-tracking) data based on a pilot experiment conducted in the author's laboratory (gray ribbon indicates SE). Middle: TRACE model predicted fixation probabilities based on simulations (reported by Mirman et al., 2011). Right: SRN predicted fixation probabilities (replotted with permission from Magnuson et al., 2003).

the bottom-up weights from the hidden layer, and, indeed, the rhyme effect evolved over the course of learning. Initially, the rhyme effect was as large as the cohort effect, indicating that the model had not yet learned its lexicon well enough to take complete advantage of the early input. As learning continued, the rhyme effect was gradually reduced, which is an important developmental progression (a point that is revisited later in the chapter). Additional training led to the complete elimination of the rhyme effect as the model learned to take advantage of its simplified lexicon and perfectly clear input in order to rule out words that did not match at onset.

Statistical learning

As previously mentioned, the speech signal does not contain invariant cues to word boundaries, so word segmentation requires combining multiple imperfect cues (e.g., Christiansen, Allen, & Seidenberg, 1998). One of those cues is lexical information: even without marked word boundaries, it is sometimes possible to infer boundary locations based on the constraint that the resulting segments have to be real words. For example, there is only one way to segment the printed sequence "silencesbe-tweenwords" to produce a sensible sequence of words. The lexical competition dynamics of the TRACE model produce this sort of lexically based word segmentation (a clear and detailed discussion with simulations is provided by McClelland & Elman, 1986, pp. 61–69).

Another cue is the transitional probability between speech segments: the likelihood of a particular segment (e.g., syllable) given the preceding segment (syllable). Within-word transitional probabilities tend to be high, and between-word transitional probabilities tend to be low. In a landmark study, Saffran and colleagues found that infants and adults are sensitive to such transitional probabilities and can use them to segment a speech stream that has no other cues to word boundaries (for a simple review, see Saffran, 2003). Subsequent studies have shown that this kind of statistical learning facilitates learning of word meanings in infants (Graf Estes, Evans, Alibali, & Saffran, 2007) and adults (Mirman, Magnuson, Graf Estes, & Dixon, 2008). Although these behavioral observations had not yet been made, Elman's (1990) original description of SRNs demonstrated that SRNs are sensitive to transitional probabilities and that this information could be used to segment words. Later simulations specifically showed that SRNs also exhibit the facilitative effect of transitional probability on word learning and that this effect arises because syllables with higher transitional probabilities develop hidden-layer representations that are more distinctive and therefore easier to map to lexical-semantic representations (Mirman et al., 2010).

Lexically guided tuning

One consequence of interactive processing in spoken word recognition is that lexical activation feeds back to affect speech perception (for reviews, see McClelland, Mirman, Bolger, & Khaitan, 2014; McClelland, Mirman, & Holt, 2006). A particularly important recent example is lexically guided tuning (for a review, see Samuel & Kraljic, 2009): if an ambiguous speech sound is consistently presented in disambiguating lexical contexts, it will come to be perceived in the lexically consistent way even without the context. For example, an ambiguous sound between /f/ and /s/ that is presented in words like "sheri_" will come to be identified as /f/ even when presented in isolation (or will be identified as /s/ if it had been presented in words like "Pari_").

The addition of a simple Hebbian learning algorithm was sufficient to produce this lexically guided tuning effect in the TRACE model (Mirman, McClelland, & Holt, 2006): an ambiguous input initially activates both possible phoneme units, but lexical feedback provides direct excitatory input to the lexically consistent phoneme unit. The Hebbian learning algorithm implemented by Mirman and colleagues strengthened the connection between concurrently active units; since the lexically consistent phoneme unit was more active (due to lexical feedback), it developed stronger connections to the input pattern. As a result, after the exposure/learning period, the previously ambiguous input pattern activated the lexically consistent phoneme more strongly even when there was no lexical context.

Individual differences

Understanding individual differences in speech perception and spoken word recognition has important theoretical and practical implications, but these efforts are often marginalized. On the practical side, understanding individual differences may help to develop more effective treatment strategies for developmental and acquired language deficits and may help adults learn a second language. On the theoretical side, individual differences reveal the structure of the cognitive system under investigation. The individual differences approach has deep roots, from the work of nineteenth-century neurologists, which formed the foundation of cognitive neuroscience, to research on chess and memory experts at the dawn of the cognitive revolution, though its appeal may have waned with the advent of functional neuroimaging and undergraduate participant pools. Nevertheless, the combination of computational modeling and case series studies of individuals with acquired language deficits (Patterson & Plaut, 2009; Schwartz & Dell, 2010) has had a tremendous impact on theories of semantic memory (e.g., Lambon Ralph, 2014; Rogers et al., 2004) and spoken word production (Dell, Schwartz, Nozari, Faseyitan, & Coslett, 2013; Schwartz, Dell, Martin, Gahl, & Sobel, 2006). Note that these computational models are instantiations of general theories of semantic memory and spoken word production, not theories of deficits per se. The neuropsychological data provide additional constraints on those theories and a potential link between cognitive theories and the neural implementation (e.g., Dell et al., 2013; Lambon Ralph, 2014). There have been far fewer systematic efforts to use computational models to account for individual differences in spoken word recognition. However, there have been a few important and promising successes.

Yee (2005) found that individuals with Broca's aphasia exhibited reduced cohort competition and increased rhyme competition, whereas individuals with Wernicke's aphasia exhibited the opposite pattern – increased cohort competition and reduced rhyme competition. Mirman and colleagues (2011) reanalyzed these data and found that, in addition to the apparent double dissociation, the participants with aphasia also exhibited a negative correlation between cohort and rhyme competition effect size. Mirman and associates then manipulated TRACE model parameters to implement six different competing accounts of spoken word recognition deficits in aphasia. Only one implementation accounted for both the double dissociation and the negative correlation between cohort and rhyme effect sizes: a response selectivity parameter that controls how activation of lexical representations drives responses. Low selectivity meant less sensitivity to activation differences, which predicted relatively more selection (fixation) of weak competitors (rhymes) and less selection (fixation) of strong competitors (cohorts), as observed for individuals with Broca's aphasia. High selectivity meant increased sensitivity to activation differences, which predicted relatively more selection (fixation) of strong competitors (cohorts) and less selection (fixation) of weak competitors (rhymes), as observed for individuals with Wernicke's aphasia. Regardless of whether this specific claim holds as more data are collected, computational models provide a common ground for testing theories. Creating concrete instantiations of the competing accounts makes it easier to make predictions from individual theories, to test theories, and to improve them. Similar approaches have also been applied to individual differences within the relatively homogeneous population of college students (Mirman, Dixon, & Magnuson, 2008) and in children with specific language impairment (McMurray, Samelson, Lee, & Tomblin, 2010).

These successes represent just first steps toward computational models of individual differences in spoken word recognition. There are far more behavioral data about individual differences in speech perception and spoken word recognition than have been addressed computationally, from bilingualism (Chapter 8 of this volume) to atypical development (specific language impairment, autism spectrum disorders, etc.; Chapter 9 of this volume) to acquired language disorders. It is not uncommon to attribute such individual differences to constructs, such as inhibitory control or language experience, that have relatively direct computational implementations in TRACE and/or SRNs (e.g., lexical inhibition parameter, number of training epochs). Therefore, such theoretical claims are readily testable using these computational models.

Development

An extremely important and very common source of individual differences in spoken word recognition is simply development. Mayor and Plunkett (2014) conducted simulations of the TRACE model using lexicons based on published norms of infant vocabulary development and provided new insights into how lexicon size and composition should affect spoken word recognition during development.

Examining the specific case of a proposed shift from holistic to segmental word representations (Walley, 1993), SRN simulations (Magnuson et al., 2003) offered a new theoretical perspective: a naïve (untrained) model does not know whether word onsets or offsets are going to be more informative about the identity of the word and it takes some time for the model to learn the phonological structure of its lexicon. As a result, early in learning, weak representations produce equal sensitivity to onset (cohort) and offset (rhyme) overlap. As the model's knowledge of the lexical structure develops, the model learns to take more and more advantage of the onset information, leading to larger cohort effects and smaller rhyme effects.

As these studies demonstrate, a biologically plausible model is not strictly necessary for computational investigations of spoken language development and individual differences. By providing direct access to the parameters that govern its processing dynamics, the TRACE model is a powerful framework for testing and developing computational accounts of individual differences and development. Developmental and acquired language impairments can be modeled using adjustments of these parameters; typical development can be modeled as increases in connection strengths and lexicon size. SRNs offer another framework for computational investigation of development (and individual differences), one in which both development and the parameters that govern processing dynamics are more intrinsic to the model and the results are emergent properties. Like the domain of individual differences, there are far more behavioral data on the development of spoken word recognition that have concrete computational accounts (see, e.g., Chapters 3 and 9 of this volume); however, the existing successes suggest that TRACE and SRNs are promising frameworks for future computational efforts.

Model challenges

The previous section highlighted some of the most important successes of the TRACE model and SRNs for current research in spoken word recognition. However, these successes are within the specific domain of spoken word recognition; the weaknesses are in addressing how spoken word recognition interacts with and is influenced by other cognitive domains such as semantic memory, cognitive control, and learning. Because these issues have been defined as outside the scope of models of spoken word recognition, the existing models have fallen farther and farther behind contemporary behavioral and neuroscience research on spoken word recognition. As the final section will discuss, these domains have their own computational models, so there is potential for integration, but current models of spoken word recognition have not done so.

Semantic, syntactic, and pragmatic constraints

Models of spoken word recognition typically stop at a simple localist lexical representation that does not capture any semantic information. Semantic information is activated very quickly from speech input, even before the word is complete (e.g.,

Gaskell & Marslen-Wilson, 2002) and top-down semantic influences reach down to affect speech perception (e.g., Borsky, Tuller, & Shapiro, 1998; Warren & Warren, 1970). That is, cascading and interactive processing should produce lexical activations that reflect the combination of top-down influences and bottom-up phonological influences. Indeed, like the cohort and rhyme competition effects, eye-tracking studies have revealed incidental activation of semantic competitors during spoken word-to-picture matching (e.g., Huettig & Altmann, 2005; Mirman & Graziano, 2012; Mirman & Magnuson, 2009; Yee & Sedivy, 2006), including time course differences between distinct types of semantic features or relations (e.g., Kalénine, Mirman, Middleton, & Buxbaum, 2012).

Failing to consider semantic influences when modeling spoken word recognition could lead to substantial misrepresentation or misunderstanding of the processing dynamics, especially when the core experimental paradigms often involve semantic processing (e.g., spoken word-to-picture matching requires accessing the semantic content of the word and the pictures). For example, although competition between phonological neighbors typically delays recognition of spoken words from "dense" phonological neighborhoods, Chen and Mirman (2014) found that semantic input (implemented as picture preview) could reverse this effect. This surprising facilitative effect was predicted by their model (see also Chen & Mirman, 2012) in large part because their model was designed to capture the effects of both phonological and semantic input.

Models of spoken word recognition have also ignored a growing literature showing that listeners anticipate upcoming words based on preceding semantic context (for a review, see Altmann & Mirković, 2009), which affects both target recognition and degree of competitor activation (e.g., Altmann & Kamide, 1999; Kalénine et al., 2012; Kukona, Fang, Aicher, Chen, & Magnuson, 2011). This rapidly growing literature suggests that the effects of anticipation on lexical competition are not straightforward, and there are open questions that may be fruitfully addressed by computational accounts (see also Chapter 5). For example, syntactic and pragmatic expectations about grammatical class (e.g., whether the speaker's next word is going to be an adjective or a noun) seem to constrain lexical competition such that nouns compete with nouns but not with adjectives (Magnuson, Tanenhaus, & Aslin, 2008). On the other hand, pragmatic "common ground" expectations seem to produce target anticipation without reducing competition from incompatible competitors, whereas semantic expectations produce both target anticipation and reduced competition from incompatible cohorts (Barr, 2008). Without a computational implementation, it is not clear how common ground constraints could be strong enough to produce robust anticipation effects without at least reducing (if not necessarily eliminating) competition from incompatible cohorts. There may be not yet discovered aspects of spoken word recognition dynamics that explain this, but investigating them requires a model that implements semantic, syntactic, and pragmatic constraints.

These phenomena are outside the scope of current models of spoken word recognition, but they do not necessarily require a radical overhaul of computational frameworks. For example, SRN models of sentence processing readily produce anticipation/prediction effects (Altmann & Mirković, 2009) and such effects can be captured using other approaches within the parallel distributed processing (PDP) framework (e.g., Kukona, Cho, Magnuson, & Tabor, 2014). The challenge may be integrating SRN models of spoken word recognition and sentence processing rather than developing a novel computational framework.

Auditory and acoustic realities

Just as the simplified output representations ignore the influence of higher-level factors, the simplified input to models of spoken word recognition also underestimates the way the realities of the speech signal affect spoken word recognition. Much like the semantic, syntactic, and pragmatic contexts, the phonological context also produces anticipation (e.g., DeLong, Urbach, & Kutas, 2005) and may similarly constrain the activation and competition dynamics (e.g., Tobin, Cho, Jennett, & Magnuson, 2010).

Models of spoken word recognition typically assume clear input and a cognitive-perceptual system uniquely engaged in spoken word recognition. In stark contrast, natural spoken word recognition takes place under a variety of "adverse conditions" (for a comprehensive review, see Mattys, Davis, Bradlow, & Scott, 2012): word reductions and deletions (typical of casual speech, e.g., Dilley & Pitt, 2010), accented speech, disfluencies, energetic masking (background noise) and filtering (e.g., telephone transmission filters out low and high frequencies), and listener attention/distraction (cognitive load) or imperfect hearing. Generalization of the lexically guided tuning effect previously described appears to be influenced by allophonic similarity (Kraljic & Samuel, 2006; Mitterer, Scharenborg, & McQueen, 2013), suggesting that speech sound representations preserve aspects of auditory input beyond just abstract phoneme identity (see also Chapter 1). Sensitivity to systematic sub-phonemic differences can also simplify the spoken word recognition task – the association between vowel length and word length can help to distinguish embedded and carrier words such as "ham" from "hamster" (e.g., Salverda, Dahan, & McQueen, 2003). Addressing these issues from a computational perspective requires grappling with core theoretical questions. What are the representational units of speech perception? How do abstract and episodic representations jointly contribute to spoken word recognition? If immediate speech sound recognition is not possible in adverse conditions, how is the time course of lexical activation and competition affected?

As with top-down effects of semantic, syntactic, and pragmatic context, the SRN framework is likely to be able to capture at least some of these effects. SRNs would certainly produce phonological anticipation effects, and the SRN model developed by Magnuson et al. (2003) would likely exhibit sensitivity to vowel length as a signal of word length if its input representation included this property of natural spoken words. In simulations of the TRACE model, the addition of input noise increases the size of the rhyme competition effect (Mirman et al., 2011), providing a computational prediction regarding the effects of noise in the input speech signal or peripheral auditory perceptual impairment.

Cognitive control

In models of spoken word recognition, "inhibition" is usually implemented as a domain-specific process such as inhibition between lexical representations, either by hand-coded inhibitory connections or emergent from representational overlap. In cognitive science more broadly, inhibition is typically framed as a higher-level executive or cognitive control function ("inhibitory control"). Studies that explore inhibitory control have used a mixture of non-linguistic tasks (e.g., the flanker task) and tasks that have a verbal component (e.g., the Stroop task) but have rarely made any meaningful contact with mechanisms of word processing. Instead, they seem to view inhibitory control as something that takes place outside the language system and modulates processing within the language system.

One might imagine that this is merely coincidental terminological overlap with no mechanistic implications, were it not for the fact that cognitive control is often invoked to explain aspects of spoken word processing, particularly individual differences in spoken word recognition. For example, larger inhibitory effects of lexical neighborhood density have been attributed to decreases in inhibitory control in normal aging (Sommers & Danielson, 1999; Sommers, 1996; Taler, Aaron, Steinmetz, & Pisoni, 2010), Alzheimer's type (Sommers, 1998), and aphasia (Botezatu & Mirman, 2014; Mirman & Graziano, 2013).

The role of cognitive control in spoken word recognition is also apparent in aphasic lexical-semantic "access deficits", in which word (or concept) knowledge is intact but access to this knowledge appears to be ineffective, inefficient, and inconsistent (for a detailed review, see Mirman & Britt, 2014). These effects have been demonstrated in spoken word-to-picture matching and spoken-to-written word matching (and other tasks), but substantial extensions of existing models of spoken word recognition would be required to account for all of the relevant phenomena, and there is no single account of access deficits to be integrated with models of spoken word recognition. On one view, access deficits arise from abnormal activation and deactivation (refractoriness) due to damage to neuromodulatory systems (Gotts & Plaut, 2002), but this model did not attempt to capture even basic aspects of spoken word recognition. Combining existing models of spoken word recognition with the computational model of neuromodulatory damage may provide a way toward a comprehensive account of access deficits and the role of cognitive control in spoken word recognition. As a starting point, Mirman and associates (2011) found that modulating the gain of the TRACE model's response selection mechanism (the slope of the nonlinear relationship between relative activation and response probability) provided the best account for the trade-off between rhyme and cohort competition effects in eight individuals with aphasia, consistent with the hypothesis that the deficit is related to cognitive control mechanisms outside the spoken word recognition system.

The contrast between the models of Gotts and Plaut (2002) and Mirman and colleagues (2011) is instructive. Gotts and Plaut proposed a sophisticated, biologically based model of neuromodulatory cognitive control but a highly simplified model of word recognition. Mirman and associates used a sophisticated, comprehensive model of spoken word recognition (TRACE) but a highly simplified model of cognitive control and response selection. Further efforts to bridge this gap and connect spoken word recognition with cognitive control may lead to substantial advances in our understanding of how spoken words are recognized.

Learning and memory

Although models of spoken word recognition have captured some very important aspects of the interactions between spoken word recognition and learning and memory, these accounts focus on individual phenomena and are still a long way from capturing the complexity of how learning and memory impact spoken word recognition (see Chapter 7, this volume). One particularly interesting set of phenomena involves the effect of sleep-related memory consolidation of word learning and lexical structure. The importance of sleep for memory consolidation has been known for some time (Stickgold, 2013), but recent studies have demonstrated its particular role in word learning (for a review and theoretical perspective, see Davis & Gaskell, 2009). Specifically, novel words can be learned quite quickly (e.g., Shtyrov, Nikulin, & Pulvermüller, 2010), but they do not begin to compete with known words until a period of consolidation has passed, typically overnight (Dumay & Gaskell, 2007, 2012; Henderson, Weighall, Brown, & Gaskell, 2012; Lindsay & Gaskell, 2013). Complementary learning systems' (e.g., O'Reilly, Bhattacharyya, Howard, & Ketz, 2014) accounts of memory offer a framework for understanding this pattern: newly learned words may be initially stored in a fast-learning hippocampal-dependent memory system, then more slowly integrated into the neocortical lexical-semantic system. Implementing this mechanism within models of spoken word recognition would require a more complex notion of the "mental lexicon" and would open the door to new predictions based on the complementary learning systems framework that could help to refine our understanding of how spoken word recognition interacts with learning and memory systems.

Toward a more complete model of spoken word recognition

The TRACE model and SRNs have served as very powerful computational frameworks for understanding spoken word recognition. They account for dozens of behavioral phenomena, including some that were documented after the development of these models. These successes have relied, in part, on detailed investigations of a relatively narrowly defined computational problem: identifying a lexical target from phonological input. After more than a quarter century of highly productive behavioral, computational, and neuroscience research, it may be time to expand what we mean by "spoken word recognition". This chapter has identified four particularly promising domains for expansion based on their wealth of behavioral evidence and computational tractability.

First, whether isolated lexical representations exist or not, they are certainly not the end result of spoken word recognition, which is influenced by semantic, syntactic, and pragmatic factors. The TRACE model and SRNs are part of the PDP framework, and other PDP models have already been developed for semantic (e.g., Rabovsky & McRae, 2014; Rogers & McClelland, 2004; Rogers et al., 2004) and syntactic (e.g., Altmann & Mirković, 2009; McClelland, St. John, & Taraban, 1989) processing, so integrating these models to develop a model of spoken word *comprehension* in sentence and discourse contexts is a natural next step.

Second, modeling speech input as a clear and unvarying signal has misrepresented the dynamics of real-world spoken word recognition and may have distorted our theories of spoken word recognition. There has been tremendous progress in automatic speech recognition (e.g., Cutajar, Micallef, Casha, Grech, & Gatt, 2013) and in understanding the relationship between speech perception and speech production (Hickok, 2012). A few computational modeling efforts have attempted to take advantage of perception-production links (Plaut & Kello, 1999) and insights from automatic speech recognition (Scharenborg, Norris, Bosch, & McQueen, 2005) and machine learning (Hannagan, Magnuson, & Grainger, 2013), but these approaches have not yet had widespread impact on models of spoken word recognition. The combined effort to include higher-level factors (semantic, syntactic, pragmatic) and lower-level (acoustic/auditory) factors will also move models of spoken word recognition away from stipulated representations and toward emergent representations, providing greater insights into the mechanisms involved.

Third, cognitive control functions are often invoked to explain phenomena in spoken word recognition with relatively little effort to specify these mechanisms or how they interact with spoken word recognition mechanisms. A prime example is "inhibition", which can be used to refer to a property of the spoken word recognition system (e.g., inhibitory weights in the TRACE model), a cognitive control function (i.e., inhibitory control), or a general property of cognitive processing (i.e., "interactive activation and *competition*"). Perhaps inhibition is all three of these (a general property of cognitive processing, modulated by a cognitive control system, and playing an important role in spoken word recognition), but appeals to underspecified cognitive control mechanisms are generally not falsifiable and hold back development of theories of spoken word recognition. There are already quite detailed cognitive and neural models of cognitive control and of inhibitory control in particular (e.g., Munakata et al., 2011), which could potentially be integrated with models of spoken word recognition.

Fourth, models of spoken word recognition have been remarkably successful at capturing some aspects of learning in spoken word recognition, but these efforts have been largely divorced from the broader cognitive, neurobiological, and computational research on learning and memory. TRACE models and SRN simulations have given us new insights into how learning new words affects spoken word recognition but little insight into what it means to learn new words in relation to other kinds of learning and memory.

These four "zones of proximal development" are the most promising domains for expanding models of spoken word recognition, providing new insights into the mechanisms and representations that support spoken word recognition and making connections with other domains of perceptual and cognitive processing.

References

Allopenna, P. D., Magnuson, J. S., & Tanenhaus, M. K. (1998). Tracking the time course of spoken word recognition using eye movements: Evidence for continuous mapping models. *Journal of Memory & Language, 38*(4), 419–439.

Altmann, G. T. M., & Kamide, Y. (1999). Incremental interpretation at verbs: Restricting the domain of subsequent reference. *Cognition, 73*(3), 247–264. doi:10.1016/S0010-0277(99)00059-1

Altmann, G. T. M., & Mirković, J. (2009). Incrementality and prediction in human sentence processing. *Cognitive Science, 33*(4), 583–609. doi:10.1111/j.1551–6709.2009.01022.x

Barr, D. J. (2008). Pragmatic expectations and linguistic evidence: Listeners anticipate but do not integrate common ground. *Cognition, 109*(1), 18–40. doi:10.1016/j.cognition.2008.07.005

Borsky, S., Tuller, B., & Shapiro, L. P. (1998). "How to milk a coat": The effects of semantic and acoustic information on phoneme categorization. *Journal of the Acoustical Society of America, 103*(5), 2670–2676.

Botezatu, M. R., & Mirman, D. (2014). A link between lexical competition and fluency in aphasia. *Frontiers in Psychology Conference Abstract: Academy of Aphasia – 52nd Annual Meeting.* doi:10.3389/conf.fpsyg.2014.64.00022

Chen, Q., & Mirman, D. (2012). Competition and cooperation among similar representations: Toward a unified account of facilitative and inhibitory effects of lexical neighbors. *Psychological Review, 119*(2), 417–430. doi:10.1037/a0027175

Chen, Q., & Mirman, D. (2014). Interaction between phonological and semantic representations: Time matters. *Cognitive Science, 39*(3), 538–558.

Christiansen, M. H., Allen, J., & Seidenberg, M. S. (1998). Learning to segment speech using multiple cues: A connectionist model. *Language and Cognitive Processes, 13*(2–3), 221–268. doi:10.1080/016909698386528

Cutajar, M., Micallef, J., Casha, O., Grech, I., & Gatt, E. (2013). Comparative study of automatic speech recognition techniques. *IET Signal Processing, 7*(1), 25–46. doi:10.1049/iet-spr.2012.0151

Davis, M. H., & Gaskell, M. G. (2009). A complementary systems account of word learning: Neural and behavioural evidence. *Philosophical Transactions of the Royal Society of London: Series B, Biological Sciences, 364*(1536), 3773–3800. doi:10.1098/rstb.2009.0111

Dell, G. S., Schwartz, M. F., Nozari, N., Faseyitan, O., & Coslett, H. B. (2013). Voxel-based lesion-parameter mapping: Identifying the neural correlates of a computational model of word production. *Cognition, 128*(3), 380–396. doi:10.1016/j.cognition.2013.05.007

DeLong, K. A., Urbach, T. P., & Kutas, M. (2005). Probabilistic word pre-activation during language comprehension inferred from electrical brain activity. *Nature Neuroscience, 8*(8), 1117. Retrieved from kadelong@cogsci.ucsd.edu

Dilley, L. C., & Pitt, M. A. (2010). Altering context speech rate can cause words to appear or disappear. *Psychological Science, 21*(11), 1664–1670. doi:10.1177/0956797610384743

Dumay, N., & Gaskell, M. G. (2007). Sleep-associated changes in the mental representation of spoken words. *Psychological Science, 18*(1), 35–39. doi:10.1111/j.1467–9280.2007.01845.x

Dumay, N., & Gaskell, M. G. (2012). Overnight lexical consolidation revealed by speech segmentation. *Cognition, 123*(1), 119–32. doi:10.1016/j.cognition.2011.12.009

Elman, J. L. (1990). Finding structure in time. *Cognitive Science, 14*(2), 179–211.

Gaskell, M. G., & Marslen-Wilson, W. D. (1997). Integrating form and meaning: A distributed model of speech perception. *Language and Cognitive Processes, 12*(5), 613–656. doi:10.1080/016909697386646

Gaskell, M. G., & Marslen-Wilson, W. D. (2002). Representation and competition in the perception of spoken words. *Cognitive Psychology, 45*(2), 220–266. doi:10.1016/S0010-0285(02)00003-8

Gotts, S. J., & Plaut, D. C. (2002). The impact of synaptic depression following brain damage: A connectionist account of "access/refractory" and "degraded-store" semantic impairments. *Cognitive, Affective & Behavioral Neuroscience, 2*(3), 187–213.

Graf Estes, K., Evans, J. L., Alibali, M. W., & Saffran, J. R. (2007). Can infants map meaning to newly segmented words?: Statistical segmentation and word learning. *Psychological Science, 18*(3), 254–260. doi:10.1111/j.1467–9280.2007.01885.x

Hannagan, T., Magnuson, J. S., & Grainger, J. (2013). Spoken word recognition without a TRACE. *Frontiers in Psychology, 4*(563), 1–17. doi:10.3389/fpsyg.2013.00563

Henderson, L. M., Weighall, A. R., Brown, H., & Gaskell, M. G. (2012). Consolidation of vocabulary is associated with sleep in children. *Developmental Science, 15*(5), 674–687. doi:10.1111/j.1467–7687.2012.01172.x

Hickok, G. S. (2012). Computational neuroanatomy of speech production. *Nature Reviews Neuroscience, 13*(2), 135–145. doi:10.1038/nrn3158

Huettig, F., & Altmann, G. T. M. (2005). Word meaning and the control of eye fixation: Semantic competitor effects and the visual world paradigm. *Cognition, 96*(1), B23–B32. doi:10.1016/j.cognition.2004.10.003

Kalénine, S., Mirman, D., Middleton, E. L., & Buxbaum, L. J. (2012). Temporal dynamics of activation of thematic and functional action knowledge during auditory comprehension of artifact words. *Journal of Experimental Psychology: Learning, Memory, and Cognition, 38*(5), 1274–1295. doi:10.1037/a0027626

Kraljic, T., & Samuel, A. G. (2006). Generalization in perceptual learning for speech. *Psychonomic Bulletin & Review, 13*, 262–268.

Kukona, A., Cho, P. W., Magnuson, J. S., & Tabor, W. (2014). Lexical interference effects in sentence processing: Evidence from the visual world paradigm and self-organizing models. *Journal of Experimental Psychology: Learning, Memory, and Cognition, 40*(2), 326–347.

Kukona, A., Fang, S.-Y., Aicher, K. A., Chen, H., & Magnuson, J. S. (2011). The time course of anticipatory constraint integration. *Cognition, 119*(1), 23–42. doi:10.1016/j.cognition.2010.12.002

Lambon Ralph, M. A. (2014). Neurocognitive insights on conceptual knowledge and its breakdown. *Philosophical Transactions of the Royal Society B: Biological Sciences, 369*(1634), 20120392. doi:10.1098/rstb.2012.0392

Lindsay, S., & Gaskell, M. G. (2013). Lexical integration of novel words without sleep. *Journal of Experimental Psychology: Learning, Memory, and Cognition, 39*(2), 608–622. doi:10.1037/a0029243

Magnuson, J. S., Mirman, D., & Harris, H. D. (2012). Computational models of spoken word recognition. In M. J. Spivey, M. F. Joanisse, & K. McRae (Eds.), *The Cambridge Handbook of Psycholinguistics* (pp. 76–103). New York: Cambridge University Press.

Magnuson, J. S., Mirman, D., & Myers, E. B. (2013). Spoken Word Recognition. In D. Reisberg (Ed.), *Oxford Handbook of Cognitive Psychology* (pp. 412–441). New York: Oxford University Press.

Magnuson, J. S., Tanenhaus, M. K., & Aslin, R. N. (2008). Immediate effects of form-class constraints on spoken word recognition. *Cognition, 108*(3), 866–873.

Magnuson, J. S., Tanenhaus, M. K., Aslin, R. N., & Dahan, D. (2003). The time course of spoken word learning and recognition: Studies with artificial lexicons. *Journal of Experimental Psychology: General, 132*(2), 202–227.

Mattys, S. L., Davis, M. H., Bradlow, A. R., & Scott, S. K. (2012). Speech recognition in adverse conditions: A review. *Language and Cognitive Processes, 27*(7–8), 953–978.

Mayor, J., & Plunkett, K. (2014). Infant word recognition: Insights from TRACE simulations. *Journal of Memory and Language, 71*(1), 89–123. doi:10.1016/j.jml.2013.09.009

McClelland, J. L., & Elman, J. L. (1986). The TRACE model of speech perception. *Cognitive Psychology, 18*(1), 1–86.

McClelland, J. L., Mirman, D., Bolger, D. J., & Khaitan, P. (2014). Interactive activation and mutual constraint satisfaction in perception and cognition. *Cognitive Science, 38*(6), 1139–1189. doi:10.1111/cogs.12146

McClelland, J. L., Mirman, D., & Holt, L. L. (2006). Are there interactive processes in speech perception? *Trends in Cognitive Sciences, 10*(8), 363–369. doi:10.1016/j.tics.2006.06.007

McClelland, J. L., St. John, M. F., & Taraban, R. (1989). Sentence comprehension: A parallel distributed processing approach. *Language and Cognitive Processes, 4*(3/4), 287–335.

McMurray, B., Samelson, V. M., Lee, S. H., & Tomblin, J. B. (2010). Individual differences in online spoken word recognition: Implications for SLI. *Cognitive Psychology, 60*(1), 1–39.

Mirman, D., & Britt, A. E. (2014). What we talk about when we talk about access deficits. *Philosophical Transactions of the Royal Society B: Biological Sciences, 369*(1634). doi:10.1098/rstb.2012.0388

Mirman, D., Dixon, J. A., & Magnuson, J. S. (2008). Statistical and computational models of the visual world paradigm: Growth curves and individual differences. *Journal of Memory and Language, 59*(4), 475–494. doi:10.1016/j.jml.2007.11.006

Mirman, D., Graf Estes, K., & Magnuson, J. S. (2010). Computational modeling of statistical learning: Effects of transitional probability versus frequency and links to word learning. *Infancy, 15*(5), 471–486. doi:10.1111/j.1532–7078.2009.00023.x

Mirman, D., & Graziano, K. M. (2012). Individual differences in the strength of taxonomic versus thematic relations. *Journal of Experimental Psychology: General, 141*(4), 601–609. doi:10.1037/a0026451

Mirman, D., & Graziano, K. M. (2013). The neural basis of inhibitory effects of semantic and phonological neighbors in spoken word production. *Journal of Cognitive Neuroscience, 25*(9), 1504–1516. doi:10.1162/jocn

Mirman, D., & Magnuson, J. S. (2009). Dynamics of activation of semantically similar concepts during spoken word recognition. *Memory & Cognition, 37*(7), 1026–1039. doi:10.3758/MC.37.7.1026

Mirman, D., Magnuson, J. S., Graf Estes, K., & Dixon, J. A. (2008). The link between statistical segmentation and word learning in adults. *Cognition, 108*(1), 271–280. doi:10.1016/j.cognition.2008.02.003

Mirman, D., McClelland, J. L., & Holt, L. L. (2006). An interactive Hebbian account of lexically guided tuning of speech perception. *Psychonomic Bulletin & Review, 13*(6), 958–965. doi:10.3758/BF03213909

Mirman, D., Yee, E., Blumstein, S. E., & Magnuson, J. S. (2011). Theories of spoken word recognition deficits in aphasia: Evidence from eye-tracking and computational modeling. *Brain and Language, 117*(2), 53–68. doi:10.1016/j.bandl.2011.01.004

Mitterer, H., Scharenborg, O., & McQueen, J. M. (2013). Phonological abstraction without phonemes in speech perception. *Cognition, 129*(2), 356–361. doi:10.1016/j.cognition.2013.07.011

Munakata, Y., Herd, S. A., Chatham, C. H., Depue, B. E., Banich, M. T., & O'Reilly, R. C. (2011). A unified framework for inhibitory control. *Trends in Cognitive Sciences, 15*(10), 453–459. doi:10.1016/j.tics.2011.07.011

O'Reilly, R. C., Bhattacharyya, R., Howard, M. D., & Ketz, N. (2014). Complementary learning systems. *Cognitive Science, 38*(6), 1229–1248. doi:10.1111/j.1551–6709.2011.01214.x

Patterson, K. E., & Plaut, D. C. (2009). "Shallow draughts intoxicate the brain": Lessons from cognitive science for cognitive neuropsychology. *Topics in Cognitive Science, 1,* 39–58.

Plaut, D. C., & Kello, C. T. (1999). The emergence of phonology from the interplay of speech comprehension and production: A distributed connectionist approach. In B. MacWhinney (Ed.), *The Emergence of Language* (pp. 381–416). Mahwah, NJ: Erlbaum.

Rabovsky, M., & McRae, K. (2014). Simulating the N400 ERP component as semantic network error: Insights from a feature-based connectionist attractor model of word meaning. *Cognition, 132*(1), 68–89. doi:10.1016/j.cognition.2014.03.010

Rogers, T. T., Lambon Ralph, M. A., Garrard, P., Bozeat, S., McClelland, J. L., Hodges, J. R., & Patterson, K. E. (2004). Structure and deterioration of semantic memory: A neuropsychological and computational investigation. *Psychological Review, 111*(1), 205–235.

Rogers, T. T., & McClelland, J. L. (2004). *Semantic Cognition: A Parallel Distributed Processing Approach.* Cambridge, MA: MIT Press.

Rumelhart, D. E., Hinton, G. E., & Williams, R. J. (1986). Learning internal representations by error propagation. In D. E. Rumelhart & J. L. McClelland (Eds.), *Parallel Distributed Processing: Explorations in the Microstructure of Cognition* (Vol. 1, pp. 318–362). Cambridge, MA: MIT Press.

Saffran, J. R. (2003). Statistical language learning: Mechanisms and constraints. *Current Directions in Psychological Science, 12*(4), 110–114. Retrieved from jsaffran@wisc.edu

Salverda, A. P., Dahan, D., & McQueen, J. M. (2003). The role of prosodic boundaries in the resolution of lexical embedding in speech comprehension. *Cognition, 90*(1), 51–89.

Samuel, A. G., & Kraljic, T. (2009). Perceptual learning for speech. *Attention, Perception, & Psychophysics, 71*(6), 1207–1218. doi:10.3758/APP

Scharenborg, O., Norris, D., Bosch, L., & McQueen, J. M. (2005). How should a speech recognizer work? *Cognitive Science, 29*(6), 867–918. doi:10.1207/s15516709cog0000_37

Schwartz, M. F., & Dell, G. S. (2010). Case series investigations in cognitive neuropsychology. *Cognitive Neuropsychology, 27*(6), 477–494. doi:10.1080/02643294.2011.574111

Schwartz, M. F., Dell, G. S., Martin, N., Gahl, S., & Sobel, P. (2006). A case-series test of the interactive two-step model of lexical access: Evidence from picture naming. *Journal of Memory and Language, 54*(2), 228–264. doi:10.1016/j.jml.2005.10.001

Shtyrov, Y., Nikulin, V. V., & Pulvermüller, F. (2010). Rapid cortical plasticity underlying novel word learning. *The Journal of Neuroscience, 30*(50), 16864–16867. doi:10.1523/JNEUROSCI.1376–10.2010

Sommers, M. S. (1996). The structural organization of the mental lexicon and its contribution to age-related declines in spoken-word recognition. *Psychology and Aging, 11*(2), 333–341.

Sommers, M. S. (1998). Spoken word recognition in individuals with dementia of the Alzheimer's type: Changes in talker normalization and lexical discrimination. *Psychology and Aging, 13*(4), 631–646.

Sommers, M. S., & Danielson, S. M. (1999). Inhibitory processes and spoken word recognition in young and older adults: The interaction of lexical competition and semantic context. *Psychology and Aging, 14*(3), 458–472.

Stickgold, R. (2013). Parsing the role of sleep in memory processing. *Current Opinion in Neurobiology, 23*(5), 847–853. doi:10.1016/j.conb.2013.04.002

Strauss, T. J., Harris, H. D., & Magnuson, J. S. (2007). jTRACE: A reimplementation and extension of the TRACE model of speech perception and spoken word recognition. *Behavior Research Methods, 39*(1), 19–30.

Taler, V., Aaron, G. P., Steinmetz, L. G., & Pisoni, D. B. (2010). Lexical neighborhood density effects on spoken word recognition and production in healthy aging. *The Journals of*

Gerontology: Series B, Psychological Sciences and Social Sciences, 65(5), 551–560. doi:10.1093/geronb/gbq039

Tobin, S. J., Cho, P. W., Jennett, P. M., & Magnuson, J. S. (2010). Effects of anticipatory coarticulation on lexical access. *Proceedings of the 33rd Annual Cognitive Science Society Meeting.* Retrieved from http://csjarchive.cogsci.rpi.edu/proceedings/2010/papers/0517/paper0517.pdf

Walley, A. (1993). The role of vocabulary development in children's spoken word recognition and segmentation ability. *Developmental Review, 13*(3), 286–350. doi:10.1006/drev.1993.1015

Warren, R. M., & Warren, R. P. (1970). Auditory illusions and confusions. *Scientific American, 223*(6), 30–36.

Weber, A., & Scharenborg, O. (2012). Models of spoken-word recognition. *WIREs Cognitive Science, 3*(3), 387–401. doi:10.1002/wcs.1178

Yee, E. (2005). *The Time Course of Lexical Activation during Spoken Word Recognition: Evidence from Unimpaired and Aphasic Individuals.* Providence, RI: Brown University.

Yee, E., & Sedivy, J. C. (2006). Eye movements to pictures reveal transient semantic activation during spoken word recognition. *Journal of Experimental Psychology: Learning, Memory, and Cognition, 32*(1), 1–14.

7

LEARNING AND INTEGRATION OF NEW WORD-FORMS

Consolidation, pruning, and the emergence of automaticity

Bob McMurray, Efthymia C. Kapnoula, and M. Gareth Gaskell

Bob McMurray is the corresponding author.

Learning a new word appears simple. One must learn the phonological form of the word (the word-form), the concept to which it refers, and an association between them. However, individually these are not trivial problems. Most concepts require integrating multiple perceptual and semantic features. Similarly, determining a novel word's referent is challenging since a novel word could refer to anything present or implied in the discourse context, its properties, or the speakers' intentions.

Learning a word-form is no less complicated. Word-forms unfold over time, necessitating activation and memory mechanisms to build a representation that abstracts over time (cf. Gupta & Tisdale, 2009). New words must also be embedded in a network of thousands of existing words, many of which are similar to the new word. Thus, learning a new word-form is not merely a matter of "knowing" the word's phonological pattern and storing it for retrieval later. Rather, this information must be embedded in the connections over which processing (real-time recognition and production) occurs (cf. Elman, 2009; Gupta & Tisdale, 2009).

Such information is embedded in pathways serving distinct functions. First, *bottom-up pathways* map acoustic or phonological information to lexemes (a term we borrow to refer to a word-form representation that is independent of its meaning). These mappings (what Leach & Samuel [2007], term a word's configuration) are required to recognize a word (activate its lexeme). Second, during recognition, lexemes inhibit one another (Dahan, Magnuson, Tanenhaus, & Hogan, 2001; Luce & Pisoni, 1998) and can feed back to affect perception, either in real-time (Samuel & Pitt, 2003) or over the course of learning (Norris, McQueen, & Cutler, 2003). These latter pathways (lateral inhibition and feedback, what Leach & Samuel [2007] term engagement) may not be strictly necessary for a word to be recognized after learning. However, they benefit word recognition, and the formation of these mappings is a crucial part of integrating new words into the lexical network. And of course these mappings are part of a much larger set of mappings to support orthographic, semantic, and articulatory processes.

This chapter examines the conditions under which new words are integrated into the lexicon. We initially focus on inhibitory linkages between lexemes, but we later broaden our discussion to consider the other related pathways. With respect to lexeme↔lexeme inhibition, a number of studies raise the possibility that multiple learning/memory systems may be engaged in the acquisition and integration of new phonological word-forms (see Dumay & Gaskell [2007] and Davis & Gaskell [2009] for a review and theoretical model). This work suggests a rather straightforward dichotomy in which the configuration (bottom-up mappings) of a word is learned rapidly, whereas sleep-based consolidation is required for integration (lexeme↔lexeme inhibitory links). However, recent studies challenge aspects of this account for both word-form integration (Coutanche & Thompson-Schill, 2014; Fernandes, Kolinsky, & Ventura, 2009; Kapnoula, Gupta, Packard, & McMurray, 2015; Kapnoula & McMurray, 2016; Lindsay & Gaskell, 2013), as well as integration into the semantic network (Borovsky, Elman, & Kutas, 2012; Borovsky, Kutas, & Elman, 2010). This prompts new thinking about how words are acquired and integrated, as well as the function of consolidation.

Here, we attempt to resolve some of these questions and propose new ideas on lexical integration and consolidation. We start by reviewing the initial work on consolidation in lexeme↔lexeme inhibition and then extend our discussion to semantics and orthography. We then describe more recent work challenging the necessity of consolidation for integration. Finally, we offer several speculative ideas for how integration is achieved and how different learning systems may contribute to word learning.

Consolidation and lexical integration

Evidence that consolidation is required for lexical integration: Lexical inhibition

Gaskell and Dumay (2003) investigated the conditions under which new lexemes form inhibitory links with existing ones. They exposed participants to novel words like *daffodat* that overlapped with real words (*daffodil*). Immediately after training, participants accurately recognized the newly acquired words (in a simple discrimination task), suggesting they had acquired the bottom-up mappings. However, the newly learned words did not interfere with recognizing the familiar competitors until after three days of training. Such results suggested that bottom-up mappings may be acquired sooner than inhibitory ones, implying a potentially different learning mechanism. These results also raised the possibility that the emergence of lexeme↔lexeme inhibition may not derive solely from additional experience – participants slept between sessions, creating an opportunity for consolidation.

A follow-up study (Dumay & Gaskell, 2007) pinned these effects more directly on sleep. They rigorously controlled the time of acquisition and test (Figure 7.1A). As Figure 7.1B shows, after a 12-hour delay without sleep (the AM group), there

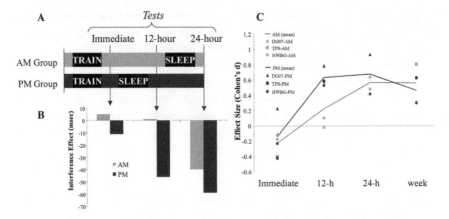

FIGURE 7.1 (A) Design of typical sleep study (e.g., Dumay & Gaskell, 2007). Comparing the evening test of the AM group to the Day 2 morning test for the PM group introduces the same 12-hour delay with or without sleep-based consolidation. (B) Results from Dumay and Gaskell: interference effect (change in RT) for familiar words with and without a newly learned competitor as a function of time of test. (C). Effect size (Cohen's d) of the magnitude of inhibition at each testing point for three studies adopting this design. (DG07: Dumay & Gaskell, 2007; TPS: Tamminen et al., 2010; HWGB: Henderson et al., 2012.)

were no interference effects, but if the delay included a night of sleep (the PM group), effects were robust. This suggests that interference may rely on overnight consolidation (see Henderson, Weighall, Brown, & Gaskell, 2012 for a similar pattern in children). This suggestion was confirmed by Tamminen, Payne, Stickgold, Wamsley, and Gaskell (2010), who measured sleep spindle activity using EEG after an evening session of word learning. They found a robust correlation between the number of spindles and the degree of lexical interference, supporting some mechanistic role for sleep-based consolidation in establishing lexical inhibition (see Figure 7.1C for results from all three studies).

Dumay and Gaskell (2012) present intriguing data suggesting that lexical representations may be fundamentally different before consolidation than after. They suggest that initial encoding of new words may be largely episodic and only later integrated into the lexicon. Supporting this, they find that immediately after training, newly learned words enhance participants' ability to detect real words embedded in them (e.g., detecting *muck* in *lirmuckt*). However, after sleep, recognition of the familiar words was slowed (though this was observed only for offset-embedded words, not onset-embedded words). They suggest the early facilitation derived from the fact that participants are likely to have noticed the familiar word during training and encoded this as part of their episodic representation, while the later interference derives from true inhibition.

The reversal of the effect between immediate and post-sleep performance suggests a potential shift in the representation of new lexemes. Building on seminal accounts of *complementary learning systems* (CLS; McClelland, McNaughton, & O'Reilly, 1995), Dumay and Gaskell (2012) (see also Davis & Gaskell, 2009) argued that catastrophic interference may be a problem during word learning; acquiring new words could interfere with similar-sounding words already in the lexicon. One solution is to "protect" long-term lexical mappings by initially encoding new words via a separate hippocampal system, and gradually incorporating them into the long-term cortical store using hippocampal replay during sleep. According to this account, the hippocampal route rapidly accommodates new words using sparse representations that mediate the mapping from auditory areas to lexical and semantic areas. These mediators are used during early stages of word learning, until direct cortical mappings can be gradually built via consolidation. This explains the consolidation-driven changes in the strength of lexical competition: the hippocampal route does not allow newly learned words to be activated quickly enough to compete against the much swifter activation of the known words (which are accessed more directly). Systems consolidation gradually strengthens the direct cortical links for novel words, leading to heightened competition effects. Indeed, supporting such an account, Davis, Di Betta, MacDonald, and Gaskell (2009) showed hippocampal activity associated with new word learning, plus changes in activity in the superior temporal gyrus (phonological/lexical encoding) after consolidation.

The time course and nature of consolidation

A number of studies further clarify the nature of consolidation addressing (1) the time course over which it occurs and (2) whether consolidation is purely sleep-based.

First, with respect to the time course, the dramatic findings of some recent studies (Dumay & Gaskell, 2007, 2012; Tamminen et al., 2010) might appear to suggest that a single night of sleep is sufficient for fully lexicalized representations. This is clearly false. For example, consistent with broader work in memory (Squire & Zola-Morgan, 1991), Gaskell and Dumay (2003) observed no significant interference effects until the fourth day of training.

Bakker, Takashima, van Hell, Janzen, and McQueen (2014) suggest a protracted time course. They asked how words learned in one modality (speech or print) interfered with familiar words when tested in a different modality. After training in either modality, interference was observed after one night of sleep (but not immediately) and grew with more consolidation. However, when words were learned via written presentation, interference was not observed in spoken testing until after a week. Thus consolidation effects are gradual and emerge over multiple days. This study also underscores that full integration of a lexeme requires linking multiple representations – phonology, lexemes, and orthography (not to mention meaning) – and that each mapping may be established with a different time course.

The second question is whether consolidation is entirely dependent on sleep or whether the passage of time or other experiences participate. It is well known in the memory literature that a variety of mechanisms exist for awake consolidation (e.g., Stickgold & Walker, 2005). A handful of the aforementioned studies adopted rigorous designs to look for the presence of non-sleep-based consolidation (see Figure 7.1A; Dumay & Gaskell, 2007; Henderson et al., 2012; McGregor, 2014). While these studies offer clear evidence for a unique effect of sleep, there is also evidence for improvement with time alone.

For example, Tamminen and colleagues (2010) showed evidence of integration after a 12-hour delay without sleep (even though sleep spindle activity was correlated with integration). Similarly, Szmalec, Page, and Duyck (2012) showed that words acquired from print exposure (using a Hebb learning task) did not show immediate interference with familiar words when tested auditorily but did so 12 hours later, whether or not the participants slept. Finally, Lindsay and Gaskell (2013) demonstrated evidence for competition between newly learned words and familiar words after a 5-hour delay (with no sleep) but not earlier. Intriguingly, this was only found when the training interleaved both the to-be-learned words and their familiar word competitors. They suggest that interleaved training avoids the catastrophic interference that necessitates sleep-based consolidation (McClelland et al., 1995). It is not clear whether all of these findings require some form of non-sleep consolidation or other factors are also involved (e.g., repeated direct cortical learning or further learning during test), but none of these studies showed immediate integration, suggesting non-sleep-based mechanisms for integration.

Other mappings

Phonological knowledge

While the focus of our review is on inhibition, the aforementioned studies also offer evidence that consolidation improves knowledge of a word's phonology (even as this can be established without it). Dumay and Gaskell (2007) found improvement in free recall performance for novel words with sleep (though not in a two-alternative forced-choice recognition task). Henderson and colleagues (2012) also found sleep-associated improvements in children in two recognition tasks (see also Henderson, Weighall, Brown, & Gaskell, 2013). Therefore, over and above the issue of "knowledge" (e.g., number of words correctly recalled or identified), consolidation also appears to improve the efficiency of recognizing and producing novel words (McGregor, 2014; Tamminen et al., 2010). However, not all gains in word knowledge over time are related to sleep. McGregor and associates (2013) examined sleep effects on a newly learned word's configuration (via free recall) in a similar sleep-study design as Dumay and Gaskell (2007, Figure 7.1A). Free recall improved after 12 hours (with or without sleep) and again at 24 hours. Taken as a whole, these data provide evidence that knowledge of a word's form is built during immediate learning but can be strengthened through sleep-based consolidation, as well as by other mechanisms such as retrieval practice (at the immediate test) or non-sleep-based consolidation.

Semantics

McGregor and colleagues (2013) also examined knowledge of a word's semantics using a semantic associate task immediately after training, as well as 12 and 24 hours later. Similarly to the phonological free recall task, learners recalled more semantic associates (of the newly learned word) after consolidation, but this was only for those who slept immediately after learning. Similarly, Coutanche and Thompson-Schill (2014) showed that when listeners were trained using a "fast-mapping" task (in which the referent of the novel word had to be inferred from a display containing a novel object and a known one), listeners showed semantic priming but only after consolidation. Thus, sleep may play an important role in fleshing out a lexeme's links to the semantic network (see also Tamminen & Gaskell, 2013; van der Ven, Takashima, Segers, & Verhoeven, 2015).

While these studies focus on the semantic network, a complementary question is how learning and consolidation affect the speed at which a newly learned word can activate its own meaning. Geukes, Gaskell, and Zwitserlood (2015) taught learners color terms (orthographically) in a fictitious second language and used Stroop interference to determine whether newly learned written words activated their meanings (the colors) automatically. They found evidence for automatic activation (Stroop interference) immediately after training but only if the Stroop test included both newly learned words and their first-language translations. When testing contained only the newly learned terms, Stroop interference wasn't observed until after sleep. This suggests that access to meaning may be more strongly automatic and task-independent after consolidation. Tham, Lindsay, and Gaskell (2015) also found evidence for graded automaticity in semantic access for new words using size congruency and semantic distance paradigms. Some of these indicators of automaticity were present after a 12-hour delay without intervening sleep (there was no immediate test), but a wider range was present after sleep, and automaticity effects were stronger after sleep. Thus, consolidation appears to affect how automatically a newly learned word's *own meaning* can be accessed.

However, Borovsky and colleagues (Borovsky et al., 2012; Borovsky et al., 2010) suggest that sleep is not required: new words can be linked into semantic networks immediately after one exposure, with clear effects on neural responses. Borovsky and associates (2010) showed that words acquired in an incidental learning paradigm show an N400 effect when embedded in semantically anomalous sentences immediately after training. This suggests that a word's semantics (thematic role structure) is available immediately after learning and can be automatically accessed. Borovsky and colleagues (2012) extend this to show semantic priming (also measured using an N400 paradigm) immediately after training, suggesting immediate linkage with the semantic network.

On top of these immediate effects, consolidation may still alter the neural circuits involved in accessing semantics. Bakker, Takashima, van Hell, Janzen, and McQueen (2015) trained participants on novel words and meanings, comparing words learned with and without sleep. Although performance on semantic decisions to these words was equivalent with and without sleep, the associated EEG responses differed somewhat. Early (300- to 500-ms) oscillatory power in the lower beta band was indistinguishable between existing words and consolidated words, whereas unconsolidated words behaved similarly to untrained words. This effect was taken to be an indicator of the semantic retrieval process. Later effects in the theta band around 500 ms were more graded but once again suggested a fully word-like neural response only for the consolidated items (see also Hawkins, Astle, & Rastle, 2015).

Thus, there is evidence that soon after learning a new word, learners can rapidly access both its own meaning and the rich semantic network with which it is associated (Borovsky et al., 2012; Borovsky et al., 2010; Geukes et al., 2015). Nonetheless, consolidation may still play a role in facilitating semantic retrieval (Coutanche & Thompson-Schill, 2014; McGregor et al., 2013; Tamminen & Gaskell, 2013), altering neural substrates (Bakker et al., 2015), and creating a more automatic access route to meaning (Geukes et al., 2015; Tham et al., 2015).

Lexeme→phonology feedback

Finally, two studies have examined the acquisition of feedback connections between word-forms and phonological representations (e.g., lexical feedback). Lindsay, Sedin, and Gaskell (2012) examined whether newly learned words shift perceptual boundaries between phonemes. They found such shifts immediately after acquisition, which did not change after a week delay. However, consolidation did affect RT after the delay, suggesting it can augment how quickly newly acquired lexemes can be activated to feedback to perception. Similarly, Leach and Samuel (2007) examined a second-order effect of feedback, showing that newly learned words could retune listeners' phoneme categories (e.g., knowing that *marfeshick* is a word and *marfesick* is not helps listeners retune their s/ʃ boundaries to hear ambiguous sounds as an /ʃ/). In some conditions, there was a marginally significant retuning on the first day of testing, but this was coupled with stronger effects after consolidation.

Is consolidation required for lexeme↔lexeme engagement

The foregoing review suggests this consolidation may not be required to form most mappings. Learners can establish a variety of mappings immediately, including mappings between perceptual representation and lexemes, top-down feedback connections (Lindsay et al., 2012), and links to the semantic network (Borovsky et al., 2010; Borovsky et al., 2012; McGregor et al., 2013), even as consolidation enhances and expands on them. However, lexeme↔lexeme inhibition seems to emerge only with sleep.

In contrast, recent studies suggest that a similar pattern may also hold for lexeme↔lexeme inhibition, with some evidence for immediate learning, even as consolidation enhances these linkages. For example, Lindsay and Gaskell (2013) did not find interference immediately after test but did several hours later (without sleep). This could derive from either non-sleep consolidation or from re-exposure during test. The latter might suggest a form of immediate learning.

Fernandes and colleagues (2009) showed clearer evidence of immediate integration. They examined lexical integration in the context of statistical learning in which the only cue to word boundaries was transitional probabilities between syllables. After training, participants were tested on familiar word competitors of the newly learned words. Robust interference was observed immediately after training, suggesting that inhibition can emerge quickly with a different learning paradigm (that perhaps requires deeper phonological analysis). Similarly, the aforementioned study by Coutanche and Thompson-Schill (2014) examining fast-mapping found lexeme↔lexeme inhibition immediately after training (even as semantic priming emerged only after sleep) but only when the new words were taught in the fast-mapping task.

One of the reasons that lexical inhibition effects may be fragile (appearing in some studies but not others) is that the methods used to assess it are arguably best thought of as indicators of global competition (Kapnoula et al., 2015; Mattys & Clark, 2002). These measures (e.g., lexical decision, pause detection) do not isolate the effects of parallel activation of multiple words from the specific inhibition of the target word. For example, participants may make a "word" decision on the basis of activation of both the target and its newly learned competitor. If the target word is slightly slowed but the competitor is active enough, these effects may cancel out. In fact, classic studies of familiar word inhibition (Marslen-Wilson & Warren, 1994) have often failed to find evidence for interference with such tasks.

Thus, a series of studies by Kapnoula, McMurray, and colleagues (Kapnoula et al., 2015; Kapnoula & McMurray, 2016) used training procedures closer to those of Gaskell, Dumay and colleagues but tested participants in a task more sensitive to the activation of the specific familiar word. For this, they used a variant of the visual world paradigm developed by Dahan, Magnuson, Tanenhaus and associates (2001) to measure inhibition among familiar words. In this paradigm, two familiar words are cross-spliced to temporarily boost activation for a competitor. For example, if the target word is *net*, the onset portion (*ne-*) is taken from a competing word, *neck*. Consequently, the coarticulatory information in the vowel temporarily favors the competitor (*neck*), and this in turn inhibits the target (*net*), slowing its recognition when the final consonant (*-t*) arrives. This is compared to conditions in which the coarticulation favors the correct word, or a non-word (*nep*). The specific activation for the target word is estimated using the visual world paradigm, as the time course of fixations to a picture of a *net* (see Figure 7.2A, for an unpublished replication conducted by Kapnoula et al.).

Kapnoula and colleagues (2015) trained participants on a set of ten novel words. Immediately after training, they were tested using the sub-phonemic mismatch/ visual world task in which the onset was spliced from either a newly learned word or an unfamiliar one. Splicing a newly learned word onto the target led to significantly fewer looks to the target than splicing an untrained non-word (Figure 7.2B), indicating interference. Both the magnitude and the timing of the interference effect were similar to that of familiar words. Thus, this provides strong evidence for immediate inhibition between newly learned and familiar words. A follow-up study (Kapnoula & McMurray, 2016a) asked whether these immediately available lexemes are episodic rather than lexicalized. Seminal work suggests episodic memory for words is better at test if presented in the same voice as during initial exposure (Palmeri, Goldinger, & Pisoni, 1993). If immediate interference effects are based on episodic memory, they may be diminished or eliminated when the

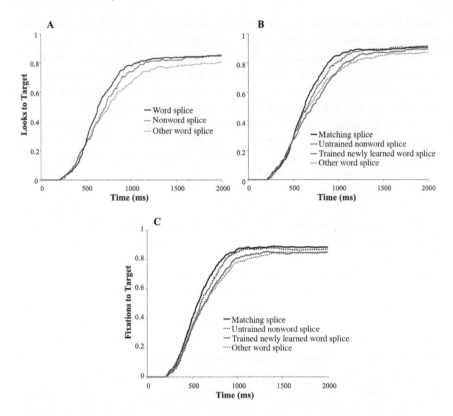

FIGURE 7.2 Results from Kapnoula and associates (2015), and Kapnoula & McMurray (2016a): looks to the target as a function of splice condition. (A) During familiar word recognition, the other-word splice shows more interference than a non-word splice. (B) After training the newly learned words exert a similar level of interference. (C) Even when the talker voice differs between training and test, robust interference is observed between newly learned and familiar words.

talker voice differs between training and test. Nonetheless, Kapnoula and McMurray (2016a) observed robust inhibition effects immediately after learning (Figure 7.2C) despite a change in talker voice. This suggests these effects do not derive from a purely exemplar-based episodic encoding.

Synthesizing the literature: Key insights

Initial work treated inhibitory links between lexemes as a critical marker of integration and offered a straightforward story (Figure 7.1B–C): while a word's sound pattern can be acquired immediately, consolidation is required for integration into the lexicon (Dumay & Gaskell, 2007, 2012; Gaskell & Dumay, 2003; Tamminen et al., 2010). This story was enriched by later evidence that consolidation affects multiple lexical mappings including semantics and orthography (Bakker et al., 2014;

McGregor, 2014) and that the passage of time may play a role as well (Lindsay & Gaskell, 2013; McGregor et al., 2013; Szmalec et al., 2012; Tamminen et al., 2010). But it is also challenged by the fact that lexical integration – including the formation of inhibitory connections and semantic associations can be seen immediately after training (Borovsky et al., 2012; Coutanche & Thompson-Schill, 2014; Fernandes et al., 2009; Kapnoula et al., 2015; Kapnoula & McMurray, 2016a).

TABLE 7.1 Key studies of word learning categorized according to mapping type and time course. For delayed effects, the studies are subcategorized in terms of whether they can be attributed specifically to sleep (but not to the passage of an equivalent amount of awake time), time (regardless of whether it was spent awake or asleep), or whether effects arose after both time and sleep (and so could have arisen from either).

		Delayed		
Mapping	*Immediate*	*Time*	*Sleep*	*Time + Sleep*
Perception → Lexeme (configuration)	McG_{13} HAR	LG	DG_{07}, TG, TPS	BTH, GD, McG_{14}
Lexeme → Perception (feedback)	LSG			LSG, LS, GHD
Lexeme ↔ Lexeme (inhibition)	FKV, KPG, KM, CTS	LG, TPS	LG, TPS, DG_{07}, HWBG	GD, BG, DG_{12}
Orthographic lexeme ↔ Orthographic lexeme (inhibition)				BDH, BTV
Orthographic lexeme ↔ Auditory lexeme (inhibition)		SPD		BTV
Lexeme → Production (recall)	McG_{13}	McG_{13}	DG_{07}, HWBG	FKV
Lexeme → Semantics	GGZ, BKE, McG_{13}, BTH			BTH, GGZ
Semantics ↔ Semantics (priming, association)	BEK	TLG	McG_{13}, TLG	TG, CTS, VTSV

Abbreviations:

BDH	Bowers et al., 2005	HWBG	Henderson et al., 2012
BEK	Borovsky et al., 2012	KM	Kapnoula & McMurray, 2016a
BKE	Borovsky et al., 2010	KPG	Kapnoula et al., 2015
BG	Brown & Gaskell, 2014	LG	Lindsay & Gaskell, 2013
BTH	Bakker et al., 2015	LS	Leach & Samuel, 2007
BTV	Bakker et al., 2014	LSG	Lindsay et al., 2012
CTS	Coutanche & Thompson-Schill, 2014	McG_{13}	McGregor et al., 2013
DG_{07}	Dumay & Gaskell, 2007	McG_{14}	McGregor, 2014
DG_{12}	Dumay & Gaskell, 2012	SPD	Szmalec et al., 2012
FKV	Fernandes et al., 2009	TG	Tamminen & Gaskell, 2012
GD	Gaskell & Dumay, 2003	TLG	Tham et al., 2015
GHD	Gagnepain et al., 2012	TPS	Tamminen et al., 2010
GGZ	Geukes et al., 2015	VTSV	van der Ven et al., 2015
HAR	Hawkins et al., 2015		

Table 7.1 offers a summary of most of the key studies, classifying each study both by the type of mapping and by whether effects were observed immediately or after a delay. There are clearly places where immediate acquisition (or consolidation) has not been shown or not tested. But broadly speaking it appears that most (if not all) of these mappings can be at least partially established during active learning. Over the course of subsequent training and consolidation, these pathways are improved and, in some cases, extended to new representations (e.g., filling in orthographic representations for auditorally learned words: Bakker et al., 2014). Across domains, these immediate effects suggest consolidation may not accomplish anything that cannot happen, at least in partial form, during some forms of active learning. This finding is underscored by a recent fMRI study by Takashima, Bakker, van Hell, Janzen, and McQueen (2014), who found that the strongest predictor of post-consolidation word learning was activation in the relevant neocortical areas during initial encoding. That is, the degree to which information is available in the right places immediately after training predicts the amount of consolidation.

These studies also do not support the idea that consolidation is required for some mappings in the lexical system but not others (as suggested by the configuration/engagement distinction). For almost all of the relevant mappings, there is evidence for both immediate and delayed effects. This again, challenges a unique role for hippocampal learning and raises the need for alternative conceptualizations.

Even if consolidation is not tied to specific pathways, this need not rule out broader notions of *systems consolidation* (replaying episodic memories to slowly and safely integrate them into neocortical areas), as described by complementary learning systems (CLS) (Davis & Gaskell, 2009; McClelland et al., 1995). Thus, we start by discussing systems consolidation and CLS more specifically. While our primary goal is not a critical evaluation of CLS, it is important to ask how CLS may yet account for this body of data. At the same time, alternative or additional processes may occur as part of consolidation. Thus, in keeping with the spirit of *complementarity*, we next turn to our more important objective of considering these mechanisms that could potentially work alongside systems consolidation (CLS) or that may offer alternatives.

Systems consolidation I: Complementary learning systems

In CLS, immediately formed hippocampal representations are not encapsulated from the rest of the lexical system. Rather they serve as a mechanism for connecting new lexemes to existing lexical, phonological, and semantic networks (Davis & Gaskell, 2009). This allows learners to rapidly form sparse representations for new words in the hippocampus that mediate between auditory areas and existing lexical and semantic knowledge. These mediators link in new knowledge rapidly during learning, while the system waits for slower neocortical connections to build. While they may be formed rapidly, however, this more indirect route may be slower during processing. Consequently, CLS does not predict that certain classes of information are encapsulated; rather, in the moment of recognition, activation takes a different and likely slower route to spread between different representations. This slower route to activation was intended to explain why newly learned words often fail to inhibit familiar words until after consolidation. The hippocampal route does not allow novel words to be activated swiftly enough to inhibit familiar neighbors. However, with systems consolidation, direct cortical links for novel words can be strengthened, leading to faster activation and more inhibition.

A challenge for this account is thus the evidence for immediate inhibition (Coutanche & Thompson-Schill, 2014; Fernandes et al., 2009; Kapnoula et al., 2015; Kapnoula & McMurray, 2016a). While immediate cortical learning is part of the CLS model, it is assumed to be relatively weak. However, perhaps the inefficiency of the hippocampal route can be overcome under some circumstances. For example, a sufficiently high level of exposure could strengthen the hippocampal route for a novel word to allow it to contribute to lexical competition even prior to sleep. This may explain the immediate interference found by Fernandes and colleagues (2009), who used more presentations of each item (63) than other studies (e.g., 36 in Gaskell & Dumay, 2003; 18 in Henderson et al., 2012). The immediate inhibitory effects of Kapnoula and associates (2015) and Kapnoula and McMurray (2016a) require a different explanation, given the close match between their training paradigms and prior studies. However, again, an inefficient hippocampal route may still be compatible with these effects. In this case, the coarticulatory mismatch favoring a newly learned word may offer a temporary boost in activation over the weakly encoded hippocampal mapping, enabling the novel word to inhibit the target word. This brief advantage for the novel word may make Kapnoula and colleagues' approach more sensitive to inhibitory effects. These two explanations suggest that systems consolidation may be consistent with immediate inhibitory effects if hippocampally mediated activation flow can influence lexical competition in certain conditions, but nonetheless systems consolidation may still alter more global properties and improve automaticity.

A second point is that the CLS model on its own may be too simplistic. Hippocampal learning and consolidation is important for word learning, explaining why hippocampal amnesics tend to remain largely unfamiliar with common words (e.g., Google) if they enter the language post-lesion (Bayley, O'Reilly, Curran, & Squire, 2008). Nonetheless, it seems likely that word learning reflects the product of multiple systems that are engaged to different degrees under different circumstances. Coutanche and Thompson-Schill's (2014) evidence for immediate inhibitory effects with fast-mapping training (but not with explicit encoding) fits with data from amnesics suggesting that fast-mapping may recruit more neocortical areas in learning new words (Sharon, Moscovitch, & Gilboa, 2011; though see Warren & Duff, 2014), leading to better learning.

Finally, traditional CLS accounts have largely assumed a sort of standard activation/ competition model of lexical processing. However, a recent study by Gagnepain, Henson, and Davis (2012) raises the possibility of other types of processes involved in word recognition that could be a product of consolidation. They studied the effects of consolidation on the MEG response to novel words and suggest that consolidation effects may not be well described by standard activation/competition models. Instead, MEG data suggested that one effect of consolidation is to update segment predictions based on new lexical knowledge. In this light, more global indicators of competition such as pause detection (which do not show immediate inhibition) may reflect changes in phonemic uncertainty after consolidation, while the visual world paradigm (which does) reflects a more direct effect of lexical uncertainty that can be due to either hippocampal or neocortical representations of novel words.

We've suggested several ways in which traditional systems consolidation (e.g., CLS) may be consistent with the findings of immediate effects. While it is premature to rule out this interpretation of immediate effects, if we accept that immediate effects may derive from rapid neocortical learning, how do we conceptualize consolidation?

Immediate engagement as rapid neocortical learning?

A key motivation for CLS is catastrophic interference, the idea that newly learned words may disrupt existing lexical representations unless integrated safely. However, recent neuroscientific and computational work suggests information can be embedded in neocortical areas soon after learning without interference when new information is added to existing schematic structures (McClelland, 2013; Tse et al., 2007). It is unclear whether word learning is analogous. Much like the schematic structures studied by Tse and McClelland, words link highly overlapping phonological and semantic networks; thus, it is possible that new items can be added to this structure without interference. These findings open the door to rapid neocortical word learning, reducing the need for the protective element of CLS (though perhaps not for other aspects of systems consolidation). If so, an important question is what sorts of learning experiences give rise to rapid neocortical learning of lexeme↔lexeme links?

A number of models argue that Hebbian learning may be part of how phonological and semantic representations are linked (Mayor & Plunkett, 2010; McMurray, Horst, & Samuelson, 2012; Mirman, McClelland, & Holt, 2006). When two representations are simultaneously coactive, their connection strengthens. While word learning – particularly in rich developmental contexts – likely entails many real-time processes to ensure that the right phonological and semantic representations are coactive, this simple principle likely underlies a number of learning phenomena.

This notion of coactivation might be relevant to the question of learning lexeme↔lexeme inhibitory connections. For a novel word like *nep* to form inhibitory connections with a known word (*net*), they must both be active. Indeed, converging evidence from several studies on lexeme↔lexeme inhibition suggest this. Three studies reporting immediate inhibition (Coutanche & Thompson-Schill, 2014; Fernandes et al., 2009; Lindsay & Gaskell, 2013) use training that should enhance coactivation among multiple novel words or among novel and familiar words. Fernandes and colleagues' (2009) statistical learning paradigm presented all of the to-be-learned words together in one unsegmented stream; Lindsay and Gaskell (2013) interleaved familiar and to-be-learned words during training; and Coutanche and Thompson-Schill's (2014) fast-mapping required learners to map novel words to novel objects in the context of familiar words/objects. In contrast, in most studies finding no immediate inhibition, novel words were taught in isolation.

If the interleaved nature of training is indeed the locus of the effect, it suggests that coactivation of two similar-sounding words leads to stronger inhibitory links between them.

So is there functional value for immediate, neocortical learning? In recent years, a number of researchers point out that listeners and talkers must rapidly adapt to new circumstances (Chang, Janciauskas, & Fitz, 2012; Kleinschmidt & Jaeger, 2015), something that would be difficult if one had to wait for consolidation. Further, these authors suggest the mechanisms of this adaptation may be based on the same mechanisms used for language acquisition (word learning). In our context, such immediate learning could be useful for ramping up inhibition when the demands on accurate word recognition are high. This predicts that if lexeme↔lexeme inhibition is built on coactivation, it may be possible to tune inhibitory links among well-learned words with appropriate experience.

A recent study by Kapnoula and McMurray (2016b) presents evidence for such adaptation. They asked whether training can change the degree of interference (and its resolution) between familiar words. Participants performed a series of tasks like lexical decision and phoneme decision on a set of familiar words. In one group, tasks were configured to enhance coactivation of pairs of familiar words and to require participants to resolve this competition to respond accurately. In the other group, training minimized coactivation. After 40 minutes of training, competition among familiar words was measured with the sub-phonemic mismatch paradigm used by

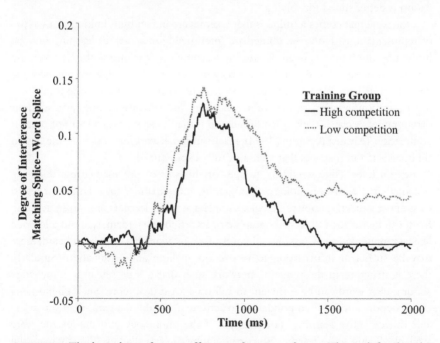

FIGURE 7.3 The lexical interference effect as a function of time. This is defined as the difference between the word-splice and matching-splice condition (e.g., the solid and gray dotted lines in Figure 7.2A).

Kapnoula and colleagues (2015). At test, participants in the high-competition group fully recovered from the interference, while those in the low-competition group did not (Figure 7.3). TRACE modeling indicated that this effect can derive from *increased* inhibition in the high-competition group, which allows the correct word (*net*) to more fully suppress the competitor (*neck*) once the final consonant is heard. This suggests that coactivation of two (familiar) lexemes yields stronger inhibitory links between words (likely via Hebbian-type mechanisms) and supports a role of coactivation for rapid learning of inhibitory connections in word learning studies. Moreover, it also helps explain the value of such rapid learning – if lexeme↔lexeme inhibitory connections can be established only with consolidation, it may not be rapid enough to help listeners tune their systems to the momentary demands of language comprehension.

Systems consolidation II: Pattern completion and collaborative learning systems

If learning can be immediate, this does not explain the dozens of experiments documenting some "boost" to various aspects of lexical representation with consolidation. What might it be doing?

While, as we described, there may be no specific content (type of mapping) that needs the hippocampal route, there may be circumstances or problems that consolidation is better suited for solving.

One issue that comes to mind is that lexemes are in fact hubs linking many types of representations. However, immediate (presumably neocortical) learning may be limited by the inputs at hand during the learning event (along with whatever else can be activated). Consequently, there may be substantial data that are not available during active learning; learners may perceive the form of a word without producing it, without various aspects of its meaning (or semantic primes), or without orthography. A classic view of consolidation is that it can serve as a form of pattern completion (Alvarez & Squire, 1994), reactivating networks used during the day to fill in association matrices that were not fully experienced.

Lexical knowledge would seem ripe for this sort of process because there are systematicities across phonology, orthography, and semantics that can be harnessed to support pattern completion. For example, for adult learners any given acoustic form can be mapped to its orthographic or its articulatory form, without a learned lexical representation. Consequently, even if a new word has only been heard, there may be sufficient information to recover its spelling and articulation. Similarly, there is structure in the semantic network such that a little semantic knowledge about a new word can be sufficient to call up a great deal more. Such phenomena create opportunities for consolidation to activate more about a word than was available during active learning. For example, if the phonology and the lexeme were available during active learning, the orthography can be called up (directly from the phonology) during consolidation; with all three types of information, coactive stronger links can be formed. Such processes likely underlie Bakker and associates' (2014) finding that consolidation can lead to inhibitory effects that can be observed in an untrained modality.

Under this view, consolidation processes are not associated with any particular type of linkage but serve to fill in missing data not present during active learning. This could play an important role in lexeme↔lexeme inhibition. In many studies, novel words were in isolation, giving learners little reason to coactivate other words in the lexicon during learning. Early in training, learners may even realize that familiar words are irrelevant and actively suppress them. This creates a missing data problem for connections between novel and familiar words. Thus, even as the appropriate coactivation during training can form inhibitory links, consolidation may also help complete the lexical network during such spare training regimes, using the same Hebbian principles at reactivation.

The mystery of the missing inhibition

If we accept that lexeme↔lexeme inhibitory connections can be acquired via active neocortical learning processes (even as consolidation may also help build them), it also begs the question of why immediate effects were not observed in older paradigms (e.g., Dumay & Gaskell, 2007; Dumay & Gaskell, 2012; Gaskell & Dumay, 2003)? Clearly, the learning paradigm may contribute; in many studies words are taught in isolation, minimizing the coactivation needed to build inhibitory links. However, this doesn't explain the fact that both Kapnoula and associates (2015) and Kapnoula and McMurray (2016a) studies used similar learning paradigms.

A second factor, then, is likely the task used to measure inhibition. As described, the VWP task used by Kapnoula and associates targets inhibition between specific pairs of words more precisely than tasks like word spotting, pause detection, and lexical decision, which are sensitive to activation dynamics more broadly. Therefore, by considering how inhibition plays out in interactive models, we may be able to determine why effects are not consistently seen and what kind of changes in the system are achieved via consolidation that give rise to enhanced interference.

In typical interactive models, lexeme↔lexeme inhibition is instantiated independently of other mappings, as inhibitory connections among words. However, measures of interference (like lexical decision or the visual world paradigm) do not isolate these specific pathways. They always require activation flow over multiple pathways, which must also be established during learning; a new word cannot inhibit a familiar word unless it is activated by the bottom-up input. Consequently, the interference that one word exerts on another is a function of multiple learned components of the system. In this light, the presence (or absence) of interference may arise from complex interactions among multiple components of the system.

We conducted preliminary simulations to see how this might play out in word learning. We simulated results analogous to Gaskell and Dumay (2003) by adding a new word (*suitabit*) to the standard TRACE lexicon that was similar to another word already in it (*suitable*).[1] To simulate word learning, we used the frequency multiplier on the phoneme→word connections for *suitabit* (as in, Dahan, Magnuson, &

Tanenhaus, 2001) and gradually ramped up the frequency of the novel word from 0 (word not present) to 150 (for comparison, the familiar word's frequency was 100). This is a pure measure of configuration; inhibitory links were present throughout learning. Figure 7.4 shows familiar word activation as a function of frequency. At low frequencies, the newly learned competitor exerts little interference on the target – even though the level of inhibition (or integration) in the model is constant. The newly learned word does not get active enough (via bottom-up mechanisms) to exert much interference. But, as the frequency of the newly learned word increases, it exerts increasingly large interference on the known word, again without any direct change to the inhibitory strength.

This suggests that increases in interference observed in behavioral paradigms (via consolidation or active learning) may also derive from changes in bottom-up learning (configuration), not just from changes in integration or inhibitory links. Such interference could not be observed if there were no inhibitory connections, so this does not challenge a positive finding of interference. However, it does make it more difficult to interpret changes in the magnitude of interference; an increase in interference could derive from stronger inhibitory connections or from more robust bottom-up activation (phoneme→lexeme links). Moreover, if we permit multiple factors to vary (e.g., both bottom-up connections and lateral inhibition), null effects could easily arise. Methodologically, this suggests that disentangling

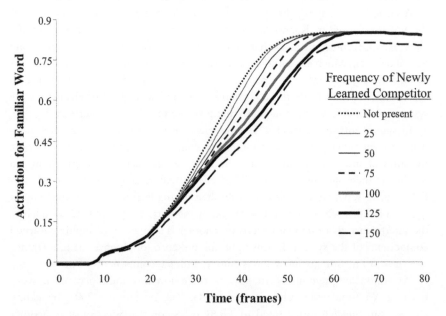

FIGURE 7.4 Activation (from TRACE) of a familiar word, *suitable*, as a function of the frequency of a newly learned competitor, *suitabit*.

these factors could be difficult, especially in tasks like lexical decision and pause detection, which are rather indirect measures of an individual word's activation. However, these simulations raise the possibility that the function of consolidation may not be to create specific kinds of mappings (e.g., lexeme↔lexeme) but rather to tune up the connections within a class of mappings or to align connections across them.

Synaptic consolidation: Pruning and tuning to achieve automaticity

As described, the various mappings involved in linking a word to its phonological, orthographic, and semantic representations are not stored "knowledge" but rather pathways over which processing occurs. Processes like word recognition, production, or semantic priming do not occur by encoding the input and retrieving lexical entries. Rather, phonological inputs are activated, and activation flows directly to relevant lexical units. The pathways over which this activation flows are where the "knowledge" of a word's properties are stored. As a result, word learning is not about acquiring knowledge and organizing it in the lexicon; it is about acquiring automatic skills for using words flexibly. This was quite apparent in the previous simulations where the strength of the bottom-up mappings shaped the model's ability to show effects of the lateral inhibitory pathways.

In this framing, learning is not simply about establishing pathways but also about refining them so that words can be recognized, produced, and spelled efficiently. Our TRACE simulations suggest that developing this automaticity (across multiple pathways) is critical for effects like interference to emerge. The question then becomes how do these mappings change (with learning, consolidation) to pass activation more quickly and precisely? That is, how do they become automatic? In CLS, one important avenue for automaticity is a stronger reliance on direct neocortical connections for word recognition, rather than hippocampal mediation between disparate cortical regions. However, changes may also occur *within* the neocortical pathways (or the hippocampal route) to increase efficiency.

In interactive models, a critical way to speed interactive processing is to strengthen the associative link between representations. For example, stronger links between perceptual representations and lexemes allow lexemes to become more active more quickly on the basis of bottom-up input (as in the preceding simulations). Similarly, stronger inhibitory connections lead to more rapid suppression of competitors. The converse of this is that automaticity may also be enhanced by *pruning* unnecessary connections. This has a close developmental analogue to the widely known finding that early in development there is an over-proliferation of synapses followed by a dramatic reduction (Greenough, Black, & Wallace, 1987; Huttenlocher, 1979). In the context of word learning, the notion of pruning suggests that learners must learn not only that a word like *dog* contains a /d/ (and strengthen the corresponding association) but also that it does not contain a /t/ (and weaken that connection).

Such pruning can also lead to more automatic and precise spreading of activation. When connections are noisy, a phonological input like a /d/ may partially activate a large number of words, some of which may not even contain a /d/. These would need to be suppressed to achieve recognition, slowing down the process. Similarly, noisy or unpruned inhibitory connections *between* words could cause a single word to spread inhibition too widely rather than targeting it to specific competitors. Pruning is essential to make patterns of activation more targeted and specific and therefore capable of being resolved more quickly.

One recent model of word learning (McMurray et al., 2012) attempted to disentangle the effects of building and pruning connections on automaticity. This model instantiated a set of associative links between words and objects (Figure 7.5A). Consistent with most connectionist models, weights started from small random values, and, over training, the correct ones are strengthened, and the irrelevant ones are weakened. On any individual encounter with a word, multiple potential referents are activated and compete using a simple competition architecture that captures the process of a listener settling on the interpretation of a word (given an array of possible referents). As words are learned in this model, they show faster processing time (fewer competition cycles to settle, Figure 7.5B); that is, recognition becomes more automatic. An analysis of the predictors of these gains suggested that the growth of the positive connections (Figure 7.5C) had little relationship (if any) to speed of processing, while the elimination of the irrelevant connections (pruning) was clearly related to how automatically referents could be activated (Figure 7.5D).

This suggests that an important route to achieving automaticity is to clean up lexical pathways, eliminating small spurious associations – associations that are either left over from development or formed from spurious correlations encountered during learning. This may happen during active learning. For example, learning novel words in the presence of a semantic foil (fast-mapping, as in Coutanche & Thompson-Schill, 2014) may create more opportunities for pruning.

However, this kind of tuning *within lexical pathways* may also be something that consolidation can assist in. Alongside systems consolidation, the neuroscience of memory and learning also highlights *synaptic consolidation*, the idea that consolidation acts to strengthen and weaken individual synapses both within the hippocampus and throughout the neocortex (Abel & Lattal, 2001; Diekelmann & Born, 2010; Tononi & Cirelli, 2014; Yang et al., 2014). These two forms of consolidation are thought to occur during different phases of sleep, with systems consolidation more associated with slow wave sleep and synaptic consolidation with REM sleep (Diekelmann & Born, 2010; though see Stickgold & Walker, 2005), a dissociation hinted at by differential effects of slow-wave sleep and spindle activity in word learning (Tamminen et al., 2010; Tham et al., 2015).

If pruning – rather than building – associations is more important for achieving automaticity, one of the challenges faced by eliminativist learning is that they must rely on negative evidence. One learns that the word *dog* does not refer to the object *fork* by noticing that they rarely co-occur. While positive evidence (the

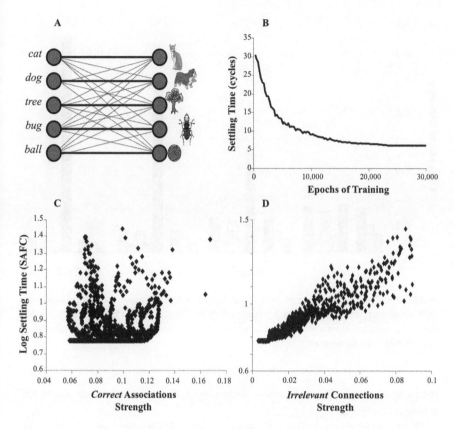

FIGURE 7.5 (A) In a word/referent mapping situation, learners must simultaneously build connections between words and their referents (thick solid lines) and avoid building or pruning connections to other objects (thin dashed lines). (B) Settling time (number of processing cycles) to recognize a familiar word over the course of training. (C) The relationship between the strength of the correct (positive) associations and settling time across a number of runs in the model. (D) The relationship between the strength of the irrelevant connections and settling time.

word *dog* paired with the concept *dog*) is unambiguous in the input, negative evidence is difficult to be certain of, particularly with only a few learning instances. In some cases, negative evidence can be obtained during active learning. For example, the fast-mapping tasks used by Coutanche and Thompson-Schill (2014) may promote pruning of connections between new words and incorrect meanings; similarly, interleaving newly learned and familiar words during training, the system can highlight distinctions between them. But in other cases (e.g., new words presented in isolation and decontextualized), such negative information may not be available. In these cases, consolidation may help accomplish some of the pruning. In this way, even though the pruning is happening within a pathway (synaptic, not systems consolidation), it is responding to a similar problem as systems consolidation (at least

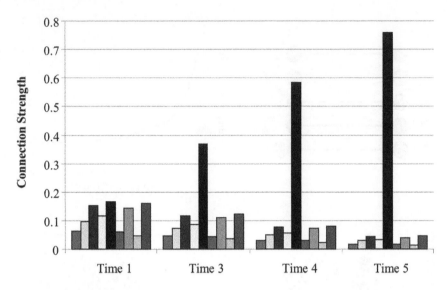

FIGURE 7.6 Associative weights over time (active learning and/or consolidation). At each time step, the central (black) association receives a small boost (it is growing); the other weights shrink when the whole set is normalized to sum to 1.0 (simulating homeostatic mechanisms).

the pattern completion version previously proposed) in that it is motivated by the problem of missing data.

Work on the psychobiology of sleep supports a link between pruning and consolidation. Data by Maret, Faraguna, Nelson, Cirelli, and Tononi (2011) suggest that in adolescent mice (but not adults), synaptic spine density in sensorimotor areas decreases during sleep and increases during waking, with concomitant changes in both neuro-receptors and electrophysiological properties (Vyazovskiy, Cirelli, Pfister-Genskow, Faraguna, & Tononi, 2008) that have been associated with long-term synaptic depression. Such processes have usually been explained as a component of maintaining an overall even level of post-synaptic activity, as a form of homeostasis (see Tononi & Cirelli, 2014 for review). However, this is difficult to distinguish from the more active sense of pruning described by McMurray et al. (2012). Figure 7.6, for example, shows a hypothetical set of weights connecting one word to nine others (within a cluster, each bar represents one connection between words). At Time 0, weights are random. At each subsequent time, a small amount has been added to the correct weight (the central one) to simulate building of connections during awake active learning. We then normalized all nine weights to sum to 1.0 in order to simulate homeostatic mechanisms during sleep. The consequence is that at each time step, we see both the building of the correct connection and the pruning of the incorrect ones, creating a situation in which these mappings support more efficient and automatic processing. Thus sleep may help overcome "missing data" during the day (negative evidence) to contribute to synaptic pruning.

Importantly, the synaptic downscaling hypothesis is not likely the whole story regarding synaptic consolidation. There is also clear evidence for increases in spine density in various brain areas with sleep (Yang et al., 2014). Our point here is not to embrace downscaling per se. Rather, we emphasize the need for synaptic tuning (both building as we saw in the TRACE simulations, and pruning as we see here) to support automaticity, and the possibility that synaptic consolidation could augment this. We also point out a perhaps unique role of pruning in achieving automaticity. To the extent that the neural evidence for downscaling mirrors this, it suggests an analogy. However, unlike many approaches to pruning (including downscaling), we argue that the irrelevant connections may not be mere noise; they reflect actual content (in this case, a negative link between representations).

Conclusions

Words are a critical nexus in the language system linking sound, semantics, syntax, spelling, and speech production. This necessitates a dense network of pathways by which information in each part of the lexical system can access others. Learning a new word is thus more than learning information about it. It is a process of embedding this information in a dense network of pathways over which automatic processing must eventually occur.

The initial work on plasticity within this system started with a straightforward model: bottom-up pathways can be established rapidly during active learning, while subtler connections (lexeme↔lexeme inhibition, feedback, etc.) may require consolidation (Gaskell & Dumay, 2003; Leach & Samuel, 2007). However, as research broadened to include more pathways, and as data accumulated with different measures of learning, a new picture emerged: for virtually every pathway within the lexical system, we see both immediate formation (after active learning) and robust consolidation effects (Table 7.1). This demands fresh thinking. We see a variety of ways to think about these issues.

First, much of what we have observed may yet be consistent with a CLS account in which immediate learning is supported by hippocampal mediation and later changes by systems consolidation. That said, the empirical data show little evidence of a sharp dissociation between certain types of lexical processing that are apparent immediately and others that are only acquired after a delay. Consolidation-related changes are often more subtle and/or graded. We need to know more about the speed and plasticity of hippocampally mediated representations; there may be multiple learning systems at work simultaneously, and there are clear task differences to be understood. It is possible that recent findings suggesting swift lexeme↔lexeme engagement imply rapid neocortical learning, but, nonetheless, the application of some form of systems consolidation is clearly supported by behavioral and neuroimaging data and will likely be important for understanding lexical plasticity. We may also need to broaden our view of systems consolidation. Pattern completion is clearly relevant given the richness of lexical learning, and there may be functions like predictive coding that have not yet been considered.

Second, we need more mechanistic models of how mappings like lexeme↔lexeme engagement are formed. We suggest that the coactivation of each word (e.g., the novel and familiar words) may play a role. This is something that may be engaged via active learning (e.g., with interleaved novel and familiar words) and even among familiar words (Kapnoula & McMurray, 2015). However, at the same time, coactivation (and the resulting Hebbian learning) may also be engaged by consolidation as a form of pattern completion or filling in of missing data to strengthen (or establish) these pathways.

Third, we also need a more complete understanding of how underlying activation states map onto the tasks used to assess learning. TRACE simulations suggest that the magnitude of interference is a product of the strength of multiple pathways within the system (both bottom-up and lateral-inhibitory), and this may make it challenging to isolate pathways using existing behavioral techniques. Similarly, Gagnepain and colleagues (2012) suggest a whole new set of processes that tasks like pause detection may be sensitive to (even as they have been classically used as measures of inhibition). We need a linking function to tie underlying activation states to behavioral responses.

Fourth, we must also consider the structure of connections *within* a pathway (e.g., within the lexeme↔lexeme inhibitory pathway). Such pathways do not just store knowledge about a word; they must also support automatic processing. In this regard, a critical factor may be the degree to which irrelevant connections within a pathway can be pruned, and the McMurray et al. (2012) model shows that this can be highly predictive of processing efficiency. This raises the possibility that *synaptic consolidation* (which may include pruning) can enhance automaticity within lexical pathways.

At the broadest level, these ideas are not mutually exclusive: systems consolidation of various kinds can clearly coexist with synaptic consolidation, and indeed each may take place during different phases of sleep (Diekelmann & Born, 2010). Similarly, coactivation, as a condition for learning, could be engaged via both active learning situations and as part of pattern completion during consolidation. Where theories may differ is in the limits placed on immediate neocortical learning and hippocampal consolidation: are there things that one or the other simply cannot accomplish?

In looking to the future of this research, we must also consider what we do not yet know. Our understanding of neocortical learning and consolidation in the brain is poor at best. Most of our understanding of these neural processes comes from either highly simplified animal learning experiments or from simplified computational models. Factors like the speed of hippocampally mediated representations, the plasticity of the neocortex, or the risks of catastrophic interference have not been investigated in model systems that approach word learning. This is because few animal learning models even approach the complexity of human word learning in terms of the number of simultaneous associations to be formed or because of the fact that associations span so many knowledge systems. Though recent work like Wasserman, Brooks, and McMurray (2015) may offer a start, it remains to be seen whether behavioral neuroscience will develop sufficient richness to address how problems analogous to word learning play out in the brain. Similarly, as McClelland (2013) makes clear, problems like catastrophic interference – which motivated the original versions of CLS – can change dramatically depending how to-be-learned material overlaps with existing knowledge structures. Models examining interference in the context of real words could be crucial for understanding catastrophic interference and the necessity of systems consolidation for mitigating it.

Perhaps more importantly, it is easy to oversimplify the distinction between hippocampal consolidation and neocortical learning. The hippocampus is not solely about acquiring knowledge. It is also involved in the processing and/or representation of inputs. This is shown by emerging work with humans (Warren, Duff, Jensen, Tranel, & Cohen, 2012) but also by classic work in animals on things like place representations (Moser, Kropff, & Moser, 2008). In this capacity, the hippocampus may also help structure immediate learning, both within hippocampal representations and in the neocortex (Tse et al., 2007; Warren & Duff, 2014). Clearly a greater understanding of the variety of roles of this important brain structure is needed before we can understand the cognitive neuroscience of word learning.

Until then, we propose complementarity. Lexical plasticity across multiple mappings is built on both active learning and consolidation. And consolidation may both complete lexical representations across pathways and tune associations within pathways to achieve more automatic processing.

Note

1 This word had only two other cohort competitors in the 214 lexicon, *sue* and *suit,* making it nearly a hermit.

References

Abel, T., & Lattal, K.M. (2001). Molecular mechanisms of memory acquisition, consolidation and retrieval. *Current Opinion in Neurobiology, 11*(2), 180–187.

Alvarez, P., & Squire, L.R. (1994). Memory consolidation and the medial temporal lobe: A simple network model. *Proceedings of the National Academy of Sciences, 91*(15), 7041–7045.

Bakker, I., Takashima, A., van Hell, J.G., Janzen, G., & McQueen, J.M. (2014). Competition from unseen or unheard novel words: Lexical consolidation across modalities. *Journal of Memory and Language, 73,* 116–130.

Bakker, I., Takashima, A., van Hell, J.G., Janzen, G., & McQueen, J.M. (2015). Changes in Theta and beta oscillations as signatures of novel word consolidation. *Journal of Cognitive Neuroscience, 27*(7), 1286–1297.

Bayley, P.J., O'Reilly, R.C., Curran, T., & Squire, L.R. (2008). New semantic learning in patients with large medial temporal lobe lesions. *Hippocampus, 18*(6), 575–583.

Borovsky, A., Elman, J.L., & Kutas, M. (2012). Once is enough: N400 indexes semantic integration of novel word meanings from a single exposure in context. *Language Learning and Development, 8*(3), 278–302.

Borovsky, A., Kutas, M., & Elman, J. (2010). Learning to use words: Event-related potentials index single-shot contextual word learning. *Cognition, 116*(2), 289–296.

Bowers, J.S., Davis, C.J., & Hanley, D.A. (2005). Interfering neighbours: The impact of novel word learning on the identification of visually similar words. *Cognition, 97*(3), B45–B54.

Brown, H., & Gaskell, M.G. (2014). The time-course of talker-specificity and lexical competition effects during word learning. *Language, Cognition and Neuroscience, 29*(9), 1163–1179.

Chang, F., Janciauskas, M., & Fitz, H. (2012). Language adaptation and learning: Getting explicit about implicit learning. *Language and Linguistics Compass, 6*(5), 259–278.

Coutanche, M.N., & Thompson-Schill, S.L. (2014). Fast mapping rapidly integrates information into existing memory networks. *Journal of Experimental Psychology: General, 143*(6), 2296–2303.

Dahan, D., Magnuson, J.S., & Tanenhaus, M.K. (2001). Time course of frequency effects in spoken-word recognition: Evidence from eye movements. *Cognitive Psychology, 42*, 317–367.

Dahan, D., Magnuson, J.S., Tanenhaus, M.K., & Hogan, E. (2001). Subcategorical mismatches and the time course of lexical access: Evidence for lexical competition. *Language and Cognitive Processes, 16*(5/6), 507–534.

Davis, M.H., & Gaskell, M.G. (2009). A complementary systems account of word learning: Neural and behavioural evidence. *Philosophical Transactions of the Royal Society B: Biological Sciences, 364*(1536), 3773–3800.

Davis, M.H., Di Betta, A.M., MacDonald, M.J.E., & Gaskell, M.G. (2009). Learning and consolidation of novel spoken words. *Journal of Cognitive Neuroscience, 21*(4), 803–820.

Diekelmann, S., & Born, J. (2010). The memory function of sleep. *Nature Reviews Neuroscience, 11*(2), 114–126.

Dumay, N., & Gaskell, M.G. (2007). Sleep-associated changes in the mental representation of spoken words. *Psychological Science, 18*(1), 35–39.

Dumay, N., & Gaskell, M.G. (2012). Overnight lexical consolidation revealed by speech segmentation. *Cognition, 123*(1), 119–132.

Elman, J.L. (2009). On the meaning of words and dinosaur bones: Lexical knowledge without a lexicon. *Cognitive Science, 33*, 547–582.

Fernandes, T., Kolinsky, R., & Ventura, P. (2009). The metamorphosis of the statistical segmentation output: Lexicalization during artificial language learning. *Cognition, 112*(3), 349–366.

Gagnepain, P., Henson, R.N., & Davis, M.H. (2012). Temporal predictive codes for spoken words in auditory cortex. *Current Biology, 22*(7), 615–621.

Gaskell, M.G., & Dumay, N. (2003). Lexical competition and the acquisition of novel words. *Cognition, 89*(2), 105–132.

Geukes, S., Gaskell, M.G., & Zwitserlood, P. (2015). Stroop effects from newly learned color words: Effects of memory consolidation and episodic context. *Frontiers in Psychology, 6*, 1–16.

Greenough, W.T., Black, J.E., & Wallace, C.S. (1987). Experience and brain development. *Child Development, 58*(3), 539–559.

Gupta, P., & Tisdale, J. (2009). Does phonological short-term memory causally determine vocabulary learning? Toward a computational resolution of the debate. *Journal of Memory and Language, 61*(4), 481–502.

Hawkins, E., Astle, D.E., & Rastle, K. (2015). Semantic Advantage for learning new phonological form representations. *Journal of Cognitive Neuroscience, 27*(4), 775–786.

Henderson, L.M., Weighall, A., Brown, H., & Gaskell, M.G. (2013). Online lexical competition during spoken word recognition and word learning in children and adults. *Child Development, 84*(5), 1668–1685.

Henderson, L.M., Weighall, A.R., Brown, H., & Gaskell, M.G. (2012). Consolidation of vocabulary is associated with sleep in children. *Developmental Science, 15*(5), 674–687.

Huttenlocher, P.R. (1979). Synaptic density in human frontal cortex – Developmental changes and effects of aging. *Brain Research*, *163*(2), 195–205.

Kapnoula, E., Gupta, P., Packard, S., & McMurray, B. (2015). Immediate lexical integration of novel word forms. *Cognition*, *134*(1), 85–99.

Kapnoula, E., & McMurray, B. (2016a). Newly learned word-forms are abstract and integrated immediately after acquisition. *Psychonomic Bulletin and Review*, *23*(2), 491–499.

Kapnoula, E.C., & McMurray, B. (2016b). Training alters the resolution of lexical interference: Evidence for plasticity of competition and inhibition. *Journal of Experimental Psychology: General*, *145*(1), 8–30.

Kleinschmidt, D. F., & Jaeger, T.F. (2015). Re-examining selective adaptation: Fatiguing feature detectors, or distributional learning? *Psychonomic Bulletin & Review*, 1–14.

Leach, L., & Samuel, A.G. (2007). Lexical configuration and lexical engagement: When adults learn new words. *Cognitive Psychology*, *55*(4), 306–353.

Lindsay, S., & Gaskell, M.G. (2013). Lexical integration of novel words without sleep. *Journal of Experimental Psychology: Learning, Memory, and Cognition*, *39*(2), 608.

Lindsay, S., Sedin, L.M., & Gaskell, M.G. (2012). Acquiring novel words and their past tenses: Evidence from lexical effects on phonetic categorisation. *Journal of Memory and Language*, *66*(1), 210–225.

Luce, P.A., & Pisoni, D.B. (1998). Recognizing spoken words: The neighborhood activation model. *Ear and Hearing*, *19*(1), 1–36.

Maret, S., Faraguna, U., Nelson, A.B., Cirelli, C., & Tononi, G. (2011). Sleep and waking modulate spine turnover in the adolescent mouse cortex. *Nature Neuroscience*, *14*(11), 1418–1420.

Marslen-Wilson, W., & Warren, P. (1994). Levels of perceptual representation and process in lexical access: Words, phonemes, and features. *Psychological Review*, *101*(4), 653–675.

Mattys, S.L., & Clark, J.H. (2002). Lexical activity in speech processing: Evidence from pause detection. *Journal of Memory and Language*, *47*(3), 343–359.

Mayor, J., & Plunkett, K. (2010). A neurocomputational account of taxonomic responding and fast mapping in early word learning. *Psychological Review*, *117*(1), 1–31.

McClelland, J.L. (2013). Incorporating rapid neocortical learning of new schema-consistent information into complementary learning systems theory. *Journal of Experimental Psychology: General*, *142*(4), 1190–1210.

McClelland, J.L., McNaughton, B.L., & O'Reilly, R.C. (1995). Why there are complementary learning systems in the hippocampus and neocortex: Insights from the successes and failures of connectionist models of learning and memory. *Psychological Review*, *102*(3), 419.

McGregor, K.K. (2014). What a difference a day makes: Change in memory for newly learned word forms over twenty-four hours. *Journal of Speech, Language, and Hearing Research*, *57*, 1842–1850. doi:10.1044/2014_JSLHR-L-13-0273

McGregor, K.K., Licandro, U., Arenas, R., Eden, N., Stiles, D., Bean, A., & Walker, E. (2013). Why words are hard for adults with developmental language impairments. *Journal of Speech, Language, and Hearing Research*, *56*, 1845–1856. doi:10.1044/1092-4388(2013/12-0233)

McMurray, B., Horst, J.S., & Samuelson, L. (2012). Word learning emerges from the interaction of online referent selection and slow associative learning. *Psychological Review*, *119*(4), 831–877.

Mirman, D., McClelland, J.L., & Holt, L.L. (2006). An interactive Hebbian account of lexically guided tuning of speech perception. *Psychonomic Bulletin & Review*, *13*(6), 958–965.

Moser, E.I., Kropff, E., & Moser, M.-B. (2008). Place cells, grid cells, and the brain's spatial representation system. *Annual Review of Neuroscience*, *31*, 69–89.

Norris, D., McQueen, J., & Cutler, A. (2003). Perceptual learning in speech. *Cognitive Psychology*, *47*(2), 204–238.

Palmeri, T.J., Goldinger, S.D., & Pisoni, D.B. (1993). Episodic encoding of voice attributes and recognition memory for spoken words. *Journal of Experimental Psychology: Learning, Memory, and Cognition, 19*(2), 309.

Samuel, A.G., & Pitt, M.A. (2003). Lexical activation (and other factors) can mediate compensation for coarticulation. *Journal of Memory and Language, 48*(2), 416–434.

Sharon, T., Moscovitch, M., & Gilboa, A. (2011). Rapid neocortical acquisition of long-term arbitrary associations independent of the hippocampus. *Proceedings of the National Academy of Sciences, 108*(3), 1146–1151.

Squire, L., & Zola-Morgan, S. (1991). The medial temporal lobe memory system. *Science, 253*(5026), 1380–1386.

Stickgold, R., & Walker, M. P. (2005). Memory consolidation and reconsolidation: What is the role of sleep? *Trends in Neurosciences, 28*(8), 408–415.

Szmalec, A., Page, M., & Duyck, W. (2012). The development of long-term lexical representations through Hebb repetition learning. *Journal of Memory and Language, 67*(3), 342–354.

Takashima, A., Bakker, I., van Hell, J.G., Janzen, G., & McQueen, J.M. (2014). Richness of information about novel words influences how episodic and semantic memory networks interact during lexicalization. *Neuroimage, 84*(0), 265–278.

Tamminen, J., & Gaskell, M.G. (2013). Novel word integration in the mental lexicon: Evidence from unmasked and masked semantic priming. *The Quarterly Journal of Experimental Psychology, 66*(5), 1001–1025.

Tamminen, J., Payne, J.D., Stickgold, R., Wamsley, E.J., & Gaskell, M.G. (2010). Sleep spindle activity is associated with the integration of new memories and existing knowledge. *The Journal of Neuroscience, 30*(43), 14356–14360.

Tham, E.K.H., Lindsay, S., & Gaskell, M.G. (2015). Markers of automaticity in sleep-associated consolidation of novel words. *Neuropsychologia, 71*(0), 146–157.

Tononi, G., & Cirelli, C. (2014). Sleep and the price of plasticity: From synaptic and cellular homeostasis to memory consolidation and integration. *Neuron, 81*(1), 12–34.

Tse, D., Langston, R.F., Kakeyama, M., Bethus, I., Spooner, P.A., Wood, E.R., . . . Morris, R.G.M. (2007). Schemas and memory consolidation. *Science, 316*(5821), 76–82.

van der Ven, F., Takashima, A., Segers, E., & Verhoeven, L. (2015). Learning word meanings: Overnight integration and study modality effects. *PLoS ONE, 10*(5), e0124926.

Vyazovskiy, V.V., Cirelli, C., Pfister-Genskow, M., Faraguna, U., & Tononi, G. (2008). Molecular and electrophysiological evidence for net synaptic potentiation in wake and depression in sleep. *Nature Neuroscience, 11*(2), 200–208.

Warren, D.E., & Duff, M.C. (2014). Not so fast: Hippocampal amnesia slows word learning despite successful fast mapping. *Hippocampus, 24*(8), 920–933.

Warren, D.E., Duff, M.C., Jensen, U., Tranel, D., & Cohen, N.J. (2012). Hiding in plain view: Lesions of the medial temporal lobe impair online representation. *Hippocampus, 22*(7), 1577–1588.

Wasserman, E.A., Brooks, D.I., & McMurray, B. (2015). Pigeons acquire multiple categories in parallel via associative learning: A parallel to human word learning? *Cognition, 136*, 99–122.

Yang, G., Lai, C.S.W., Cichon, J., Ma, L., Li, W., & Gan, W.-B. (2014). Sleep promotes branch-specific formation of dendritic spines after learning. *Science, 344*(6188), 1173–1178.

8

BILINGUAL SPOKEN WORD RECOGNITION

Peiyao Chen and Viorica Marian

Viorica Marian is the corresponding author.
The authors would like to thank the members of the *Bilingualism and Psycholinguistics Research Group* at Northwestern University for helpful comments. Preparation of this chapter was supported in part by grant NICHD R01 HD059858 to Viorica Marian.

Bilinguals are capable of understanding and speaking two different languages. Interestingly, behavioral and neural evidence suggests that, even when only one language is being used overtly, both languages are being accessed in parallel (Blumenfeld & Marian, 2013; Kroll, Dussias, Bogulski, & Valdés Kroff, 2012; Kroll, Gullifer, & Rossi, 2013; Marian & Spivey, 2003a). This means that, when listening to words from a single language, words from the bilingual's other language also become activated. For example, a Korean-English bilingual may look for flowers when asked "Did you see the goat?" because the word "goat" means *flower* in Korean (꽃, /k͈ot̚/). In order to correctly select "goat" from the mental lexicon, the bilingual must use auditory and visual cues from the available context (e.g., the sentence is in English, and no flowers are nearby). As this process of selection is continuously experienced across a variety of situations, it may have long-term consequences for the cognitive system.

The current chapter reviews behavioral and neural evidence on how knowing more than one language (i.e., being bilingual or multilingual) changes the cognitive and linguistic demands of spoken word recognition. We explore how linguistic and cognitive constraints influence the presence and the extent of language coactivation by examining factors such as language proficiency, between-language phonological and lexical similarities, and sentence context. We then consider bilingual speech perception under adverse listening conditions. We finally discuss how bilinguals use internal resources (e.g., cognitive control) and external cues (e.g., language environment) to overcome parallel language activation and successfully recognize words in a spoken context.

Constraints on parallel activation during bilingual spoken word recognition

Research on bilingual language processing indicates that bilinguals activate both languages during listening (Marian & Spivey, 2003a, 2003b; Spivey & Marian, 1999), reading (Van Heuven, Dijkstra, & Grainger, 1998), and speaking (Colomé, 2001). While some early evidence suggested that bilinguals accessed each of their languages selectively (Gerard & Scarborough, 1989; Scarborough, Gerard, & Cortese, 1984), this language-specific access has been shown to occur only under certain task demands, types of instructions, and material list compositions (e.g., Dijkstra, Timmermans, & Schriefers, 2000; Van Heuven, Dijkstra, & Grainger, 1998). Most recent evidence supports a non-selective, parallel-access account of bilingual language processing (see Kroll, Bobb, & Wodniecka, 2006 for a review).

Convincing support for the simultaneous coactivation of both languages comes from bilingual research employing the visual world paradigm (VWP). Marian and Spivey (2003b) tracked bilinguals' and monolinguals' eye movements while instructing them to pick up a target item (e.g., *marker*) while the display also included either a within-language phonological competitor (e.g., *marbles*), a between-language phonological competitor (e.g., *stamp*, the Russian word for which is /markə/), or both a within-language and a between-language competitor simultaneously (see Figure 8.1). While both bilinguals and monolinguals experienced within-language competition, only bilinguals showed between-language competition, suggesting that the observed parallel activation was indeed due to the bilinguals' second language experience.

The bilingual version of the VWP has since been frequently used to investigate cross-linguistic activation in bilingual spoken word recognition (e.g., Chambers & Cooke, 2009; Ju & Luce, 2004; Weber & Cutler, 2004; Wu, Cristino, Leek, & Thierry, 2013), and a number of linguistic and cognitive factors have been found to modulate the extent of coactivation. For instance, in bilingual spoken word recognition, the degree of phonological similarity between two languages can influence the extent to which the non-target language becomes activated (e.g., Blumenfeld & Marian, 2007). In addition, the bilingual's own perception of phonetic categories has a pronounced effect: a bilingual with broader, less accurate L2 phonetic categories will activate a larger set of phonological competitors (e.g., Broersma & Cutler, 2008). Next, we discuss how language proficiency and age of acquisition, bilinguals' phonemic representations, sentence context, and phonological and lexical similarity influence language coactivation. These linguistic and cognitive factors can be grouped into two categories according to whether they affect (a) bottom-up or (b) top-down processing (note, however, that this dichotomy is for heuristic purposes only and does not capture the full complexity of the dynamic interaction within the cognitive system).

FIGURE 8.1. An example display using the visual world paradigm (adapted from Marian & Spivey, 2003b), showing a target (*marker*, upper right corner), a within-language competitor (*marbles*, lower right corner), a between-language competitor (*stamp*, upper left corner, Russian word /markə/) and a control item (*key*, lower left corner). (*Credits:* The pictures of *key* and /markə/ were taken by Evan-Amos as part of Vanamo Media, which creates public domain works for educational purposes. The picture of *marbles* was obtained from a collection of marbles within the permanent collection of the Children's Museum of Indianapolis [http://commons.wikimedia.org/wiki/File:The_Childrens_Museum_of_Indian apolis _-_Marbles.jpg]; the original photo was cropped and transformed into grayscale in GIMP [photo credit: Black Market, licensed under Creative Commons Attribution 3.0 Unported, http://creativecommons.org/licenses/by-sa/3.0/deed.en]. The picture of *stamp* was obtained from https://www.flickr.com/photos/barrydahl/337642359/in/photostream/; the original photo was resized and transformed into grayscale by GIMP 2; the text in the original photo was also removed [photo credit: Barry Dahl, licensed under Creative Commons Attribution 2.0 Generic, https://creativecommons.org/licenses/by-sa/2.0/].)

Language proficiency and age of acquisition

Language proficiency (see Van Hell & Tanner, 2012 for a review) and age of acquisition (e.g., Canseco-Gonzalez et al., 2010) have both been shown to influence the degree of cross-linguistic activation in bilingual word recognition. Although these two factors are both related to bilinguals' language profile and experience and thus exert top-down influences, they seem to impact language coactivation in different ways: while language proficiency modulates the baseline level of activation for each language, age of acquisition affects the strength of connection between two languages.

A bilingual's relative proficiency in his or her two languages influences the degree of cross-linguistic activation. Specifically, when the target language (i.e., the language that is required for completing the current task) is the less proficient language, bilinguals consistently activate phonological competitors from their more proficient language (Blumenfeld & Marian, 2007; Marian & Spivey, 2003a, 2003b; Weber & Cutler, 2004), a finding that has been demonstrated by tracking eye movements using the VWP.

Blumenfeld and Marian (2007) examined the effect of proficiency on language coactivation in German-English bilinguals (with high proficiency in German) and English-German bilinguals (with low proficiency in German) using the VWP. The name of the target object (e.g., *desk*) shared a similar phonological onset with one of the non-target objects' names in German (the between-language competitor: e.g., *lid*, "deckel" in German). Even though only English was heard during the task, German-English bilinguals looked at the between-language competitors more often than at control objects, indicating that the German names (the more proficient language) of the objects were activated. However, English-German bilinguals did not look at the between-language competitor more often than at the control object, suggesting that competition from the non-target language is modulated by relative proficiency in the two languages.

Indeed, when target words are from the more proficient language, evidence of language coactivation of the non-target language is less consistent. While some studies find activation of phonological competitors from the less proficient language (Marian & Spivey, 2003b; Spivey & Marian, 1999), others do not (Blumenfeld & Marian, 2007; Ju & Luce, 2004; Marian & Spivey, 2003a; Weber & Cutler, 2004). Additionally, proficiency in the non-target language has been shown to modulate the extent of coactivation. When high- and low-proficiency bilinguals were directly compared, high-proficiency bilinguals looked more often at between-language competitors than did low-proficiency bilinguals (Blumenfeld & Marian, 2013). These asymmetrical findings reflect the crucial role that proficiency plays in determining the presence of parallel activation of the phonological competitors from the non-target language.

Language proficiency also influences whether translation equivalents (i.e., words that have the same meaning in both the target and the non-target languages) become activated. One way to explore this issue is through the use of event-related potentials (ERPs), which are a measure of neural responses that are time-locked to the stimulus onset. Several distinct ERP components have been used to index discrete stages of cognitive processing (Luck, 2005), including the widely studied N400 component. While the N400 is associated with several different cognitive processes (for a review, see Kutas & Federmeier, 2011), in language research it is frequently used to index the ease of semantic integration as well as phonological and semantic repetition effects, including sensitivity of the N400 amplitude to phonological overlap (Praamstra & Stegeman, 1993; Radeau, Besson, Fonteneau, & Castro, 1998). Thierry and Wu (2007) exploited this property of the N400 to investigate the coactivation of translation equivalents. Participants were asked to make semantic relatedness judgments on English word pairs they saw or heard. Some of the presented word pairs shared the same phonological onset in Chinese translation equivalents (e.g., *train* – *ham*, 火车/*huǒ chē*/ – 火腿/*huǒ tuǐ*/). While Chinese-English bilinguals and English monolinguals showed similar behavioral patterns, responding to semantically unrelated word pairs more slowly than to related word pairs, ERPs showed that bilinguals and monolinguals processed the stimuli differently. Specifically, only Chinese-English bilinguals elicited a reduced N400 to semantically unrelated word pairs that shared the same phonological onset in Chinese translations, when compared to word pairs that shared no phonological onset. This result indicates that bilinguals automatically activate translation equivalents from the non-target language.

This activation of translation equivalents is dependent upon a bilingual's relative proficiencies across his or her two languages. For example, Phillips, Klein, Mercier, and de Boysson (2006) showed that translation equivalents became activated only when bilinguals processed their less dominant language (L2). More importantly, when bilinguals were divided into relatively high- and low-proficiency groups according their L2, only highly proficient bilinguals showed activation of L2 translation equivalents when listening in their L1 (Phillips et al., 2006). Activation of L2 translation equivalents has also been demonstrated when bilinguals are highly proficient in both of their languages. In a VWP study of balanced bilinguals, Shook (2014) found that Spanish-English bilinguals who were highly proficient in both languages always activated translation equivalents from the non-target language, regardless of which language they were listening to (Shook, 2014). These results together indicate that language proficiency not only influences the activation of the non-target language but also affects the activation of translation equivalents from the non-target language: the more proficient a language is, the more likely it is to become activated.

These effects of language proficiency on parallel activation are compatible with predictions made by computational models of bilingual language processing. For example, the Bilingual Interactive Activation model (BIA and BIA+, Dijkstra & Van Heuven, 1998, 2002) and the Bilingual Model of Lexical Access model (BIMOLA, Grosjean, 1997; Léwy & Grosjean, 2008) both propose a resting activation or pre-activation level for a language, which determines the ease and speed of accessing or activating that language. The BIA model employs the subjective frequency of words in each of a bilingual's languages (a measure related to proficiency in each language) as the resting activation level of word units. Words from a more proficient language with higher subjective frequencies have a higher resting activation level than words from a less proficient language. Therefore, these words become activated more easily and can therefore more readily compete for selection in a spoken context.

Age of acquisition, though often confounded with language proficiency, has also been shown to be an important factor that mediates the degree of parallel activation. In an eye-tracking experiment, Canseco-Gonzalez and colleagues (2010) tested three groups of bilinguals who varied in the ages at which they acquired their L2. They found that only bilinguals who learned an L2 before the age of 6 showed between-language competition from the L2. However, in this study, bilinguals who acquired their L2 earlier were also more proficient in the L2. Therefore, it is not clear whether the effect seen by Conseco-Gonzalez and associates is attributed to differences in age of acquisition or proficiency. Nevertheless, a recent ERP study confirmed that age of acquisition seems to affect parallel language activation. When examining parallel activation in early and late bilinguals who did not differ in L2 proficiency, Altvater-Mackensen and Mani (2013) found that only early bilinguals who acquired the L2 before the age of 6 showed a reduced N400-like response for words that were phonologically similar across the two languages. This finding is consistent with the notion that an early-acquired language is integrated more closely with the native language (i.e., the native language and early-acquired L2 share more common cortical areas) than a language learned later in life (e.g., Kim, Relkin, Lee, & Hirsch, 1997; Perani et al., 1998; Perani et al., 2003).

In sum, age of acquisition seems to modulate the connection strength between two languages, which affects language coactivation independently from the effect of language proficiency. That is, for bilinguals with equal proficiency in their two languages, bilinguals with an early age of L2 acquisition seem to have a more integrated language system than bilinguals with a late age of L2 acquisition. Thus, the activation of one language is more likely to induce coactivation of the other language in bilinguals with an early age of L2 acquisition. Meanwhile, language proficiency affects the baseline activation level of bilinguals' two languages during bilingual spoken word recognition, and the baseline activation level influences the presence of parallel activation via top-down processing. When proficiency in a language is high, the baseline activation of that language is high. The higher the baseline activation of a language, the more likely that language is to become activated.

Phonemic representations in the non-native language

Another top-down influence on language coactivation during spoken word recognition is bilinguals' internal representation of phonemes from their two languages. Even within a single language, spoken word recognition requires selecting a target word from all activated word candidates (Dahan & Magnuson, 2006). Because non-native speakers often have smaller vocabularies in their L2 compared to monolingual speakers of that language (Bialystok, Craik, & Luk, 2008), one would expect non-native speakers to experience less competition during L2 word recognition, as fewer lexical candidates would be activated. However, increasing evidence has shown that non-native speakers experience more within-language competition than native speakers, partly because of non-native speakers' L2 phonetic categories (Broersma, 2002; Broersma & Cutler, 2008, 2011). For example, native Japanese speakers have difficulty distinguishing between the English sounds /r/ and /l/ due to their inaccurate representations of these two non-native sounds. When hearing target words (e.g., *rocket*) in their non-native language (i.e., English), Japanese-English bilinguals activate both the target word and unrelated competitors that contain the phoneme /l/ in place of /r/ (e.g., *locker*). This results in increased competition compared to native speakers of English (Cutler, Weber, & Otake, 2006; Weber & Cutler, 2004). The inaccurate phonemic representation also causes greater between-language competition. For example, Dutch native speakers easily confuse the English phoneme /æ/ (which does not exist in Dutch) with /ɛ/ (which exists in both Dutch and English). Therefore, hearing an L2 target word (e.g., *carrot*, /kærət/) that contains a confusable phoneme activates between-language competitors (e.g., *kerk*, / kɛrk/, means *church* in Dutch) from the native language (Weber & Cutler, 2004).

Bilinguals' inaccurate representations of L2 phonologies may be due to a limited ability to incorporate phonological variants from the non-native language into an already formed phonological space. In an ERP study, Sebastián-Gallés, Rodríguez-Fornells, de Diego-Balaguer, and Díaz (2006) had Spanish-Catalan and Catalan-Spanish bilinguals perform a Catalan lexical decision task that included Catalan-like non-words. These non-words replaced one vowel from a Catalan word with a similar, Catalan-specific phoneme (e.g., /ɛ/, which is distinguished from /e/ in Catalan). To native Spanish speakers, this phonetic difference was difficult to perceive, and the Spanish-Catalan bilinguals were worse at rejecting these non-words than were the Catalan-Spanish bilinguals. In addition, only the Catalan-Spanish bilinguals showed an enhanced error-related negativity (ERN) when they incorrectly accepted non-words. Because the ERN is related to either explicit or implicit awareness of making an error (Nieuwenhuis, Ridderinkhof, Blom, Band, & Kok, 2001), these results suggest that Catalan-Spanish bilinguals remained sensitive to a phonetic contrast in their native language, whereas Spanish-Catalan speakers had greater difficulty perceiving the non-native contrast. Spanish-Catalan bilinguals who learned Catalan around the age of 3 failed to develop the non-native phoneme representation, even after a long period of immersion (i.e., around 20 years) (Sebastián-Gallés et al., 2006).

To summarize, bilinguals' imperfect representations of non-native phonemes can be strong and persistent, becoming a significant source of increased within- and between-language competition. Ambiguous phonemes activate similar-sounding phonemes from both the non-native and native languages, resulting in greater difficulty during non-native spoken word recognition.

Sentence context

We have reviewed how bilinguals recognize spoken words in isolation, but what happens to words embedded in a meaningful sentence context? Previous research on bilingual *visual* word recognition has shown that high-constraint sentences, which provide a meaningful semantic context that serves to reduce the numbers of possible word candidates, can eliminate cross-language competition (e.g., Schwartz & Kroll, 2006). During bilingual *spoken* word recognition, sentence context has a similar effect on restricting parallel activation via top-down influences (e.g., Chambers & Cooke, 2009).

Attending to sentence context helps to reduce the between-language competition experienced by bilinguals. During non-native spoken sentence comprehension in the visual world paradigm, bilinguals have been found to greatly reduce their fixations to between-language competitors when sentence context was highly constraining (e.g., "Marie will *feed* the chicken") but not when sentence context was low constraint (e.g., "Marie will *describe* the chicken") (Chambers & Cooke, 2009; Lagrou, Hartsuiker, & Duyck, 2013a). Similarly, FitzPatrick and Indefrey (2010) tested coactivation of the non-target language in a sentence context using ERPs. They manipulated the final words to construct sentences that were either semantically congruent (e.g., "The goods from Ikea arrived in a large cardboard *box*"), semantically incongruent (e.g., "He unpacked the computer, but the printer is still in the *towel*"), semantically incongruent but initially congruent due to sharing the onset of the words in the congruent condition (within-language competitors; e.g., "When we moved house, I had to put all my books in a *bottle*"), or semantically incongruent but sharing the onset of the L1 translation of the words in the congruent condition (between-language competitors; e.g., "My Christmas present came in a bright-orange *doughnut*", which shares the onset with the Dutch word for box, *doos*). As expected, the fully incongruent condition elicited an enhanced N400 compared to the fully congruent condition, reflecting more difficult semantic integration. The within-language competitors also elicited a larger N400 because of their semantic incongruity, but the peak was delayed relative to the incongruent condition. This delay suggests that semantically incongruent lexical items that matched the partial phonological input (e.g., *bottle*) were considered for semantic integration initially and then were recognized as semantic violations as the spoken word unfolded. Interestingly, unlike within-language competitors, between-language competitors were not considered for semantic integration. Instead, the elicited N400 from the between-language competition condition had a similar amplitude and peak as in the fully incongruent condition.

The constraining effect of sentence context on parallel language activation is consistent with predictions made by the BIA+ model (Dijkstra & Van Heuven, 2002). The BIA+ contains a word identification system that incorporates linguistic representations (e.g., lexical phonology, sublexical phonology, and semantics) from both of a bilingual's languages and is affected by linguistic context such as the semantic content of sentences. When presented with sentences, the semantic information from a particular language sends feedback to the word identification system; in turn, the activation of words in the unused language is gradually decreased, resulting in less parallel language activation. Through this feedback from the semantic level, sentence context can eliminate or attenuate parallel activation by exerting influence on the word identification system via top-down processing.

Phonological and lexical similarity

In previous sections, we considered how a bilingual's language profile or sentence context affects bilingual spoken word recognition. Next, we will examine the role of linguistic features of the auditory input. These linguistic features include phonological similarity (how the sounds of words in one language resemble the sounds of words from the other language) or whether words from the two languages share form and meaning (i.e., cognates). These kinds of linguistic characteristics may be a source of ambiguity during word recognition, thereby increasing non-target language activation.

Words that share auditory form but not meaning across languages (i.e., interlingual homophones) are particularly likely to produce bottom-up ambiguity during spoken word recognition. For example, the word /li:f/ means *leaf* in English but *sweet* in Dutch. Homophones provide a unique opportunity for studying parallel activation during spoken word recognition because their identical or highly similar phonology is likely to activate the word's meaning in both languages. Indeed, when bilinguals performed simple lexical decisions on spoken words in two languages, regardless of whether the tasks were in L1 or L2, bilinguals took longer to respond to homophones than to non-homophones. Monolinguals showed no difference in responses to the two word types, suggesting that bilinguals accessed the meanings of the homophones in the other language (Lagrou, Hartsuiker, & Duyck, 2011). Results of interlingual homophone studies are consistent with studies using interlingual homographs, which also find that bilinguals respond more slowly to homographs than to non-homographs in lexical decision tasks (e.g., Dijkstra, Moscoso del Prado Martín, Schulpen, Schreuder, & Harald Baayen, 2005; Dijkstra, Timmermans, & Schriefers, 2000).

Beyond words that share form, which constitute a special case in the bilingual lexicon, the degree of phonological similarity between word pairs has also been shown to affect the magnitude and duration of parallel activation during spoken word recognition of non-homophone words (Blumenfeld & Marian, 2007; Lagrou et al., 2013a). The finding that phonological features of perceived words affect the degree to which cross-linguistic competition occurs is consistent with computational models of spoken word recognition such as BIMOLA (Grosjean, 1997; Léwy & Grosjean, 2008) and the Bilingual Language Interaction Network for Comprehension of Speech model (BLINCS, Shook & Marian, 2013). While both models predict that phonological similarity increases language coactivation, they differ in whether the phonological representation of each language is shared or separate. According to BLINCS, activated phonemes in a shared phonological representation activate words from both languages at the phono-lexical level (see Figure 8.2). In BIMOLA, the incoming auditory input can be mapped onto separate phonological representations for each language, and activated phonemes can then activate words in that language. In both models, when an auditory stream contains shared or similar phonemes in bilinguals' two languages, similar-sounding words from both languages become activated. Therefore, increased phonological similarity across languages increases the extent of language coactivation.

In addition to form overlap, overlap in meaning (as in the case of cognates) also increases parallel activation. For example, Blumenfeld and Marian (2007) examined spoken word recognition in bilingual speakers of German and English when the target word was either a cognate or a non-cognate. They found that the

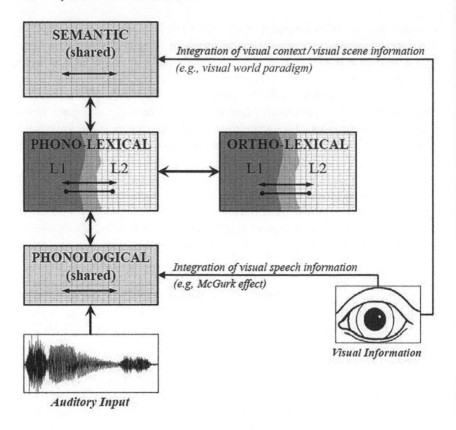

FIGURE 8.2 The Bilingual Language Interaction Network for Comprehension of Speech model (BLINCS, from Shook and Marian, 2013).

cognate status of the target word boosted parallel activation for the bilingual speakers. One possible mechanism behind increased language coactivation with cognate targets is via semantic feedback, as predicted by the BLINCS model (Shook & Marian, 2013). Within BLINCS, the representations of words at different levels (e.g., phonological, phono-lexical, orthographic, and semantic) are linked through bidirectional, excitatory Hebbian connections, which allow the different levels to communicate during spoken word recognition (see Figure 8.2). Furthermore, in BLINCS, cognates are represented closely at the phono-lexical level and also share meaning at the semantic level. As a result, cognates are activated both by overlapping phonological information (i.e., bottom-up input from the phonological level to the phono-lexical level), as well as top-down feedback from a shared semantic representation (semantic to phono-lexical level). This simultaneous activation from both bottom-up and top-down sources within the BLINCS serves to increase language coactivation for cognates relative to non-cognates.

Interaction between bottom-up input and top-down influences

Studies that use interlingual homophones in a sentence context provide us with an opportunity to understand how bottom-up (e.g., the degree of phonological overlap) and top-down (e.g., constraining sentence context) information may interact during bilingual spoken word recognition. When homophones were used in sentences and the sentence context was constructed so that the homophones' meanings fit semantically in the target language only, Dutch-English bilinguals were found to activate their non-target language (Vandeberg, Guadalupe, & Zwaan, 2011). Similarly, when bilinguals were asked to make lexical decisions on interlingual homophones that were the final word in either high (e.g., "The boy wanted a dog or a cat as a new *pet*") or low (e.g., "The boy's birthday present was a new *pet*") semantic-constraint sentences, sentence context did not completely eliminate the homophone interference effect (Lagrou, Hartsuiker, & Duyck, 2013b). Although the interference effect was smaller in high semantic-constraint sentences, cross-linguistic activation still occurred. These findings suggest that semantic contextual cues reduce competition from the non-target language, but might not be able to completely override the strong effects of bottom-up linguistic input (i.e., homophones).

A recent ERP study examined the time course of the activation of homophones' meanings in the non-target language within sentences. FitzPatrick and Indefrey (2014) found that when a cross-linguistic homophone was embedded into a sentence in participants' L2, the homophone's meaning in the non-target language was available after a short delay. When the homophone was embedded into a sentence in participants' L1, the homophone's meaning in the non-target language was available immediately. These ERP findings are consistent with behavioral evidence suggesting that, in some contexts (e.g., homophones), bottom-up linguistic input still activates the non-target language even when embedded in a meaningful sentence context.

However, whether a homophone's meaning in the non-target language is available immediately or in a delayed manner may be affected by bilinguals' language proficiency. It is likely that bilinguals associate homophone meanings from the less dominant language more closely with pronunciations in the more dominant language because the probability of hearing these homophones in the more dominant language is higher. Therefore, when bilinguals hear the homophone in the more proficient language, they are faster to activate homophone meanings from the less proficient language (FitzPatrick & Indefrey, 2014).

Furthermore, interactions among language proficiency, sentence context, and phonological similarity reveal an intricate pattern of how bilinguals simultaneously respond to top-down and bottom-up information. For example, when sentence context within the less dominant language was highly constraining, Chambers and Cooke (2009) found that bilinguals did not coactivate their more dominant language regardless of their proficiency in the non-dominant language. Additionally, when sentence constraint was low within the non-dominant language, coactivation could occur even when phonological overlap was slight. However, low-constraint sentences within the dominant language led to coactivation only when the target and between-language competitor shared a large degree of phonological overlap (Lagrou et al., 2013a).

These interactions between top-down and bottom-up factors suggest that sentence context has a stronger influence on language coactivation than does language proficiency. However, the top-down influence from sentence context might be limited when the bottom-up input maximally activates both languages (e.g., interlingual homophones). While no computational models are currently equipped to predict these complex patterns, models that allow bidirectional interactivity (such as BLINCS) can be modified to accommodate this finding. In the future, computational models will need to specifically account for the interactivity among top-down and bottom-up influences during parallel activation in bilingual spoken word recognition.

Consequences of bilingualism for spoken word recognition

In the previous sections, we reviewed some of the factors that influence parallel activation during bilingual spoken word recognition and showed that bilinguals experience an additional source of competition (i.e., between languages). Next, we will consider how this increased competition affects bilingual speech perception in a difficult listening context (e.g., background noise). We will then provide evidence that bilinguals use both internal resources (e.g., cognitive control) and external resources (e.g., language environment and linguistic cues) to optimize spoken word recognition outcomes. We suggest that the challenge of bilingual spoken word recognition leads to the development of a more flexible cognitive system.

Speech perception disadvantages under adverse conditions

As a result of bilinguals' less accurate L2 phonemic representations, one might expect bilinguals to perform worse in L2 speech perception tasks compared to native speakers. Surprisingly, bilinguals usually recognize words and sentences in their L2 as accurately as monolinguals in quiet listening environments (e.g., Mayo, Florentine, & Buus, 1997). However, when bilinguals are placed under adverse listening conditions such as noisy background environments, they do indeed show difficulties in speech perception.

In previous studies, the Speech Perception in Noise Test (SPIN; Kalikow, Stevens, & Elliott, 1977) has been used to compare speech perception across monolinguals and bilinguals. In the SPIN test (e.g., Mayo et al., 1997), participants are asked to repeat target words from a list of complete sentences, which are presented auditorily at a fixed loudness within different levels of background noise. When there is no noise, bilinguals and monolinguals are equally able to recognize the target words. However, as the noise level increases, bilinguals experience a steeper decrease in accuracy than do monolinguals (Rogers, Lister, Febo, Besing, & Abrams, 2006; Rosenhouse, Haik, & Kishon-Rabin, 2006). Similarly, in the Hearing in Noise Test (HINT; distributed by Starkey Laboratories, Koch, Nilsson, & Soli, n.d.), which measures the hearing threshold at which participants are able to accurately recognize words, bilinguals show comparable thresholds to monolinguals in a quiet listening condition. However, when the noise level increases, bilinguals require higher thresholds than monolinguals to achieve the same recognition accuracy (Von Hapsburg, Champlin, & Shetty, 2004). Bilinguals, as shown in these speech perception studies, seem to be more vulnerable to adverse listening conditions.

This greater vulnerability of speech perception under adverse condition holds true for both bilinguals who acquired their L2 at an early age (Mayo et al., 1997; Shi, 2010; Tabri, Chacra, & Pring, 2011) and for bilinguals who learned the L2 at a later age (Mayo et al., 1997; Meador, Flege, & Mackay, 2000; Nakamura & Gordon-Salant, 2011; Shi, 2010; Von Hapsburg et al., 2004) compared to monolinguals. A plausible source of this greater vulnerability is that bilinguals' relatively low competence of processing their non-native language causes them to suffer more under noise conditions. However, this is unlikely the case for early bilinguals, who either acquired their L2 since birth (Shi, 2010), were very proficient in their L2 (Mayo et al., 1997), or were L2 dominant (Rogers et al., 2006). Instead, the disadvantage of listening to speech in noise might be attributed to increased cognitive demands that are required for managing interactions between two languages.

Under quiet conditions, bilinguals must select words from their larger lexicon (as L1 and L2 are combined), possibly requiring more cognitive resources compared to monolinguals. When listening conditions worsen, additional cognitive resources are needed to extract speech from noise, resulting in declined performance for both monolinguals and bilinguals. For bilinguals, these additional cognitive demands could reduce available resources to manage the competition arising between languages. Therefore, bilinguals demonstrate a steeper decline than monolinguals when perceiving speech in noise. This explanation is supported by the finding that bilinguals' accuracy in L1 speech perception in noise also decreases as their L2 proficiency increases (von Hapsburg & Bahng, 2009).

Under suboptimal listening conditions, bilinguals are also less efficient at making use of semantic information than are monolinguals. Recent evidence suggests that under adverse listening conditions, bilinguals do not benefit as much as monolinguals from the semantic cues provided by sentences (Shi, 2014). Whereas bilinguals can utilize semantic information only from sentences when there is no background noise, monolinguals can rely on semantic context even when the speech signal is not clear (Bradlow & Alexander, 2007). This is supported by neuroimaging evidence that cortical regions implicated in semantic processing are recruited only for the processing of L1 (but not L2) sentences under noise conditions (Hervais-Adelman, Pefkou, & Golestani, 2014).

Cognitive flexibility in bilingual spoken word recognition

Although bilinguals have greater difficulties in perceiving speech in noise, many studies do report comparable performance (e.g., overall accuracy) for bilinguals compared to monolinguals under a quiet listening environment. Considering the fact that bilinguals experience more competition than monolinguals during spoken word recognition (because competition can occur both within and across a bilingual's languages), it is somewhat unexpected that they do not show any apparent difficulties in spoken word recognition. In the next section, we review how bilinguals use both internal and external resources to successfully resolve the additional competition that they experience during spoken word recognition.

Inhibitory control

Behavioral evidence suggests that inhibitory control ability might modulate the extent to which bilinguals coactivate their two languages, and may determine bilinguals' effectiveness in managing competition from the non-target language. Blumenfeld and Marian (2013) were the first to investigate the effect of individuals' inhibitory control abilities on parallel activation during bilingual spoken word recognition. In a visual world paradigm task, they found that bilinguals with better inhibitory control showed decreased coactivation of competitors immediately before selection of the target word. This phenomenon was not observed in bilinguals with weaker inhibitory control abilities, suggesting that bilinguals with better inhibitory control are able to reduce language coactivation and select target words more effectively. Furthermore, better inhibitory control has also been associated with decreased between-language competition among relatively low-proficiency bilinguals (Mercier, Pivneva, & Titone, 2014); therefore, inhibitory control may be particularly important when competition interferes with comprehension.

Over time, the frequent recruitment of inhibitory control enables bilinguals to develop a more efficient cognitive control system. In fact, the finding that bilinguals have overall better inhibitory control than their monolingual peers has been well documented in recent research (e.g., Bialystok et al., 2008; Costa, Hernández, & Sebastián-Gallés, 2008; but see Paap & Greenberg, 2013) and has been attributed to bilinguals' unique experience managing coactivation of both languages (Blumenfeld & Marian, 2011; see Kroll & Bialystok, 2013 and Kroll, Bobb, Misra, & Guo, 2008 for reviews).

This inhibitory control advantage, in turn, results in less effortful language processing for bilinguals. In a recent fMRI study, Marian and colleagues (2014) examined bilingual-monolingual differences in recruiting neural resources to resolve within-language phonological competition during spoken word recognition. Whereas monolinguals relied more on areas thought to underlie executive control (including right anterior cingulate and left superior frontal gyrus), bilinguals did not recruit those areas more when processing phonologically competing words. These findings suggest that competition resolution is more automated in bilinguals and that the bilingual cognitive system has become tuned over time to be more efficient at resolving competition.

Linguistic cues and language environment

In addition to inhibitory control, bilinguals also use available cues from linguistic input and the language environment to make spoken word recognition more efficient. For example, when linguistic input strongly indicates the involvement of one of a bilingual's two languages, bilinguals are better able to restrict language activation to only one language. Ju and Luce (2004) found that Spanish-English bilinguals were able to use subtle differences in Spanish and English voice onset time (VOT) to limit activation of the non-target language. This suggests that bilinguals use sub-phonemic cues to restrict lexical activation, thereby reducing word competition. Similarly, bilinguals can use linguistic cues to facilitate word recognition. In a cross-modal priming task, bilinguals listened to interlingual homophone primes that were pronounced in either Dutch or English. They then made lexical decisions on visually presented English word targets. When targets followed the English-sounding homophone primes, lexical decisions were faster than when they followed the Dutch-sounding homophone primes (Schulpen, Dijkstra, Schriefers, & Hasper, 2003).

Furthermore, language environment, like cues from the auditory input, is also utilized as a prompt for recognizing spoken words more efficiently. For example, in an L2-dominant environment, bilinguals are more likely to show between-language competition from L2 into L1 (Marian & Spivey, 2003b); however, when the presence of L1 in the environment is boosted (for example, by playing L1 music), between-language competition from L1 into L2 increases (Marian & Spivey, 2003a). It has been shown that the experimental language environment in which bilinguals are tested affects bilinguals' awareness of their two languages' involvement (Elston-Güttler, Gunter, & Kotz, 2005). It is likely that bilinguals become more sensitive to the language of their environment and use it to modulate the baseline activation of their two languages in order to limit cross-language competition. This sensitivity, together with better inhibitory control, is an indicator of a highly flexible cognitive system in bilinguals.

Conclusion

In this chapter, we have reviewed the influences of top-down and bottom-up factors on language coactivation during bilingual spoken word recognition. Top-down factors include bilinguals' language proficiency and age of L2 acquisition, internal phonemic representations across two languages, and sentence context. Meanwhile, phonological features of the linguistic input affect word recognition in a bottom-up fashion. We discussed how knowing a second language affects bilinguals' perception of spoken input. Whereas bilinguals recognize words as well as monolinguals under normal listening conditions, they exhibit speech perception disadvantages under adverse listening conditions such as noise. This suggests that knowing more than one language increases cognitive demands for bilinguals. In order to navigate these increased demands, bilinguals rely on inhibitory control and linguistic cues to achieve successful spoken word recognition.

The interaction between top-down (e.g., sentence context) and bottom-up (e.g., phonological similarity) influences on language coactivation is at the core of bilinguals' ability to efficiently integrate information during spoken word recognition. While blocking out unnecessary information (i.e., words from the language not currently in use) helps bilinguals focus on ongoing word recognition, maintaining both languages active allows bilinguals to match the auditory input onto either potential language more quickly. As the goal of spoken word recognition is to quickly match auditory input with mental representations, bilinguals maintain activation of both languages while at the same time regulating the extent of coactivation to maximize efficiency during language comprehension.

By comparing bilingual disadvantages in speech perception in noise to their unimpaired performance under quiet conditions, we find that the use of both internal (e.g., inhibitory control) and external (e.g., linguistic cues) resources enable bilinguals to resolve increased cognitive demands, which results in a highly flexible cognitive system. Consistent with research from other bilingual language processing domains (e.g., production: Guo, Liu, Misra, & Kroll, 2011; reading: Macizo, Bajo, & Martín, 2010), we suggest that inhibitory control is involved in the reduction of language coactivation during spoken word recognition. Although a causal relationship has not yet been empirically demonstrated, evidence indicating a bilingual inhibitory control advantage on non-linguistic tasks suggests a promising link between bilingual language experience and inhibitory control gains. Future research will need to clarify the exact way in which inhibitory control is involved during bilingual spoken word recognition (e.g., its influence on the baseline level of language activation vs. its role in the active suppression of competitors) and how recruitment of inhibitory control changes as bilinguals become more proficient in their second language (e.g., different mechanisms for high- and low-proficiency bilinguals or linear gains as proficiency increases).

To conclude, knowing and using more than one language leads to language coactivation during spoken word recognition and thus increases cognitive demands for bilinguals. Nevertheless, bilinguals are able to use cognitive resources to constrain coactivation and gain advantages in executive functions. We therefore suggest that while experience with a second language increases the difficulty of spoken word recognition, it also shapes the flexibility of the cognitive system. This flexibility, conferred through language experience, reflects the general plasticity of the human cognitive system and the dynamic relationship between language and cognition, a relationship into which bilingualism provides a unique lens.

References

Altvater-Mackensen, N., & Mani, N. (2013). Effects of pre-exposure to object and label during word-learning. In S. Baiz (Ed.), *Proceedings of the 37th Annual Boston University Conference on Language Development* (pp. 13–23). Sommerville, MA: Cascadilla Press.

Bialystok, E., Craik, F., & Luk, G. (2008). Cognitive control and lexical access in younger and older bilinguals. *Journal of Experimental Psychology: Learning, Memory, and Cognition, 34*(4), 859–873. doi:10.1037/0278–7393.34.4.859

Blumenfeld, H. K., & Marian, V. (2007). Constraints on parallel activation in bilingual spoken language processing: Examining proficiency and lexical status using eye-tracking. *Language and Cognitive Processes, 22*(5), 633–660. doi:10.1080/01690960601000746

Blumenfeld, H. K., & Marian, V. (2011). Bilingualism influences inhibitory control in auditory comprehension. *Cognition, 118*(2), 245–257. doi:10.1016/j.cognition.2010.10.012

Blumenfeld, H. K., & Marian, V. (2013). Parallel language activation and cognitive control during spoken word recognition in bilinguals. *Journal of Cognitive Psychology, 25*(5), 547–567. doi:10.1080/20445911.2013.812093

Bradlow, A. R., & Alexander, J. A. (2007). Semantic and phonetic enhancements for speech-in-noise recognition by native and non-native listeners. *The Journal of the Acoustical Society of America, 121*(4), 2339–2349. doi:10.1121/1.2642103

Broersma, M. (2002). Comprehension of non-native speech: Inaccurate phoneme processing and activation of lexical competitors [oral]. *Proceedings of the 7th International Conference on Spoken Language Processing* (pp. 261–264). Center for Spoken Language Research, University of Colorado, Boulder (CD-ROM).

Broersma, M., & Cutler, A. (2008). Phantom word activation in L2. *System, 36*(1), 22–34. doi:10.1016/j.system.2007.11.003

Broersma, M., & Cutler, A. (2011). Competition dynamics of second-language listening. *The Quarterly Journal of Experimental Psychology, 64*(1), 74–95. doi:10.1080/17470218.2 010.499174

Canseco-Gonzalez, E., Brehm, L., Brick, C. A., Brown-Schmidt, S., Fischer, K., & Wagner, K. (2010). Carpet or carcel: The effect of age of acquisition and language mode on bilingual lexical access. *Language and Cognitive Processes, 25*(5), 669–705. doi:10.1080/01690960903474912

Chambers, C. G., & Cooke, H. (2009). Lexical competition during second-language listening: Sentence context, but not proficiency, constrains interference from the native lexicon. *Journal of Experimental Psychology: Learning, Memory, and Cognition, 35*(4), 1029–1040. doi:10.1037/a0015901

Colomé, À. (2001). Lexical activation in bilinguals' speech production: Language-specific or language-independent? *Journal of Memory and Language, 45*(4), 721–736. doi:10.1006/jmla.2001.2793

Costa, A., Hernández, M., & Sebastián-Gallés, N. (2008). Bilingualism aids conflict resolution: Evidence from the ANT task. *Cognition, 106*(1), 59–86. doi:10.1016/j.cognition.2006.12.013

Cutler, A., Weber, A., & Otake, T. (2006). Asymmetric mapping from phonetic to lexical representations in second-language listening. *Journal of Phonetics, 34*(2), 269–284. doi:10.1016/j.wocn.2005.06.002

Dahan, D., & Magnuson, J. S. (2006). Spoken word recognition. In M. J. Traxler & M. A. Gernsbacher (Eds.), *Handbook of Psycholinguistics* (pp. 249–283). Amsterdam: Academic Press.

Dijkstra, T., Moscoso del Prado Martín, F., Schulpen, B., Schreuder, R., & Harald Baayen, R. (2005). A roommate in cream: Morphological family size effects on interlingual homograph recognition. *Language and Cognitive Processes, 20*(1–2), 7–41. doi:10.1080/01690960444000124

Dijkstra, T., Timmermans, M., & Schriefers, H. (2000). On being blinded by your other language: Effects of task demands on interlingual homograph recognition. *Journal of Memory and Language, 42*(4), 445–464. doi:10.1006/jmla.1999.2697

Dijkstra, T., & Van Heuven, W. J. B. (1998). The BIA model and bilingual word recognition. In J. Grainger & A. M. Jacobs (Eds.), *Localist Connectionist Approaches to Human Cognition* (pp. 189–225). Mahwah, NJ: Erlbaum.

Dijkstra, T., & Van Heuven, W. J. B. (2002). The architecture of the bilingual word recognition system: From identification to decision. *Bilingualism: Language and Cognition, 5*(3), 175–197. doi:10.1017/S1366728902003012

Elston-Güttler, K. E., Gunter, T. C., & Kotz, S. A. (2005). Zooming into L2: Global language context and adjustment affect processing of interlingual homographs in sentences. *Cognitive Brain Research, 25*(1), 57–70. doi:10.1016/j.cogbrainres.2005.04.007

FitzPatrick, I., & Indefrey, P. (2010). Lexical competition in nonnative speech comprehension. *Journal of Cognitive Neuroscience, 22*(6), 1165–1178.

FitzPatrick, I., & Indefrey, P. (2014). Head start for target language in bilingual listening. *Brain Research, 1542,* 111–130. doi:10.1016/j.brainres.2013.10.014

Gerard, L. D., & Scarborough, D. L. (1989). Language-specific lexical access of homographs by bilinguals. *Journal of Experimental Psychology: Learning, Memory, and Cognition, 15*(2), 305.

Grosjean, F. (1997). Processing mixed languages: Issues, findings and models. In A. M. B. de Groot & J. F. Kroll (Eds.), *Tutorial in Bilingualism: Psycholinguistic Perspectives* (pp. 225–254). Mahwah, NJ: Erlbaum.

Guo, T., Liu, H., Misra, M., & Kroll, J. F. (2011). Local and global inhibition in bilingual word production: fMRI evidence from Chinese–English bilinguals. *NeuroImage, 56*(4), 2300–2309. doi:10.1016/j.neuroimage.2011.03.049

Hervais-Adelman, A., Pefkou, M., & Golestani, N. (2014). Bilingual speech-in-noise: Neural bases of semantic context use in the native language. *Brain and Language, 132,* 1–6. doi:10.1016/j.bandl.2014.01.009

Ju, M., & Luce, P. A. (2004). Falling on sensitive ears: Constraints on bilingual lexical activation. *Psychological Science, 15*(5), 314–318.

Kalikow, D. N., Stevens, K. N., & Elliott, L. L. (1977). Development of a test of speech intelligibility in noise using sentence materials with controlled word predictability. *The Journal of the Acoustical Society of America, 61*(5), 1337–1351.

Kim, K. H. S., Relkin, N. R., Lee, K. M., & Hirsch, J. (1997). Distinct cortical areas associated with native and second languages. *Nature, 388*(6638), 171–174.

Koch, D. B., Nilsson, M. J., & Soli. S. D. (n.d.). *Using the HINT Test on Compact Disk – Manual Two.* Eden Prairie, MN: House Ear Institute, Licensed to Starkey Laboratories.

Kroll, J. F., & Bialystok, E. (2013). Understanding the consequences of bilingualism for language processing and cognition. *Journal of Cognitive Psychology, 25*(5), 497–514. doi:10.1080/20445911.2013.799170

Kroll, J. F., Bobb, S. C., Misra, M., & Guo, T. (2008). Language selection in bilingual speech: Evidence for inhibitory processes. *Acta Psychologica, 128*(3), 416–430. doi:10.1016/j.actpsy.2008.02.001

Kroll, J. F., Bobb, S. C., & Wodniecka, Z. (2006). Language selectivity is the exception, not the rule: Arguments against a fixed locus of language selection in bilingual speech. *Bilingualism: Language and Cognition, 9*(02), 119–135. doi:10.1017/S1366728906002483

Kroll, J. F., Dussias, P. E., Bogulski, C. A., & Valdés Kroff, J. R. (2012). Juggling two languages in one mind: What bilinguals tell us about language processing and its consequences for cognition. In B. Ross (Ed.), *The Psychology of Learning and Motivation, 56* (pp. 229–262). San Diego: Academic Press. doi:10.1016/B978-0-12-394393-4.00007-8

Kroll, J. F., Gullifer, J., & Rossi, E. (2013). The multilingual lexicon: The cognitive and neural basis of lexical comprehension and production in two languages. In C. Polio (Ed.), *Annual Review of Applied Linguistics on Multilingualism, 33* (pp. 102–127). Cambridge: Cambridge University Press. doi:10.1017/S0267190513000111

Kutas, M., & Federmeier, K. D. (2011). Thirty years and counting: Finding meaning in the N400 component of the event-related brain potential (ERP). *Annual Review of Psychology, 62,* 621–647. doi:10.1146/annurev.psych.093008.131123

Lagrou, E., Hartsuiker, R. J., & Duyck, W. (2011). Knowledge of a second language influences auditory word recognition in the native language. *Journal of Experimental Psychology: Learning, Memory, and Cognition, 37*(4), 952–965. doi:10.1037/a0023217

Lagrou, E., Hartsuiker, R. J., & Duyck, W. (2013a). Interlingual lexical competition in a spoken sentence context: Evidence from the visual world paradigm. *Psychonomic Bulletin & Review, 20*(5), 963–972. doi:10.3758/s13423–013–0405–4

Lagrou, E., Hartsuiker, R. J., & Duyck, W. (2013b). The influence of sentence context and accented speech on lexical access in second-language auditory word recognition. *Bilingualism: Language and Cognition, 16*(03), 508–517. doi:10.1017/S1366728912000508

Léwy, N., & Grosjean, F. (2008). The Léwy and Grosjean BIMOLA model. In F. Grosjean, *Studying Bilinguals* (pp. 201–208). Oxford, New York: Oxford University Press.

Luck, S. J. (2005). *An Introduction to the Event-Related Potential Technique* (pp. 34–49). Cambridge, MA: MIT press.

Macizo, P., Bajo, T., & Martín, M. C. (2010). Inhibitory processes in bilingual language comprehension: Evidence from Spanish-English interlexical homographs. *Journal of Memory and Language, 63*(2), 232–244. doi:10.1016/j.jml.2010.04.002

Marian, V., Chabal, S., Bartolotti, J., Bradley, K., & Hernandez, A. (2014). Differential recruitment of executive control regions during phonological competition in monolinguals and bilinguals. *Brain & Language, 139*, 108–117. doi:10.1016/j.bandl.2014.10.005

Marian, V., & Spivey, M. (2003a). Competing activation in bilingual language processing: Within- and between-language competition. *Bilingualism Language and Cognition, 6*(2), 97–115. doi:10.1017/S1366728903001068

Marian, V., & Spivey, M. (2003b). Bilingual and monolingual processing of competing lexical items. *Applied Psycholinguistics, 24*(2), 173–193. doi:10.1017.S0142716403000092

Mayo, L. H., Florentine, M., & Buus, S. (1997). Age of second-language acquisition and perception of speech in noise. *Journal of Speech, Language, and Hearing Research, 40*(3), 686–693.

Meador, D., Flege, J. E., & Mackay, I. R. A. (2000). Factors affecting the recognition of words in a second language. *Bilingualism: Language and Cognition, 3*, 55–67.

Mercier, J., Pivneva, I., & Titone, D. (2014). Individual differences in inhibitory control relate to bilingual spoken word processing. *Bilingualism: Language and Cognition, 17*(1), 89–117. doi:10.1017/S1366728913000084

Nakamura, K., & Gordon-Salant, S. (2011). Speech perception in quiet and noise using the hearing in noise test and the Japanese hearing in noise test by Japanese listeners. *Ear and Hearing, 32*(1), 121–131.

Nieuwenhuis, S., Ridderinkhof, K. R., Blom, J., Band, G. P. H., & Kok, A. (2001). Error-related brain potentials are differentially related to awareness of response errors: Evidence from an anti-saccade task. *Psychophysiology, 38*(5), 752–760.

Paap, K. R., & Greenberg, Z. I. (2013). There is no coherent evidence for a bilingual advantage in executive processing. *Cognitive Psychology, 66*(2), 232–258. doi:10.1016/j.cogpsych.2012.12.002

Perani, D., Abutalebi, J., Paulesu, E., Brambati, S., Scifo, P., Cappa, S. F., & Fazio, F. (2003). The role of age of acquisition and language usage in early, high-proficient bilinguals: An fMRI study during verbal fluency. *Human Brain Mapping, 19*(3), 170–182. doi:10.1002/hbm.10110

Perani, D., Paulesu, E., Galles, N. S., Dupoux, E., Dehaene, S., Bettinardi, V., . . . Mehler, J. (1998). The bilingual brain: Proficiency and age of acquisition of the second language. *Brain, 121*(10), 1841–1852.

Phillips, N. A., Klein, D., Mercier, J., & de Boysson, C. (2006). ERP measures of auditory word repetition and translation priming in bilinguals. *Brain Research, 1125*(1), 116–131. doi:10.1016/j.brainres.2006.10.002

Praamstra, P., & Stegeman, D. F. (1993). Phonological effects on the auditory N400 event-related brain potential. *Cognitive Brain Research*, *1*(2), 73–86.

Radeau, M., Besson, M., Fonteneau, E., & Castro, S. L. (1998). Semantic, repetition and rime priming between spoken words: Behavioral and electrophysiological evidence. *Biological Psychology*, *48*(2), 183–204.

Rogers, C. L., Lister, J. J., Febo, D. M., Besing, J. M., & Abrams, H. B. (2006). Effects of bilingualism, noise, and reverberation on speech perception by listeners with normal hearing. *Applied Psycholinguistics*, *27*(3), 465–485. doi:10.1017.S014271640606036X

Rosenhouse, J., Haik, L., & Kishon-Rabin, L. (2006). Speech perception in adverse listening conditions in Arabic-Hebrew bilinguals. *International Journal of Bilingualism*, *10*(2), 119–135.

Scarborough, D. L., Gerard, L., & Cortese, C. (1984). Independence of lexical access in bilingual word recognition. *Journal of Verbal Learning and Verbal Behavior*, *23*(1), 84–99.

Schulpen, B., Dijkstra, T., Schriefers, H. J., & Hasper, M. (2003). Recognition of interlingual homophones in bilingual auditory word recognition. *Journal of Experimental Psychology: Human Perception and Performance*, *29*(6), 1155–1178. doi:10.1037/0096–1523.29.6.1155

Schwartz, A. I., & Kroll, J. F. (2006). Bilingual lexical activation in sentence context. *Journal of Memory and Language*, *55*(2), 197–212. doi:10.1016/j.jml.2006.03.004

Sebastián-Gallés, N., Rodríguez-Fornells, A., de Diego-Balaguer, R., & Díaz, B. (2006). First- and second-language phonological representations in the mental lexicon. *Journal of Cognitive Neuroscience*, *18*(8), 1277–1291.

Shi, L. F. (2010). Perception of acoustically degraded sentences in bilingual listeners who differ in age of English acquisition. *Journal of Speech, Language, and Hearing Research*, *53*(4), 821–835.

Shi, L. F. (2014). Measuring effectiveness of semantic cues in degraded English sentences in non-native listeners. *International Journal of Audiology*, *53*(1), 30–39. doi:10.3109/14992 027.2013.825052

Shook, A. (2014). Bilingual spoken language comprehension: A computational and empirical study of lexical-semantic. (Unpublished doctoral dissertation.) Northwestern University, Evanston, Illinois.

Shook, A., & Marian, V. (2013). The bilingual language interaction network for comprehension of speech. *Bilingualism: Language and Cognition*, *16*(2), 304–324. doi:10.1017/ S1366728912000466

Spivey, M., & Marian, V. (1999). Crosstalk between native and second languages: Partial activation of an irrelevant lexicon. *Psychological Science*, *10*(3), 281–284. doi:10.1111/1467–9280.00151

Tabri, D., Chacra, K. M. S. A., & Pring, T. (2011). Speech perception in noise by monolingual, bilingual and trilingual listeners. *International Journal of Language & Communication Disorders*, *46*(4), 411–422. doi:10.3109/13682822.2010.519372

Thierry, G., & Wu, Y. J. (2007). Brain potentials reveal unconscious translation during foreign-language comprehension. *Proceedings of the National Academy of Sciences*, *104*(30), 12530–12535. doi:10.1073pnas.0609927104

Van Hell, J. G., & Tanner, D. (2012). Second language proficiency and cross language lexical activation. *Language Learning*, *62*(s2), 148–171.

Van Heuven, W. J., Dijkstra, T., & Grainger, J. (1998). Orthographic neighborhood effects in bilingual word recognition. *Journal of Memory and Language*, *39*(3), 458–483.

Vandeberg, L., Guadalupe, T., & Zwaan, R. A. (2011). How verbs can activate things: Cross-language activation across word classes. *Acta Psychologica*, *138*(1), 68–73. doi:10.1016/j. actpsy.2011.05.007

Von Hapsburg, D., & Bahng, J. (2009). Effects of noise on bilingual listeners' first language (L1) speech perception. *Perspectives on Hearing and Hearing Disorders: Research and Diagnostics*, *13*(1), 21–26. doi:10.1044/hhd13.1.21

Von Hapsburg, D., Champlin, C. A., & Shetty, S. R. (2004). Reception thresholds for sentences in bilingual (Spanish/English) and monolingual (English) listeners. *Journal of the American Academy of Audiology, 15*(1), 88–98.

Weber, A., & Cutler, A. (2004). Lexical competition in non-native spoken-word recognition. *Journal of Memory and Language, 50*(1), 1–25. doi:10.1016/S0749-596X(03)00105-0

Wu, Y. J., Cristino, F., Leek, C., & Thierry, G. (2013). Non-selective lexical access in bilinguals is spontaneous and independent of input monitoring: Evidence from eye-tracking. *Cognition, 129*(2), 418–425. doi:10.1016/j.cognition.2013.08.005

9

THE EFFECT OF SPEECH SOUND DISORDERS ON THE DEVELOPING LANGUAGE SYSTEM

Implications for treatment and future directions in research

Breanna I. Krueger and Holly L. Storkel

The hallmark characteristic of children with speech sound disorders (SSDs) is a delay in speech sound production characterized by significantly more errors in production than same-aged peers (Gierut, 1998). SSD refers to a variety of disorders that can affect sound development. Examples of SSD include phonological disorders (difficulty learning the sounds of language), motor speech disorders (difficulty physically producing the sounds of the language), structural disorders (e.g., difficulty learning speech due to a cleft or gap in the palate) and sensory-based disorders (e.g., difficulty learning speech due to hearing impairment). In this chapter, we focus on children with developmental phonological disorders (DPDs). In these children, delays in sound production occur in the absence of any obvious motor, structural, sensory, or neurologic cause and in the context of normal hearing and nonverbal intelligence. In contrast, the language skills of children with DPD – beyond phonology – are open to debate. For example, comorbidity of language impairment is estimated at 11–15% at 6 years of age (Shriberg, Tomblin, & McSweeny, 1999) but much higher at 40–60% for preschool children with DPD (Shriberg & Austin, 1998). Likewise, comorbidity with reading impairment is estimated at 30% (Pennington, 2006). Thus, at least some children with DPD have broader deficits that affect other aspects of language, including the ability to learn the mapping between phonology and orthography.

Children with DPD eventually do master phonological production, typically during the elementary school years. Thus, the hallmark deficit appears to resolve. However, when long-term follow-ups use sensitive measures, it is evident that the underlying deficit has not completely resolved. For example, Lewis and Freebairn (1992) examined preschool children (age 4–6), school-age children (age 7–11), adolescents (age 12–17), and adults (age 18–45) with either current DPD (i.e., the younger children) or a history of DPD (i.e., older children and adults). At all ages, participants with DPD scored significantly worse than participants without DPD on measures of phonological processing (e.g., non-word repetition, production of tongue twisters). Although children with DPD do master phonological production, albeit at a later age than their peers, weak phonological processing appears to remain throughout life (see also Preston, Hull, & Edwards, 2013). A major issue then is what is the underlying deficit in DPD? On the surface, it appears to be a production deficit, but these long-term outcome data hint that there may be other deficits that don't resolve with current treatments and/or maturation. Understanding the nature of the deficit has implications for theories of phonology as well as for clinical treatment. At issue here is what does it mean to know a phonology, and how can phonological learning be accelerated?

Nature of phonological deficit

It is clear that children with DPD do not produce speech sounds with comparable accuracy to their peers. However, it is unclear what the underlying mechanisms are that lead to these incorrect productions because the mechanisms cannot be observed directly. Several prevailing theories suggest the mechanisms that may contribute to DPD. For example, Munson, Edwards, and Beckman (2005) propose that phonology can be decomposed into four types of knowledge: (1) perceptual, (2) articulatory, (3) higher-level phonological categories, namely abstract representations, and (4) social-indexical. *Perceptual knowledge* encompasses the acoustic-perceptual characteristics of sounds and words. *Articulatory knowledge* relates to motor plans for sounds across a variety of contexts, as well as the relationship between articulation and acoustics. *Abstract representations* correspond to multiple types of information, such as how changes in sounds relate to changes in meaning and how sounds can be combined to form words. *Social-indexical knowledge* captures a person's understanding of language variation (e.g., regional dialects). This area has received limited attention in the study of child speech. Thus, there is limited evidence related to DPD. However, for the other three areas, the question becomes whether children with DPD have deficits in all of these areas or just a subset. A complicating issue is that each type of knowledge interacts with and influences the others, resulting in an interactive system. For example, if we identify the formation of abstract representations as an impairment, is that impairment really the result of underlying perceptual processing difficulties? It is crucial to unpack this complex system to understand the nature of the deficit in children with DPD so that appropriate remediation programs can be designed. As a result, recent efforts have focused on testing these three types of knowledge in children with DPD.

Perception

Children are born with the ability to categorize consonants according to their acoustic features and have the ability and preference to segment what they hear in terms of syllables, rather than individual phonemes (Eimas, Siqueland, Jusczyk, & Vigorito, 1971; Liberman, Harris, Hoffman, & Griffith, 1957; Werker, Gilbert, Humphrey, &

Tees, 1981; Werker & Tees, 1983). The ability to segment rapid speech into smaller units, such as phonemes, refines and improves as the child develops and accumulates experience hearing speech. Children with DPD present with difficulties with segmentation of the speech signal, and this has a broad impact on later word recognition, learning, and articulation. In children with DPD, there is a diminished ability to categorize sounds that have been manipulated along a spectral continuum, indicating a deficit in the ability to categorize sounds based on acoustic information (Hoffman, Daniloff, Bengoa, & Schuckers, 1985; Ohde & Sharf, 1988). This difficulty reflects a lack of perceptual refinement that would allow for efficient categorization. This deficit further extends to the ability to discriminate between two sounds (e.g., "s" in "seat" vs. "sh" in "sheet") by preschoolers with DPD (Rvachew & Jamieson, 1989). Again, the categorization and discrimination of phonemes is one of the earliest means for acquiring information about spoken language for infants and young children. Many children with DPD seem to experience a breakdown at this basic level, and this may drive later difficulties in other linguistic domains. In children as young as 3 years of age, production is consistent with the ability to discriminate between and identify phonemes. That is, if a child has difficulty with producing a phoneme, s/he is likely to also have difficulty discriminating and identifying it (Thomas & Sénéchal, 1998). However, children with DPD do show variation in this area, complicating the interpretation. For example, Rvachew and Jamieson (1989) reported that five children with DPD showed normal sound discrimination functions for "s" in "seat" vs. "sh" in "sheet," whereas seven children with DPD showed deviant sound discrimination functions in the same task. There are several possible explanations for this variation. One possibility is that the tasks typically used to evaluate perceptual processing by children may not be sensitive enough to identify more subtle deficits. For example, if reaction times were used, differences might be observed for children who show appropriate accuracy in sound discrimination. A second possibility is that children's perceptual abilities are likely improving as listening experience accumulates and improvements in perception may precede improvements in production (Rvachew, Rafaat, & Martin, 1999). Thus, a child with DPD who can discriminate between sounds that s/he normally misarticulates may be ready to acquire the correct production. Furthermore, if that child's perception had been sampled at an earlier point, a deficit might have been identified. A final possibility is that not all children with DPD have deficits in sound discrimination, although they still could show deficits in other areas of perception. While there is some support for these hypotheses, systematic testing of each alternative in the same sample of children has yet to be undertaken.

Perceptual processing deficits may lead to weaker phonological representations in children with DPD. As a result, children with DPD may struggle with any variation in acoustic information (Edwards, Fourakis, Beckman, & Fox, 1999; Edwards, Fox, & Rogers, 2002; Hoffman et al., 1985). Edwards and colleagues (1999) found that children with DPD identified fewer words with removed final consonants than typically developing peers and identified significantly fewer words when the vowel was removed. Children with DPD also identified fewer words, on average, than typically developing children in conditions where any acoustic information was removed – regardless of how much or how little remained (Edwards et al., 1999). Taken together, these findings suggest that there may be a difficulty with low-level perceptual processing, which spreads to cause difficulty with the processing of variation in the acoustic signal. Furthermore, these detrimental effects may spread upward to the perception of words and phrases. This basic struggle and its larger impact are reflected in decreased performance on tasks where any alteration of the acoustic signal results in lowered word recognition. A logical conclusion is that children with DPD may store their acoustic representations in a manner that cannot easily accommodate variation. It appears that perceptual processing deficits may contribute to the phonological deficit observed in children with DPD, however, most of the perceptual evidence is based on the perception of real words. Real words have an abstract representation in Munson's theoretical model. Thus, when perceptual processing deficits are identified using real word stimuli it is difficult to clearly determine whether the deficit arises from perceptual processing, abstract representations, or a combination of the two. More research systematically manipulating the lexical status of the stimuli in perceptual processing tasks is needed to further disentangle the contribution of perceptual processing and abstract representations to the phonological deficits observed in children with DPD.

Articulation

The production pattern of children with DPD is the defining characteristic of the disorder and leads to a potential interpretation that DPD is exclusively an issue with motor-speech execution. In fact, there is a general imprecision of articulation in children with DPD, but, as seen in perception, there is also a difficulty with the storage and retrieval of a more abstract articulatory gesture. The articulatory abilities of children with DPD have been explored by examining differences in children's error patterns, acoustic parameters, speech rate, and electropalatographic measures. In terms of general motor-speech abilities, children with DPD lack articulatory lingual precision. A review of electropalatography studies found that children with DPD do not make fine movements with the tongue and have difficulty producing the control required to differentiate between alveolar sounds, which are formed with the tip of the tongue (e.g., /t/), and sounds that are formed with other parts of the tongue, such as the back (e.g., /k/) (Gibbon, 1999). As with perceptual processing, the presence of undifferentiated tongue movements in children with DPD is variable with some children showing normal fine motor movements but others showing a pattern of undifferentiated movements (Gibbon, 1999). Even within the population of children with DPD, there is variability, with some children showing difficulty with only certain movements and others showing broader deficits across a range of movements. Acoustic analyses provide similar evidence that children with DPD lack precision and coordination in moving the jaw and tongue during speech and that this difficulty is variable across children with DPD (Edwards et al., 1999). Generally, children with DPD have difficulty moving their articulators independently, leading to more ballistic oral gestures.

A result of these difficulties with articulatory precision is that children with DPD tend to have a slower speaking rate than their peers, and they tend to make more errors when asked to perform rapid-syllable production tasks, such as diadochokinetic repetition (Cohen & Waters, 1999). Diadochokinetic repetition requires the speaker to produce syllables in rapid succession, varying place of articulation to determine precision of tongue movements (e.g., [pa ta ka]). A slowed speaking rate could indicate either that (1) there is a deficit in the actual movement of the tongue (i.e., the tongue can't move fast enough to support a faster speaking rate), or (2) there is a difficulty accessing the representation of the movements themselves (i.e., retrieving the appropriate motor plan is slow such that a faster speaking rate can't be achieved), or (3) both of these difficulties contribute to slow speech. These explanations implicate fundamentally different problems with articulation. The first account could be thought of as a pure motor deficit where the child knows the movement to make but simply cannot make the articulators move quickly. In contrast, the second account implicates representations of speech movements. Here, the imprecision or slowing is a result of imprecise representations of how a particular sound is to be made and/or slow retrieval of that representation. In this case, poor execution reflects a problem with the representation (i.e., the motor plan) of the movement. The fact that this slowed rate is observed even after remediation of production errors motivates future research to separate these potential explanations to better understand the deficit and to further improve treatment outcomes for children with DPD.

It is important to note that although articulatory deficits may be present in children with DPD, they are likely not sufficiently severe enough to fully explain the production patterns observed. Specifically, many children with DPD are capable of producing sounds that they normally misarticulate when provided with support in the form of production cues. This is referred to as stimulability testing where a speech-language pathologist provides a model of correct production of a sound as well as articulatory instructions to guide the child's production. With this support, some children with DPD are able to produce some erred sounds well enough that an adult would interpret the production as the target sound. The production may lack motor precision, but it is "good enough" to be interpreted as the target. Thus, it is not the case that a child with DPD is incapable of moving his/her muscles to make a particular sound and that accounts for the child's misarticulation of that sound. Rather, the motor deficits observed are more subtle but still could be a contributing factor to the nature of the deficit as well as a limiting factor in treatment.

Abstract representations: Phonological awareness

One common approach to evaluating abstract phonological representations is to examine performance on phonological awareness tasks. Phonological awareness is the knowledge that spoken words are made up of segments, or phonemes, and refers to the ability to identify these segments as individual abstract units. Through observation of these skills, the quality of the child's representations can be inferred, and predictions about later success in reading can be made. The current methods involve behavioral tasks, such as matching sounds, which do not have the ability to separate perceptual or productive skills from those of the abstract representation. These tasks, do, however capture behavior as it relates to the integrative functioning of these systems.

Researchers have long established a relationship between DPD, phonological awareness, and later success in literacy (Bird, Bishop, & Freeman, 1995). The connection between DPD and phonological awareness is tied to a decreased ability to segment and store sounds into representations that are easily and readily accessed and manipulated. Since there is a close connection between phonological awareness and vocabulary size in reading, it is difficult to predict reading success based on only one of these, particularly since children who have DPD often have deficits in both (Catts, 2009). When 4-year-olds with DPD are matched in receptive language and compared to typically developing peers, their scores are significantly worse on tests of phonological awareness, such as onset matching and segmentation of words; however, the children with DPD demonstrate age-appropriate early literacy knowledge, such as knowing the names of letters and identifying words (Rvachew, Ohberg, Grawburg, & Heyding, 2003). This pattern suggests that the orthographic but not phonological part of reading is unaffected by DPD. Gernand and Moran (2007) examined this outcome in more detail in 6-year-olds who varied in phonological skills: typical, mild DPD, moderate DPD. The results indicated that the children with DPD performed significantly poorer on standardized and non-standardized phonological awareness tasks, regardless of the severity of phonological impairment (mild vs. moderate). That is, both groups were equally impaired (Gernand & Moran, 2007). To summarize, children with DPD have deficits in the formation of abstract representations of phonemes as indexed by poor phonological awareness, which later impacts reading.

Abstract representations: Non-word repetition

Another way of investigating the status of abstract phonological representations is to examine performance on tasks involving non-words. In initial studies of non-word repetition, inclusion of misarticulated sounds in the stimuli to be repeated complicated interpretation, making it difficult to determine whether poorer non-word repetition by children with DPD was due to their more frequent misarticulations or the perceptual and memory skills required for non-word repetition. However, when non-words are adequately controlled to contain only early acquired sounds that children with DPD correctly produce, the difficulty with non-word repetition is still observed (Shriberg et al., 2009). Importantly, problems with non-word repetition remain evident when language skills are controlled (Shriberg et al., 2009). Thus, poor non-word repetition by children with DPD does not seem to be attributable to comorbid language impairments. A descriptive items analysis indicated that poorer non-word repetition performance by children with DPD was not attributable to articulatory factors. Instead, it was hypothesized that children with

DPD had difficulty with non-word repetition due to difficulty with processing and storage of novel acoustic-perceptual information (Shriberg et al., 2009).

Additional patterns from non-word repetition provide further insight. In particular, typically developing children are influenced by the phonotactic probability of the non-words. Phonotactic probability refers to the likelihood of occurrence of a sound sequence in a language. Thus, non-words can be composed of commonly or rarely occurring sound sequence. Typically developing children tend to repeat common sound sequences more accurately than rare sound sequences due to the greater support from abstract phonological representations in long-term memory. In contrast, children with DPD demonstrate reduced effects of phonotactic probability in non-word repetition tasks (Munson, Edwards, & Beckman, 2005), suggesting lesser support from abstract representations. In addition, children with DPD do not appear to benefit from prior exposure to the non-words (i.e., repetition priming). Munson and colleagues (Munson, Baylis, Krause, & Yim, 2010), exposed children to non-words during a listening phase and then had children repeat non-words: half that had been pre-exposed and half that had not been pre-exposed. Typically developing children repeated pre-exposed non-words better than novel non-words; whereas children with DPD showed reduced repetition priming, with the amount of priming being inversely proportional to the severity of their DPD (e.g., milder DPD was associated with greater priming). This pattern indicates that children with DPD have difficulty with rapid perceptual learning of non-words. Finally, children with DPD show difficulty with a receptive version of non-word repetition. Specifically, children with DPD have difficulty identifying errors in others' repetition of non-words (Sutherland & Gillon, 2005). Taken together, these data suggest that problems with non-word repetition by children with DPD indicate deficits in abstract representations as well as perceptual processing or learning of novel phonological sequences. Performance on non-word repetition can be used to differentiate between children with DPD and those with typical speech, suggesting that abstract representations are a key factor in the deficit (Preston & Edwards, 2007).

Abstract representations: Real words

Turning to real words, two issues can be examined: (1) whether learning of new words is appropriate; (2) whether access to known words is intact. In terms of word learning, children with DPD learn the same number of words as their peers (McDowell & Carroll, 2012; Storkel, 2004), yet they learn different types of words. In terms of types of words, both phonotactic probability and neighborhood density have been manipulated. Neighborhood density refers to the number of known words that are phonologically similar to a given word, in this case, a new word to-be-learned. Children with DPD learn non-words more often when phonotactic probability is rare and neighborhood density is sparse, whereas children who are typically developing show optimal performance in the aforementioned condition and when phonotactic probability is common and neighborhood density is dense (Storkel, Maekawa, & Hoover, 2010). Even when vocabulary size is matched, children who have DPD and typically developing children both seem to learn non-words that are rare in phonotactic probability or that are sparse in their neighborhood density, but only typically developing children are able to then create a full lexical entry that can be used and integrated into other parts of communication (Storkel et al., 2010). Word learning by children with DPD may be facilitated by rare phonotactic probability and sparse neighborhoods due to the lower number of known words with which to confuse the new word (Storkel, 2004). Taken together, these findings from word learning suggest that weaknesses in perceptual processing and/or abstract representations dictate the words that are readily learned by children with DPD.

In terms of access to already known words, children with DPD tend to show appropriate performance. For example, children with DPD perform similarly to typically developing children on rapid automatic naming tasks, which require access to well-known words (Anthony et al., 2011). Likewise, children with DPD perform comparably to peers on delayed picture-naming tasks, indicating normal abilities to access known words and hold them in memory over a brief delay (Munson et al., 2010). Lastly, cross-modal picture-word interference paradigms show similar results for children with DPD and typically developing children (Munson et al., 2010). In cross-modal picture-word interference, children hear a word and name a picture. The timing between the auditory word and picture can be varied, as well as the relationship between the auditory word and the name of the picture. When the auditory word and picture are the same, responses tend to be fast, whereas when the auditory word and picture are different, responses tend to be slowed, with the amount of slowing depending on the phonological overlap between the word and picture. Comparable performance by the children with DPD suggests that they are able to access abstract phonological information when the stimuli are well-known real words and retrieval cues are strong (e.g., picture support, unaltered speech). When combined with the findings from word learning, this suggests that long-term learning of words may help to overcome initial challenges in word learning, yet the previously reviewed evidence on perceptual difficulties suggests that representations of words may be vulnerable when retrieval conditions are challenging (e.g., altered speech). These findings fit well with the idea that representations of words can be gradient (McGregor, Friedman, Reilly, & Newman, 2002; McGregor, Sheng, & Ball, 2007). Likewise, adults experience difficulty with word recognition under challenging conditions (Mattys, Brooks, & Cooke, 2009; Mattys & Wiget, 2011), so it is not surprising that children, particularly those whose learning is strained as a result of DPD, experience difficulties in less than optimal conditions. Initial learning of words may be challenging for children with DPD, but greater exposure to words allows children with DPD to overcome this initial challenge and gain a representation that is sufficient for certain tasks. However, when tasks are more challenging, representations of words may not be sufficient to support performance that is as accurate or as fast as typically developing children.

Treatment

Understanding the nature of the deficit in DPD can guide treatment methods to remediate both the immediate and long-term consequences of DPD. That is, treatments designed to target the underlying deficit should lead to better outcomes than treatments that fail to consider the nature of the deficit. In complement, experimental manipulation of treatment can further inform our understanding of DPD and provide unique insights into phonological acquisition. That is, different parameters can be manipulated in treatment, and subsequent phonological change can be observed, providing an understanding of the parameters that facilitate acquisition.

In general, the goal of treatment for children with DPD is to promote the greatest change possible in the phonological system to allow these children to catch up to their peers and normalize their speech sooner than they would without treatment. Because the hallmark characteristic of DPD is a delay in speech sound production, most treatment studies focus exclusively on measures of production as the primary outcome. As noted previously, this may be a somewhat narrow view of phonology. A broader view may be needed to truly remediate the full set of deficits present in DPD. However, much is known about how to improve speech production through treatment (Baker & McLeod, 2011; Gierut, 2001, 2007).

Typically, treatment for children with DPD begins with selection of a target sound(s) (Baker & McLeod, 2011; Gierut, 2001, 2007). Sound selection is crucial to treatment success (Gierut, 2007). If the "correct" sound is selected for treatment, the child will not only learn the treated sound but will gain broader insights into the phonological system, making changes in multiple sounds that were previously produced in error (see Baker & McLeod, 2011; Gierut, 2001, 2007). In addition, the clinician must consider how to teach the selected target sound(s). This consideration relates to the nature of the deficit in terms of whether perceptual, production, or abstract representations are tapped by treatment activities.

Various methods that target perception have been incorporated into treatment of DPD with mixed results. For example, Rvachew (1994), developed a computer program called Speech Assessment and Interactive Learning Systems (Innovations, 1995). In this program, children are presented with correct and incorrect productions of target words and asked to identify whether the production is correct. Feedback is provided. Wolfe, Presley, and Mesaris (2003) showed that this type of perceptual training facilitated treatment progress for sounds that were poorly perceived prior to treatment. Moreover, when perceptual training was not included as a component of treatment, pretreatment identification scores predicted treatment outcomes. That is, sounds that were perceived well prior to treatment showed good treatment progress without perceptual training, whereas sounds that were poorly perceived prior to treatment showed poorer treatment progress without perceptual training. This finding reinforces the prior claim of variability in perceptual processing by children with DPD but also highlights the importance of perception for phonological learning.

Turning to production, treatment involves production of the sound, thereby targeting motor skills to some degree. However, we know of no studies that have targeted the fine-grained aspects of motor coordination that have been shown to be problematic for at least some children with DPD. Thus, it is unclear whether a focus on more fine-grained aspects of motor coordination would enhance outcomes. Likewise, we know of no studies that have examined fine-grained aspects of motor coordination pre- and post-treatment, making it unclear whether more subtle aspects of production improve with current treatment approaches. Although this is an interesting question for understanding the nature of the deficit, the instrumentation needed would likely preclude use in clinical settings.

Some treatments attempt to target abstract representations by incorporating phonological awareness activities, such as the production of alliterations and rhymes and segmenting sentences and words (Bernhardt & Major, 2005; Dean, Howell, Waters, & Reid, 1995; Major & Bernhardt, 1998). These activities seem to improve phonological awareness. Each of these methods promotes growth and change above and beyond having no therapy, but comparative studies of these methods indicate that improvement in articulation is observed whether phonological awareness activities are included or not (Hesketh, Adams, Nightingale, & Hall, 2000; Tyler, Edwards, & Saxman, 1987). As in perceptual processing, assessment of the child's weaknesses across phonological areas prior to treatment is important in identifying the best treatment approach.

A final issue in treatment of DPD relates to the treatment stimuli. Treatment of DPD rarely exclusively involves practice articulating sounds in isolation, although some treatments include isolated sound production as a component. Rather, treatment stimuli typically incorporate target sounds in non-words or real words during the majority of the treatment. Given that non-words and real words tap different types of processing, this raises the question of which approach is best. Recently, the issue has been addressed through a retrospective examination of treatment outcomes (Gierut, Morrisette, & Ziemer, 2010), as well as a prospective experimental manipulation of treatment (Gierut & Morrisette, 2010). When treatment progress was measured during or immediately following treatment, children showed greater phonological learning with non-words than with real word stimuli. However, when outcomes were examined at a longitudinal follow-up point, children showed equivalent long-term phonological learning for both non-word and real word treatment. That is, phonological learning in treatment of real words was slower during treatment but gains continued to be made even when treatment was withdrawn, leading to similar long-term outcomes for both types of stimuli. It may be that the lack of an existing lexical representation for non-words served to better highlight the new phonological structure being taught, producing immediate gains in production. In contrast, the existing lexical representation of real words may have obscured the new phonological structure being taught, slowing gains in production. However, similarities and contrasts between the targeted real words and other known words might continue to emerge after treatment was withdrawn. In this way, the use of real words supported diffusion of the phonological change throughout the lexicon after treatment withdrawal, facilitating additional phonological learning. Thus, both approaches appear efficacious but through different mechanisms of change.

When treatment of DPD focuses on real word stimuli, there are other factors that promote phonological learning. These factors include neighborhood density (Gierut & Morrisette, 2012b; Gierut, Morrisette, & Champion, 1999; Morrisette & Gierut, 2002) and word frequency (Gierut & Morrisette, 2012a, 2012b; Gierut et al., 1999; Morrisette & Gierut, 2002). Word frequency refers to the number of times a word occurs in a speech corpus. Earlier studies manipulated these variables in isolation, but more recent work has considered the combinations that promote phonological learning. In particular, high density, when combined with high frequency, promotes the greatest phonological learning when compared to other possible pairings (Gierut & Morrisette, 2012b). Here, it is thought that dense neighborhoods may highlight phonological structure by providing evidence of a wide array of minimal pair words that contrast the treated sound with other sounds of the language. Within this high contrast condition, it is crucial that the treated words be high frequency, arguably, so that the treated word is salient relative to the contrasting words. This pattern suggests that contrasts within the lexicon may facilitate phonological acquisition.

Initial studies of word frequency in phonological treatment did not consider the relationship with age-of-acquisition (AoA). AoA is the age when a word is typically learned. In terms of the relationship to frequency, high-frequency words tend to be early acquired, whereas low-frequency words tend to be late acquired. Prior psycholinguistic research has suggested that AoA may have stronger effects than word frequency for at least some aspects of language processing (e.g., Morrison & Ellis, 1995; Morrison, Ellis, & Quinlan, 1992). When word frequency is pitted against AoA in phonological treatment, AoA has a stronger effect than word frequency, with AoA essentially washing out the effect of frequency (Gierut & Morrisette, 2012a). Specifically, greater phonological learning was observed when target sounds were incorporated into late acquired words than into early acquired words. In this case, early acquired words may have entrenched production patterns that impede phonological learning, whereas later acquired words may lack stable production patterns, facilitating phonological learning. This mirrors the findings from non-word vs. real word treatment. Since non-words are novel, they have no stable production pattern, which supports a greater focus on phonology. The same mechanism may be at work for later acquired words.

Opportunities for advancement

The majority of research in the area of DPD is behavioral and based upon accuracy. While these data have provided information about production differences, as well as some information about the perceptual skills of children with DPD, they are not fine-grained enough to disentangle the complexities of DPD. That is, we can identify that there is a problem but have greater difficulty identifying the underlying issues contributing to this problem. Accuracy-based data fail to provide sufficient information about the processing abilities of children with DPD. One issue is the observed heterogeneity of this population. Is this population truly heterogeneous, or is the conclusion based on insensitive data? Thanks to technological advancements that are widely used with other groups, more sensitive data can be obtained to further the understanding of DPD and to improve therapeutic approaches.

In terms of processing, several methods are applicable to DPD. Eye-tracking and mouse-tracking studies are largely behavioral but provide enhanced temporal resolution. Eye-tracking methods are often used to determine at what time identification of targeted information occurs and provides insight into abstract representation through the use of cohort competitors. For example, when presented with word sets like "beaker, beetle, speaker, and dolphin" with accompanying picture sets, where "beaker" is the target word, adults' eyes fixate on both "beetle" and "speaker" as a result of phonological similarity inducing the access of these competitors (Allopenna, Magnuson, & Tanenhaus, 1998). Most of these studies are conducted with adults and typically developing children, but it would be informative to know whether children with DPD store and access words in a similar manner. Mouse tracking is another method for measuring online processing of auditory stimuli (Freeman & Ambady, 2010). This technology allows presentation of pictures with accompanying auditory stimuli. Subjects click on a picture, and their mouse trajectory is mapped along with reaction time, accuracy, number of "flips" (much like saccades in eye tracking), and maximal deviation. Mouse movements made during visual-field tasks seem to be consistent with eye movement data from the same task (Freeman & Ambady, 2010; Freeman, Dale, & Farmer, 2011), making this technology a cheaper alternative to eye-tracking systems. This type of data could converge with EEG data, specifically event-related potentials (ERPs), to form a better understanding of how children with DPD segment and store what they hear. ERPs are electrical responses from the brain that are evoked when an expected event occurs. Specific responses (either positive or negative) at a certain duration from the stimulus onset indicate response to that stimulus. ERPs can provide fine-tuned information about speech segmentation and the categorization of sounds into phonetic units (Sharma, Kraus, Mcgee, Carrell, & Nicol, 1993).

Another issue that restricts the understanding of DPD is the lack of information about differences in how the brain processes speech. It is possible that children with DPD recruit different areas of the brain for speech perception and processing than typically developing children. If supported, this hypothesis would explain the differences seen in behavioral tasks such as those that measure phonological awareness abilities. fMRI (functional magnetic resonance imaging) is a method that can be used to view the brain's processing of input. It shows the location of activation in the response through measurement of blood oxygen levels. Additional blood is recruited to areas of high processing, and this provides a way to investigate areas of the brain responsible for specific types of input. This method can be used to locate areas of activation in the developing brain in terms of auditory learning (Ahmad, Balsamo, Sachs, Xu, & Gaillard, 2003) and reading (Brem et al., 2010; Temple et al., 2001) and has largely focused on typically developing children. Inconsistencies in brain activation have been found between typical and dyslexic readers in terms of phonological, auditory, and orthographic processing (Corina et al., 2001; Temple et al., 2001). Although this method is useful, it is quite expensive, and is not well suited to the study of children since it requires the child to hold still and is quite noisy. However, it could be useful in studying older children after overt production errors have resolved, although the noise level of fMRI machines would need to be considered.

An alternative approach for children is the less invasive and relatively new technology called near-infrared spectroscopy (NIRS). The NIRS device is a cap (much like an EEG) that is placed on the head and measures the blood at the outer level of the cerebral cortex through the scalp. Much like fMRI, NIRS indicates the location of activity in the brain by measuring changes in hemoglobin concentration and blood oxygen level and can be used across the lifespan (Bortfeld, Fava, & Boas, 2009; Bortfeld, Wruck, & Boas, 2007). This method is advantageous for infants and children because the caretaker of the child can be present, the child can be active and moving, and it allows for presentation of visual and auditory stimuli. NIRS has been used to examine sensitivity to spoken language in infants (Bortfeld et al., 2007) and to identify lateralization of language in the brain (Bortfeld et al., 2009).

Conclusion

Returning to the original question, "What does it mean to know a phonology?," the study of children with DPD provides some answers but also raises additional questions. From the evidence presented, deficits in speech perception, articulation, and abstract representations seem to contribute to the effects of DPD. It is difficult to identify which element is largely responsible, since these domains overlap and interact. Thus, knowing a phonology is not simply developing skills in isolated domains. Knowing a phonology involves the execution of complex interactions across domains. Although children with DPD seem to have difficulty perceiving segments of words, this area is further impacted by difficulty in the formation of abstract representations. Consequently, despite the obvious difficulty in production of speech sounds, this difficulty may be rooted in early perceptual difficulty and the weak state of abstract representations. This complex interchange of information leads us to conclude that DPD arises from deficits in multiple, interrelated systems. Taken together, the study of children with DPD highlights the interrelatedness of perception, production, and abstract representations in the developing phonological system, as well as the far-reaching consequences of problems in any one area. Although much is known about DPD, one limitation in studying this population has been the use of behavioral measures that may have limited resolution. Now is an opportune time to take advantage of new technologies that afford better time and spatial resolution to further advance our understanding of children with DPD and to gain new insights about the complex relationship between perception, production, and abstract representations.

Turning to the second question, "How can phonological learning be accelerated?," experimental studies of treatment of children with DPD provide a unique opportunity to manipulate the learning environment in ethically justified ways and to observe the consequences. Treatment studies of children with DPD suggest that there is a need to consider the underlying factors that may contribute to overt production errors and incorporate activities targeting these areas when there is evidence that they warrant attention. That is, it seems less effective to ignore the underlying deficit and assume that other areas of strength will compensate. Rather, it is more effective to directly target the underlying deficit, suggesting that learning is accelerated when the components of phonology can operate effectively together. Furthermore, treatment studies highlight the interrelationships between phonology and the lexicon, and effective phonological learning rests on this relationship. Specifically, the manipulation of lexical characteristics can accelerate phonological learning. As our understanding of the nature of the deficit in DPD advances through the use of more fine-grained measures, treatment methods can continue to be refined, which will improve outcomes for children with DPD but also yield additional insights into phonological learning more generally.

References

Ahmad, Z., Balsamo, L., Sachs, B., Xu, B., & Gaillard, W. (2003). Auditory comprehension of language in young children: Neural networks identified with fMRI. *Neurology, 60*(10), 1598–1605.

Allopenna, P. D., Magnuson, J. S., & Tanenhaus, M. K. (1998). Tracking the time course of spoken word recognition using eye movements: Evidence for continuous mapping models. *Journal of Memory and Language, 38*(4), 419–439.

Anthony, J. L., Aghara, R. G., Dunkelberger, M. J., Anthony, T. I., Williams, J. M., & Zhang, Z. (2011). What factors place children with speech sound disorders at risk for reading problems? *American Journal of Speech-Language Pathology, 20*(2), 146–160.

AVAAZ Innovations. (1995). *SAILS: Speech Assessment and Interactive Learning System*. London, Ontario, Canada: AVAAZ Innovations Inc.

Baker, E., & McLeod, S. (2011). Evidence-based practice for children with speech sound disorders: Part 1 narrative review. *Language, Speech, and Hearing Services in Schools, 42*(2), 102–139.

Bernhardt, B. H., & Major, E. M. (2005). Speech, language and literacy skills 3 years later: A follow-up study of early phonological and metaphonological intervention. *International Journal of Language & Communication Disorders, 40*(1), 1–27.

Bird, J., Bishop, D., & Freeman, N. (1995). Phonological awareness and literacy development in children with expressive phonological impairments. *Journal of Speech and Hearing Research, 38*(2), 446.

Bortfeld, H., Fava, E., & Boas, D. A. (2009). Identifying cortical lateralization of speech processing in infants using near-infrared spectroscopy. *Developmental Neuropsychology, 34*(1), 52–65.

Bortfeld, H., Wruck, E., & Boas, D. A. (2007). Assessing infants' cortical response to speech using near-infrared spectroscopy. *Neuroimage, 34*(1), 407–415.

Brem, S., Bach, S., Kucian, K., Guttorm, T. K., Martin, E., Lyytinen, H., . . . Richardson, U. (2010). Brain sensitivity to print emerges when children learn letter–speech sound correspondences. *Proceedings of the National Academy of Sciences, 107*(17), 7939–7944.

Catts, H. W. (2009). The narrow view of reading promotes a broad view of comprehension. *Language, Speech, and Hearing Services in Schools, 40*(2), 178–183.

Cohen, W., & Waters, D. (1999). *Measuring speech motor skills in normally developing and phonologically disordered pre-school children.* Paper presented at the Proceedings of the XIVth International Congress of Phonetic Sciences, San Francisco, 1–7 August.

Corina, D. P., Richards, T. L., Serafini, S., Richards, A. L., Steury, K., Abbott, R. D., . . . Berninger, V. W. (2001). fMRI auditory language differences between dyslexic and able reading children. *Neuroreport, 12*(6), 1195–1201.

Dean, E., Howell, J., Waters, D., & Reid, J. (1995). Metaphon: A metalinguistic approach to the treatment of phonological disorder in children. *Clinical Linguistics & Phonetics, 9*(1), 1–19.

Edwards, J., Fourakis, M., Beckman, M. E., & Fox, R. A. (1999). Characterizing knowledge deficits in phonological disorders. *Journal of Speech, Language, and Hearing Research, 42*(1), 169.

Edwards, J., Fox, R. A., & Rogers, C. L. (2002). Final consonant discrimination in children: Effects of phonological disorder, vocabulary size, and articulatory accuracy. *Journal of Speech, Language, and Hearing Research, 45*(2), 231.

Eimas, P. D., Siqueland, E. R., Jusczyk, P., & Vigorito, J. (1971). Speech perception in infants. *Science, 171*(3968), 303–306.

Freeman, J. B., & Ambady, N. (2010). MouseTracker: Software for studying real-time mental processing using a computer mouse-tracking method. *Behavior Research Methods, 42*(1), 226–241.

Freeman, J., Dale, R., & Farmer, T. (2011). Hand in motion reveals mind in motion. *Frontiers in Psychology, 2*, 59.

Gernand, K. L., & Moran, M. J. (2007). Phonological awareness abilities of 6-year-old children with mild to moderate phonological impairments. *Communication Disorders Quarterly, 28*(4), 206–215.

Gibbon, F. E. (1999). Undifferentiated lingual gestures in children with articulation/phonological disorders. *Journal of Speech, Language, and Hearing Research, 42*(2), 382–397.

Gierut, J. A. (1998). Treatment efficacy: Functional phonological disorders in children. *Journal of Speech Language and Hearing Research, 41*(1), S85.

Gierut, J. A. (2001). Complexity in phonological treatment clinical factors. *Language, Speech, and Hearing Services in Schools, 32*(4), 229–241.

Gierut, J. A. (2007). Phonological complexity and language learnability. *American Journal of Speech-Language Pathology, 16*(1), 6–17.

Gierut, J. A., & Morrisette, M. L. (2010). Phonological learning and lexicality of treated stimuli. *Clinical Linguistics & Phonetics, 24*(2), 122–140.

Gierut, J. A., & Morrisette, M. L. (2012a). Age of word acquisition effects in treatment of children with phonological delays. *Applied Psycholinguistics, 33*(01), 121–144.

Gierut, J. A., & Morrisette, M. L. (2012b). Density, frequency and the expressive phonology of children with phonological delay. *Journal of Child Language, 39*(04), 804–834.

Gierut, J. A., Morrisette, M. L., & Champion, A. H. (1999). Lexical constraints in phonological acquisition. *Journal of Child Language, 26*(2), 261–294.

Gierut, J. A., Morrisette, M. L., & Ziemer, S. M. (2010). Nonwords and generalization in children with phonological disorders. *American Journal of Speech-Language Pathology, 19*(2), 167–177.

Hesketh, A., Adams, C., Nightingale, C., & Hall, R. (2000). Phonological awareness therapy and articulatory training approaches for children with phonological disorders: A comparative outcome study. *International Journal of Language and Communication Disorders, 35*(3), 337–354.

Hoffman, P. R., Daniloff, R. G., Bengoa, D., & Schuckers, G. H. (1985). Misarticulating and normally articulating children's identification and discrimination of synthetic [r] and [w]. *Journal of Speech and Hearing Disorders, 50*(1), 46.

Lewis, B. A., & Freebairn, L. (1992). Residual effects of preschool phonology disorders in grade school, adolescence, and adulthood. *Journal of Speech, Language, and Hearing Research, 35*(4), 819–831.

Liberman, A. M., Harris, K. S., Hoffman, H. S., & Griffith, B. C. (1957). The discrimination of speech sounds within and across phoneme boundaries. *Journal of Experimental Psychology, 54*(5), 358–368.

Major, E. M., & Bernhardt, B. H. (1998). Metaphonological skills of children with phonological disorders before and after phonological and metaphonological intervention. *International Journal of Language & Communication Disorders, 33*(4), 413–444.

Mattys, S. L., Brooks, J., & Cooke, M. (2009). Recognizing speech under a processing load: Dissociating energetic from informational factors. *Cognitive Psychology, 59*(3), 203–243.

Mattys, S. L., & Wiget, L. (2011). Effects of cognitive load on speech recognition. *Journal of Memory and Language, 65*(2), 145–160.

McDowell, K. D., & Carroll, J. (2012). Manipulating word properties: Targeting vocabulary learning for children with and without speech sound inaccuracies. *Child Language Teaching and Therapy, 28*(1), 101–121.

McGregor, K. K., Friedman, R. M., Reilly, R. M., & Newman, R. M. (2002). Semantic representation and naming in young children. *Journal of Speech, Language, and Hearing Research, 45*(2), 332–346.

McGregor, K. K., Sheng, L., & Ball, T. (2007). Complexities of expressive word learning over time. *Language, Speech, and Hearing Services in Schools, 38*(4), 353–364.

Morrisette, M. L., & Gierut, J. A. (2002). Lexical organization and phonological change in treatment. *Journal of Speech, Language, and Hearing Research, 45*(1), 143–159.

Morrison, C. M., & Ellis, A. W. (1995). Roles of word frequency and age of acquisition in word naming and lexical decision. *Journal of Experimental Psychology: Learning, Memory, and Cognition, 21*(1), 116.

Morrison, C. M., Ellis, A. W., & Quinlan, P. T. (1992). Age of acquisition, not word frequency, affects object naming, not object recognition. *Memory & Cognition, 20*(6), 705–714.

Munson, B., Baylis, A. L., Krause, M. O., & Yim, D. (2010). Representation and access in phonological impairment. *Laboratory Phonology, 10*.

Munson, B., Edwards, J., & Beckman, M. E. (2005). Relationships between nonword repetition accuracy and other measures of linguistic development in children with phonological disorders. *Journal of Speech, Language & Hearing Research, 48*(1), 61–78.

Ohde, R. N., & Sharf, D. J. (1988). Perceptual categorization and consistency of synthesized /rw/ continua by adults, normal children and /r/-misarticulating children. *Journal of Speech, Language, and Hearing Research, 31*(4), 556–568.

Pennington, B. F. (2006). From single to multiple deficit models of developmental disorders. *Cognition, 101*(2), 385–413.

Preston, J. L., & Edwards, M. L. (2007). Phonological processing skills of adolescents with residual speech sound errors. *Language, Speech, and Hearing Services in Schools, 38*(4), 297–308.

Preston, J. L., Hull, M., & Edwards, M. L. (2013). Preschool speech error patterns predict articulation and phonological awareness outcomes in children with histories of speech sound disorders. *American Journal of Speech-Language Pathology, 22*(2), 173–184.

Rvachew, S. (1994). Speech perception training can facilitate sound production learning. *Journal of Speech, Language, and Hearing Research, 37*(2), 347–357.

Rvachew, S., & Jamieson, D. G. (1989). Perception of voiceless fricatives by children with a functional articulation disorder. *Journal of Speech and Hearing Disorders, 54*(2), 193–208.

Rvachew, S., Ohberg, A., Grawburg, M., & Heyding, J. (2003). Phonological awareness and phonemic perception in 4-year-old children with delayed expressive phonology skills. *American Journal of Speech-Language Pathology, 12*(4), 463–471.

Rvachew, S., Rafaat, S., & Martin, M. (1999). Stimulability, speech perception skills, and the treatment of phonological disorders. *American Journal of Speech-Language Pathology, 8*(1), 33–43.

Sharma, A., Kraus, N., Mcgee, T., Carrell, T., & Nicol, T. (1993). Acoustic versus phonetic representation of speech as reflected by the mismatch negativity event-related potential. *Electroencephalography and Clinical Neurophysiology/Evoked Potentials Section, 88*(1), 64–71.

Shriberg, L. D., & Austin, D. (1998). Comorbidity of speech-language disorder: Implications for a phenotype marker for speech delay. *The Speech-Language Connection*, 73–117.

Shriberg, L. D., Lohmeier, H. L., Campbell, T. F., Dollaghan, C. A., Green, J. R., & Moore, C. A. (2009). A nonword repetition task for speakers with misarticulations: The syllable repetition task (SRT). *Journal of Speech, Language, and Hearing Research, 52*(5), 1189–1212.

Shriberg, L. D., Tomblin, J. B., & McSweeny, J. L. (1999). Prevalence of speech delay in 6-year-old children and comorbidity with language impairment. *Journal of Speech, Language, and Hearing Research, 42*(6), 1461.

Storkel, H. L. (2004). The emerging lexicon of children with phonological delays: Phonotactic constraints and probability in acquisition. *Journal of Speech, Language, and Hearing Research, 47*(5), 1194–1212.

Storkel, H. L., Maekawa, J., & Hoover, J. R. (2010). Differentiating the effects of phonotactic probability and neighborhood density on vocabulary comprehension and production: A comparison of preschool children with versus without phonological delays. *Journal of Speech, Language, and Hearing Research, 53*(4), 933–949.

Sutherland, D., & Gillon, G. T. (2005). Assessment of phonological representations in children with speech impairment. *Language, Speech & Hearing Services in Schools, 36*(4), 294–307.

Temple, E., Poldrack, R. A., Salidis, J., Deutsch, G. K., Tallal, P., Merzenich, M. M., & Gabrieli, J. D. (2001). Disrupted neural responses to phonological and orthographic processing in dyslexic children: An fMRI study. *Neuroreport, 12*(2), 299–307.

Thomas, E. M., & Sénéchal, M. (1998). Articulation and phoneme awareness of 3-year-old children. *Applied Psycholinguistics, 19*(03), 363–391.

Tyler, A. A., Edwards, M. L., & Saxman, J. H. (1987). Clinical application of two phonologically based treatment procedures. *Journal of Speech and Hearing Disorders, 52*(393–409).

Werker, J. F., & Tees, R. C. (1983). Developmental changes across childhood in the perception of non-native speech sounds. *Canadian Journal of Psychology, 37*(2), 278–286.

Werker, J. F., Gilbert, J. H., Humphrey, K., & Tees, R. C. (1981). Developmental aspects of cross-language speech perception. *Child Development*, 349–355.

Wolfe, V., Presley, C., & Mesaris, J. (2003). The importance of sound identification training in phonological intervention. *American Journal of Speech-Language Pathology, 12*(3), 282–288.

10

SPEECH PERCEPTION BY HUMANS AND MACHINES

Matthew H. Davis and Odette Scharenborg

Matt Davis was supported by the UK Medical Research Council (MC-A060-5PQ80).
Odette Scharenborg was supported by a Vidi-grant from the Netherlands Organization for
Scientific Research (NWO; grant number: 276-89-003).

In 2009, a company called SpinVox was the subject of media controversy after it was revealed that the voicemail transcription service that it supplied was dependent on call centres in South Africa and the Philippines. Rather than the fully automated system that some had anticipated, behind the scenes they used human listeners to transcribe many or perhaps all the voicemail messages that they processed. In 2010, SpinVox was sold to a computer speech technology company, Nuance Communications, who had previously acknowledged that "Spinvox is offering something that is impossible to deliver now".[1] At the time of writing, it remains unclear whether automated transcription of voicemail messages – from any speaker, on any topic, and with the background noise and distortion that is common in telephone calls – will ever achieve the level of accuracy of human listeners.

Simply put, the most effective system for perceiving speech and recognizing words is a human who is a native speaker of the target language and has intact hearing. This advantage for human listeners is particularly pronounced for speech that is heard against background noise, contains unfamiliar words, or is degraded in other ways. The goal of the other chapters in this volume is to understand how human listeners achieve this remarkable success. This is curiosity-driven science at its most vital and informative. Despite the rise of other means of communication such as email and messaging services on smartphones, spoken language remains the primary form of human communication. The cognitive and neural processes that support successful spoken communication are unique to humans and in many ways define what it is that makes us human (Pinker, 1994).

Knowledge of how the human brain perceives and understands speech also has more pragmatic purposes, which are the focus of this chapter. Our focus here is on linking insights from human speech perception to help listeners that are not human, that is, computer speech recognition systems. This could be considered a key technological application of research on human speech perception and spoken word recognition;[2] however, in practice, engineering approaches to automatic speech recognition have been (at best) only loosely guided by knowledge gained from studying human speech perception. Indeed, perhaps the most famous comment on this topic comes from the pioneer of automatic speech recognition (ASR) systems, Fred Jelinek, who apparently remarked in the 1980s, "Anytime a linguist leaves the group the recognition rate goes up" (see Jurafsky & Martin, 2009). The development of machine speech recognition systems has proceeded in isolation from the study of human speech recognition. A goal of this chapter is to attempt to bridge this divide – both by explaining the operation of current state-of-the-art machine recognition systems to researchers studying human speech recognition and by highlighting mechanisms that allow human listeners to achieve their remarkable success in speech comprehension that are potentially useful for ASR systems. While Jelinek was perhaps right to dismiss linguists in favour of engineers at the time, we believe that our current understanding of human speech perception can offer useful insights to engineers building automatic speech recognition systems.

In this chapter we will first report on the current status of the recognition of speech by machines before describing the underlying computations by which current ASR systems operate. We will then consider three ways in which insights from human speech recognition might guide future technological advances in machine speech recognition. These proposals entail three different forms of human-inspired design in which (1) the nature of the representations, (2) the computational implementation, or (3) the functions achieved during recognition are modelled on human speech perception. Specifically, we seek inspiration from human recognition by (1) adopting articulatory feature representations modelled after the mechanics of human speech production, (2) using brain-inspired processing mechanisms (deep neural networks, DNNs), (3) incorporating forms of perceptual learning that appear to operate in human listeners.

Current status of machine speech recognition

Many of us already use speech recognition technology, such as Apple's Siri, Google Now, or Microsoft Cortana, on a daily basis when interacting with our smartphones. These systems are practical and extremely effective. However, at present none of these systems reach 100% accuracy in transcribing single sentences. Such suboptimal recognition performance is particularly noticeable in large-vocabulary ASR systems that have to deal with a wide variety of speakers, degraded speech signals, or different types of background noise. In his seminal 1997 paper, Lippmann showed that machines perform more than an order of magnitude worse than humans on a word recognition task in degraded conditions (Lippmann, 1997). But despite a large improvement of machine performance in noisy or degraded conditions in recent years, automatic systems still perform six to seven times worse than humans (e.g., Hilger & Ney, 2006 on similar material as used for the comparison by Lippmann, 1997).

Scharenborg (2007) reviewed the results of systematic comparisons of human and machine recognition systems and documented an order-of-magnitude better performance for humans, not only at the word level (Lippman, 1997; Carey & Quang, 2005; Juneja, 2012) but also at the level of individual phonemes (e.g., Cutler & Robinson, 1992; Sroka & Braida, 2005; Meyer, Wesker, Brand, Mertins, & Kollmeier, 2006) and at the level of articulatory/acoustic features (e.g., Sroka & Braida, 2005; Cooke, 2006; Meyer, Brand, & Kollmeier, 2011). This difference in performance persists even if higher-level lexical, semantic, or world knowledge is prevented from influencing perception. This is shown by a detailed comparison of human and machine performance on a corpus of logatomes, that is, CVC and VCV sequences without semantic information (e.g., Meyer et al., 2006). Thus it is not the case that human advantages in speech recognition are solely due to more effective comprehension and use of higher-level linguistic information. Artificial systems are impaired at perception as well as the comprehension of speech.

When faced with speech that is heard in a noisy background, is spoken in an unfamiliar accent, or that contains out-of-vocabulary words, automatic systems struggle even more (for a humorous illustration of Apple's Siri system struggling to respond to a Scottish English speaker, see http://bit.ly/zY3eV9). Reviews of noise-robust machine speech recognition systems document the substantial engineering effort that has been dedicated to improving the performance of these systems (Li, Deng, Gong, & Haeb-Umbach, 2014). Yet even state-of-the-art performance still falls short of human listeners on all but the simplest of listening tasks. A recent series of engineering 'challenges' for noise-robust speech recognition have shown that for small vocabulary, closed-set tasks (reporting letters and/or digits), automated systems can approach human performance (see Barker et al., 2013). Accuracy remains high (>90%) even if the speech is quieter than the masking noise (a negative signal-to-noise ratio, SNR). However, for a second challenge that involved a 5000-word vocabulary (Vincent et al., 2013), all the systems tested produced substantial numbers of errors for speech that is 9 dB louder than background noise; this SNR (+9 dB) is typically fully intelligible for healthy human listeners (Miller, Heise, & Lichten, 1951). The best system showed a 15% keyword error rate at +9-dB SNR that increased to nearly 30% (Vincent et al., 2013) for speech masked by noise of equal amplitude (i.e., 0-dB SNR). Healthy human listeners typically report connected speech with near perfect accuracy at 0-dB SNR (Miller et al., 1951).

Despite these limitations, current automatic systems are an impressive technological achievement and have reached a level of performance suitable for nearly universal deployment in modern smartphones (with recognition typically achieved by processing speech in the "cloud" rather than in the phone itself). In the following section, we will briefly describe the computational mechanisms by which these systems transcribe heard speech.

How machines recognize speech

The fundamental idea behind all successful machine speech recognition systems (following the pioneering work of Jelinek, 1976) is to treat the problem of spoken word recognition as a statistical problem – that of determining the most probable sequence of words given the acoustic speech input. This is exactly the same goal as explicitly stated in recent models of human speech perception (e.g., Norris & McQueen, 2008). In both cases, recognition is achieved by Bayesian perceptual inference with speech as the sensory input and the most likely word sequence as the desired output. However, ASR systems don't break this inference process into discrete parts (what are the most likely speech segments given the sounds heard, which are the most likely words given these speech segments, etc.), in the same way that might be assumed for a bottom-up account of human speech recognition (see Mirman, Chapter 6 of this volume). Instead, typical ASR systems are designed in such a way as to combine acoustic and higher-level information throughout the recognition process using a single, integrated search process.

Figure 10.1 shows a schematic of a typical ASR system in which speech wave-forms are first passed through an acoustic preprocessor to generate a sequence of vectors that represent the MEL-frequency spectrum (i.e., the energy profile over a frequency space similar to that of human hearing) of successive time windows of a spoken utterance. These acoustic features provide a relatively robust and compact

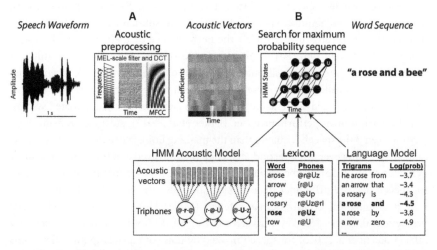

FIGURE 10.1 Block diagram of a typical machine speech recognition system. Two key processes are (A) acoustic preprocessing in which the speech signal is passed through an MEL-scale filter bank, followed by application of a discrete cosine transformation to generate sequences of acoustic vectors (MEL-frequency cepstral coefficients, MFCC) that represent the speech waveform; and (B) a search algorithm that combines information from Hidden Markov Model (HMM) acoustic models, a lexicon and a language model to estimate the probability of different word sequences having generated the observed sequence of acoustic vectors. The maximum probability sequence is then returned as the system's best assessment of the sequences of words heard.

description of the speech signal. These acoustic vectors provide the input to a search procedure (typically implemented using the Viterbi algorithm) that determines the most probable sequence of words that would have generated the observed sequence of acoustic vectors. In typical implementations, the search algorithm combines multiple sources of knowledge concerning (for instance) the probability of the sequence of acoustic vectors being generated by specific speech segments (acoustic model), which sequences of segments form real words (lexicon), and the relative likelihood of different word sequences (language model). Determining the sequence of words that is most likely to have generated an observed sequence of acoustic vectors allows an ASR system to report the most probable sequence of words contained in the speech waveform. The most probable word sequence can then be transcribed, used to drive a dialogue system, or for other purposes (see Young, 1996, for a more detailed review).

Most machine speech recognition systems achieve recognition by using several different representations for different sources of language knowledge (acoustic models, lexicon, language model); each of these components is typically chosen individually for its computational convenience and performance. An ASR system can be constructed from multiple components because all these parts represent information in terms of probabilities that can be readily combined into a single search process.

One commonly used technique for relating the acoustic signal to speech segments are Hidden Markov Models (HMMs), which model the expected variation in the signal statistically and typically represent a single phoneme or a three-phoneme sequence (triphone). These HMMs provide a useful mechanism for dealing with sequences of acoustic vectors of variable lengths (e.g., due to differences in speech rate). Words are defined in the lexicon as sequences of acoustic models. Yet another, different knowledge source is used in computing the probability of word sequences; most systems use a language model that supplies the frequency of occurrence of words and the likelihood of different two- or three-word sequences (bigrams and trigrams) using a count of the conditional probability of successive words in a large sample of text or speech. Thus, despite agreement among engineers that Bayesian perceptual inference is the key to effective machine speech recognition, a number of different components can be used to implement this process (see Scharenborg, Norris, Bosch, & McQueen, 2005, for a review from the perspective of human speech recognition).

During recognition, automatic systems typically use all these different sources of information (from the acoustic model, lexicon, and language model) at the same time. For any given utterance, the likelihood of the hypothesised word sequences (paths) is computed (e.g., using a graphical structure) that represents all the possible speech segments present in (some or all of) that utterance. Computing the likelihood of different paths involves multiplying the probabilities of sequences of segments so as to determine the probability of different words and word sequences. Thus acoustic, phonemic, and word-based uncertainty is combined into a single, integrated optimization process. The length of the word sequence that will be recognised in a single optimisation is closely related to the complexity of the language model (for instance, if a trigram language model is used, then word sequences that typically contain three words will be optimised in a single search). This delay allows automatic systems to flexibly adjust the hypothesised word sequences, ultimately selecting the word sequence with the best match (i.e., highest probability) to have generated the input speech signal. This approach also means that unlike what is often assumed about human speech perception, automatic systems do not explicitly recognise speech sounds; that is, they do not have any knowledge of which speech segments were heard, only that specific words (that plausibly contain specific segments) were heard.

Although this approach yields effective systems for large-vocabulary, continuous speech recognition, it is often acknowledged in the automatic speech recognition community that the improvements in automatic speech recognition performance over the past decades can largely be credited to an increase in computing power and the availability of increasing amounts of suitable, high-quality speech material for training automatic speech recognition systems (e.g., Bourlard, Hermansky, & Morgan, 1996; Moore & Cutler, 2001),which both directly lead to more accurate acoustic models (De Wachter et al., 2007). For some time, however, increases in performance have slowed, reaching asymptote at a level that (as described earlier in the chapter) falls short of human performance. In order to break through this barrier, simply adding more training material will not help, nor is it to be expected that adding "better" training material will help (see e.g., Kirchhoff & Schimmel, 2005, who used infant-directed speech to train automatic speech recognition systems). Instead, fundamentally new methodologies are needed (Bourlard et al., 1996; Moore, 2003; De Wachter et al., 2007). In this chapter we will discuss three recent developments in ASR that are (to varying degrees) inspired by human speech recognition and that might contribute to future progress in ASR.

Alternative representations of speech signals

In implementing automatic speech recognition systems, certain practical decisions have to be made concerning the representations used at different levels of the system. For example, as already described, speech waveforms recorded by a microphone are transformed into sequences of acoustic vectors that are used to train HMM-based acoustic models. The representations that are typically used are MEL-frequency cepstral coefficients (MFCCs, Davis & Mermelstein, 1980), based on a non-linear spectral representation for each time window of the short-term Fourier spectrum of speech (i.e., the spectrum of a spectrum, see Figure 10.1). These are often described as inspired by certain characteristics of the human auditory system (the MEL-frequency scale is based on the frequency spacing of human auditory filters at different centre frequencies). This proves to be an effective representation of the speech signal for HMM-based systems since it removes a great deal of redundant information from the speech stream and excludes information that is irrelevant for the recognition of words, such as pitch and continuous background noise. This form of data reduction is effective for HMM acoustic models working with clear speech since HMMs have only a limited ability to deal with non-linearity or redundancy. More detailed (but also more redundant) acoustic representations such as the output of an auditory filterbank can be used. For example, it has also been proposed that more robust recognition performance in difficult listening conditions might be achieved with other representations of the speech waveform (Li et al., 2014).

Another form of representation that is commonly incorporated into automatic recognition systems is the phoneme. Phonemes are commonly used as the mediating step between acoustic signals and specific words; that is, the acoustic models represent phonemes or triphones, and words are made from sequences of these units. This approach implements what is known as the beads-on-a-string model of speech perception (Ostendorf, 1999). Although this model works satisfactorily for carefully produced speech, it runs into problems with more naturalistic speech. This is mainly due to the high pronunciation variability in naturalistic speech (e.g., due to coarticulation and phonetic reduction processes, "stand back" can be pronounced /stam bak/ in connected speech, see Gaskell & Marslen-Wilson, 1996). The strict, segmental nature of phoneme-based acoustic models limits their sensitivity to the fine-grained acoustic detail of speech. For example, in deciding whether the words "grade A" or "grey day" is a better transcription of the sounds /greidei/, these systems overlook subtle acoustic cues (such as syllable duration, stress patterns, coarticulation, allophonic variation, etc.) that provide phonetic evidence to distinguish between sequences of sounds that occur within a single word or straddle word boundaries. Such cues are distributed over time and do not easily feature in phoneme-based HMM models but have nonetheless been shown to be used by human listeners (Davis, Marslen-Wilson, & Gaskell, 2002; Salverda et al., 2003; Shatzman & McQueen, 2006a/b; see Scharenborg, 2010 for a review).

To overcome these problems, alternative representations have been proposed, such as representations based on articulatory features (Kirchhoff, 1999; King & Taylor, 2000). These alternative accounts are often motivated with respect to the characteristics of the human speech recognition system in which feature representations are often proposed to mediate between acoustic and lexical representations of speech (e.g., Jakobson, Fant, & Halle, 1952; see also Marslen-Wilson & Warren, 1994; Lahiri & Reetz, 2010; Johnsrude & Buchsbaum, Chapter 1 of this volume). Articulatory or articulatory-acoustic features (AFs) describe properties of articulatory events – that is, the lip, mouth and tongue movements that speakers make when producing speech sounds. However, these are typically embodied not in detailed mechanical descriptions but rather in abstract classes that characterise the most essential aspects of the articulatory properties of speech sounds such as manner and place of articulation, tongue position, and voicing. With this type of feature, speech can be represented without necessarily assuming a sequence of discrete segments. Consequently, fine-phonetic detail such as nasalisation of a vowel preceding a nasal sound (such as in the vowel of the word "ban") can contribute to identification of nasal segments (/n/), whilst not creating difficulties for the identification of the vowel /a/ (see Lahiri & Marslen-Wilson, 1991; Hawkins, 2003).

Many different approaches have been investigated for incorporating AFs into automatic speech recognition systems, though to date none of these has been incorporated into commercial ASR systems. These include using artificial neural networks (Kirchhoff, 1999; King & Taylor, 2000; Wester, 2003), HMMs (Kirchhoff, 1999), linear dynamic models (Frankel, 2003), dynamic Bayesian networks (Livescu et al., 2003), and support vector machines (Scharenborg, Wan, & Moore, 2007) to replace HMM-based acoustic models. AF classifiers have been used to improve speech recognition performance in adverse conditions (Kirchhoff, 1998; Kirchhoff, Fink, & Sagerer, 2002) in order to build language-independent phone recognizers (Siniscalchi & Lee, 2014) and to improve computational models of human word recognition (Scharenborg, 2010). This last model is particularly helpful for illustrating how the use of articulatory features and duration representations can simulate human data on the recognition of words in which lexical segmentation creates ambiguity (as for onset-embedded words like "cap" in "captain", cf. Davis et al., 2002; Salverda, Dahan, & McQueen, 2003; or for segmenting minimal pairs like "grade A" and "grey day", cf. Nakatani & Dukes, 1977; Shatzman & McQueen, 2006a/b).

Although promising, the lack of large training corpora that label the speech signal in terms of AF values hampers the further development of AF-based systems (only one small training set is available, created during the 2004 Johns Hopkins Summer Workshop, Livescu et al., 2007). The most popular corpus for research into AF classification is the standard TIMIT database designed for comparison of more conventional ASR systems (Garofolo, 1988). This is a corpus of read American English consisting of high-quality, manually created phonetic transcriptions using a large set of phonetic labels. Consequently, training and testing of AF classifiers are generally achieved by starting from data that are labelled at the phoneme level and replacing phoneme labels with their (canonical) AF values. These AF values change synchronously at the phoneme boundaries, losing a large part of the potential for AF representations as an alternative to segmental representation (Schuppler, van Doremalen, Scharenborg, Cranen, & Boves, 2009).

An alternative or complementary proposal to using sub-phonemic, articulatory features in ASR is that articulatory features are combined into larger syllabic units during recognition (see, for instance, Greenberg, 1999 for a prominent example). It has been proposed, for instance, that many forms of pronunciation variability (such as duration changes) can be more effectively modelled using syllables rather than phonemes as the unit of representation (Greenberg, Carvey, Hitchcock, & Chang, 2003). However, to date, few viable ASR systems have been built in this way (see Kirchhoff, 1996; Puurula & Van Compernolle, 2010, for attempts). One problem with this approach is that typical ASR systems use segment-level transcriptions to link acoustic models to a lexicon of known words. A syllable-based model that eschews segmental representations would have no way to identify the syllables in low-frequency monosyllabic words other than by learning from the exemplars of these words that occur in the training set. In contrast, a system that works with segmental or AF representations can recognise low-frequency words as sequences of more frequent segments and is therefore likely to be more successful at word recognition.

These debates in the ASR literature concerning the units of representation that are most effective for speech recognition parallel long-standing debates in the literature on human speech recognition concerning the nature of speech representations (see Johnsrude and Buchsbaum, Chapter 1 of this volume, or Goldinger & Azuma, 2003). An alternative approach, however, would be to allow the automatic recognition system to determine which unit or units of representation most reliably mediate between the acoustic signal and word recognition. One way to achieve this is to have automatic systems break the input sequences of acoustic features into either predefined "units" or "units" that are automatically learned and can then be used in the recognition of words (e.g., De Wachter et al., 2007; Aimetti, ten Bosch, & Moore, 2009). An alternative approach is to use neural network learning algorithms to "discover" suitable intermediate representations between speech and words. The next section of this chapter will review historical and more recent approaches to ASR using neural networks. However, the majority of existing neural network-based ASR systems use neural networks not to achieve word recognition directly from acoustic representations but rather to replace the HMM-based acoustic models in existing systems. Thus, the flow diagram depicted in Figure 10.1, with minor modifications, remains an accurate description of most current ASR systems.

Neural networks for machine speech recognition

Neural networks are multilayer systems of simple processing units that compute the weighted sum of their inputs, which is then passed through a non-linear function and output to subsequent levels of processing (see Bishop, 1995, for an introduction). These simple, neurally inspired systems have a long history. Their adoption and capacities for tasks such as automatic speech recognition have been largely due to the development and refinement of learning algorithms that are capable of setting the weights on the connections between units so as to solve specific problems (e.g., mapping from sequences of acoustic vectors to phonemes or words). Among the earliest of these was the perceptron learning procedure of Rosenblatt (1958). However, more significant advances followed the development (or rediscovery) of learning by back-propagation of error by Rumelhart, Hinton, and Williams (1986), along with subsequent extensions of this procedure to train recurrent neural networks – that is, systems with internal states that retain a "history" of past input and that can therefore process signals (such as speech) that unfold over time (Pearlmutter, 1995). Critically, back-propagation and other, similar learning algorithms can be used to train networks with hidden units. These allow for the input to be transformed into mediating representations so that these networks can learn non-linearly separable mappings that evade simpler methods such as perceptrons or HMMs (see Bishop, 1996, for a detailed presentation of linear separability).

As part of a flurry of interest in neural networks that followed the two-volume "PDP books" in the 1980s (McClelland & Rumelhart, 1986; Rumelhart & McClelland,

1986), many researchers explored the possibility of using either static or recurrent neural networks in machine speech recognition (see Lippman, 1989, for an early review of these efforts). However, these systems often failed to achieve sufficient scale (in terms of the size of training materials) or accuracy (e.g., phoneme identification performance) to supplant existing HMM-based systems. A few notable successes were achieved by using hybrid systems in which recurrent neural networks with a single hidden layer were used to compute phoneme probabilities from speech signals that could then be interfaced with conventional Viterbi-based search procedures (see, for instance, Bourlard & Morgan, 1994; Robinson, 1994). Despite these early demonstrations, however, the neural network components of these hybrid systems were hard to train due to the limited speed of workstation computers at that time. Furthermore, the performance advantages offered by systems with a single hidden layer were not sufficient to render more conventional HMM systems obsolete, and the training procedures for multilayer systems were of limited ability. Hence, these recurrent network systems were in time replaced by more tractable HMM-based systems as described earlier in this chapter.

Recent years have seen a resurgence of interest in the use of neural networks for machine speech recognition. In part, this is the result of increases in computer processing speed, particularly by using graphics processors to perform fast vector computations during training. One striking and influential demonstration by Mohamed, Dahl, & Hinton (2009) showed that a deep neural network (DNN, i.e., a neural network with multiple layers of hidden units between the input and output) could substantially improve on state-of-the-art HMM scores on the TIMIT phoneme identification task. This success has led many groups to make updated versions of the hybrid systems that were used in the 1990s by using neural networks to replace the traditional HMM-based acoustic models (see Hinton et al., 2012, for a review). These DNN-based systems are trained using large sets of phonetically labelled speech signals to output the posterior probability of different HMM states (phonemes or triphones, for example) given a sequence of acoustic states as input. We will therefore consider the critical elements of this advance and consider the parallels between this approach and proposals made for human speech recognition – a domain in which neural network or connectionist approaches remained popular throughout the intervening decades (as exemplified by simple recurrent network models, see Gaskell & Marslen-Wilson, 1997; Mirman, Chapter 6 of this volume).

The modern resurgence of interest in DNN systems for phoneme identification arises not only from the increased speed of modern computers but also from the development of new and more robust methods for training DNNs. One reason for the success of DNNs for classification tasks (such as phoneme recognition) is the use of generative, pretraining schemes in which a DNN learns (in an unsupervised fashion) to represent the acoustic characteristics of the input. Input to these models is often supplied using the same MEL-frequency cepstral coefficient representations used in HMM-based systems, though other, more redundant auditory representations (such as the output of auditory filter banks) have been tried with some success (Hinton et al., 2012). The training procedure used is hierarchical; a single layer is trained to represent first-order dependencies in the acoustic vectors, before an additional layer is added to represent dependencies among these first-order dependencies, and then a third layer, and so on. Critically, these models are generative; connectivity is bidirectional, and typical training algorithms (e.g., the contrastive divergence algorithm, Hinton, Osindero, & Teh, 2006) alternate between "wake" phases in which the model derives internal representations from the input and "sleep" phases in which the model uses those internal representations to reconstruct input sequences similar to those that were presented (see Hinton, 2014, for a overview). These procedures provide an effective procedure for discovering compact representations of sequences of acoustic feature vectors.

For machine speech recognition, however, it is not sufficient to derive a robust and compact representation of the speech signal. These representations also have to be categorized into discrete units (such as single phonemes, N-phones, features, syllables, etc.) in order to make contact with higher-level representations such as words. Hence, the hierarchical stack of units and connections that were trained to represent and reconstruct speech signals in a DNN are interfaced with a final layer of units with an output function suitable for classifying speech signals into unique categories (typically triphones). The entire stack of units (including the lower-level stages that were originally trained in an unsupervised manner) are then subjected to discriminative or supervised training using the back-propagation learning algorithm (Rumelhart et al., 1986). The full system is then able to output the probability of different units in the acoustic signal (typically N-phone probabilities) with an accuracy unmatched by HMM-based systems (see Hinton et al., 2012). The key advance provided by DNNs, relative to both HMMs and recurrent networks with a single layer of hidden units is that these networks provide a powerful mechanism for learning multiple layers of non-linear features (see Hinton, 2014, for discussion). This success has led to the adoption of DNN methods by many of the major commercial speech recognition systems (see McMillan, 2013, for an accessible introduction).

From the perspective of computational modelling of human speech recognition, these two stages of training an acoustic model (generative pretraining and discriminative training) are reminiscent (in their goal, if not in their methods) of connectionist approaches to human spoken language acquisition (see Mirman, Chapter 6 of this volume). Building on recurrent network simulations reported in Elman (1990), a number of authors have proposed that early stages of speech acquisition (during the first year of life) are well explained by training recurrent neural networks to predict subsequent segments in extended sequences of speech sounds (Cairns, Shillcock, Chater, & Levy, 1997; Christiansen, Allen, & Seidenberg, 1998). These self-supervised neural networks develop internal representations that capture important forms of linguistic structure such as words in artificially coded speech sequences, and periods of accurate and inaccurate prediction reflect knowledge of likely words in connected speech signals. The second stage of supervised learning used in these DNN systems is also reminiscent of procedures used in training connectionist or neural network models of spoken word recognition (such as the Distributed Cohort Model, Gaskell & Marslen-Wilson, 1997, or other similar models using localist representations of spoken words, Norris, 1990; Davis, 2003, see Mirman, Chapter 6 of this volume). Interestingly, these recurrent network systems appear to perform better if both forms of learning (unsupervised prediction and supervised lexical identification) are combined in a single system (Davis, 2003; Mirman, Estes, & Magnuson, 2010).

Despite the gratifying success of neurally inspired components in machine speech recognition systems, many of these systems still make unrealistic assumptions about how the temporal structure of the speech signal should be coded. The DNNs described so far mostly use separate sets of input units to code a sequence of acoustic vectors. That is, they use different units and connections information that occur at the present and previous time points; they also retain a veridical (acoustic) representation of the preceding acoustic context. Thus, these models use an unanalysed acoustic context for the recognition of the most likely speech segment in the current acoustic vector (as in time-delay neural networks described by Waibel, Hanazawa, Hinton, Shikano, & Lang, 1989). This is a spatial method of coding temporal structure (similar to that used in the TRACE model, McClelland & Elman, 1986). Spatial coding seems unrealistic as a model of how temporal structure and acoustic context is processed during speech perception. Humans don't use different auditory nerve fibres or cortical neurons to process sounds that are presented at different points in time, but rather the same neurons provide input at all points in time, and perception is supported by internal representations that retain relevant context information.

A more appropriate method for coding temporal structure therefore involves using recurrent neural networks, in which input is presented sequentially (one acoustic vector at a time), and activation states at the hidden units provide the temporal context required to identify the current input that can be trained with variants of back-propagation (see Elman, 1990; Pearlmutter, 1995). Recurrent neural networks were initially used successfully in phoneme probability estimation (e.g., Robinson, 1994) but were found to be difficult to train, particularly when long-distance dependencies must be processed in order to identify speech signals (for instance, if input from several previous time steps must be used to inform the current input). Sequences in which there are long delays from when critical information appears in the input and when target representations permit back-propagation of error require that weight updates be passed through multiple layers of units (one for each intervening time step) during training. These additional intervening units make it more likely that error signals will become unstable (since error gradients can grow exponentially large or become vanishingly small, see Hochreiter, Bengio, Frasconi, & Schmidhuber, 2001). Various solutions to this problem of learning long-distance temporal dependencies have been proposed, including schemes for incremental learning of progressively longer-distance dependencies (e.g., Elman, 1993). Perhaps the most powerful solution, however, comes from long short-term memory networks proposed by Hochreiter & Schmidhuber (1997), in which error signals are preserved over multiple time points within gated memory circuits. These systems achieve the efficient learning of long-distance dependencies and are now being used in deep neural network systems for acoustic modelling (see Beaufais, 2015).

Despite the successful deployment of these neural networks, their incorporation into existing ASR systems has still largely come from replacing single components of existing systems with DNNs and not from an end-to-end redesign of the recognition process. For example, DNNs have been used to replace the HMM acoustic model shown in Figure 10.1. However, this still requires the phoneme classification output of a neural network to be transformed into standard HMM states (corresponding to phonemes) and a search algorithm to be used to combine these HMM states into word sequences constrained by N-gram-based language models (essentially the same hybrid connectionist approach proposed in Bourlard & Morgan, 1994). More recently, some authors have begun to explore the possibility of end-to-end neural network–based speech recognition systems (e.g., Chorowski, Bahdanau, Cho, & Bengio, 2014; Graves & Jaitly, 2014). These systems have not so far been sufficiently successful (or computationally tractable) to operate without a traditional N-gram-based language model. Furthermore, while DNN-based language models have been proposed in other contexts (e.g., for machine translation systems, Cho et al., 2014), these have rarely been interfaced to a perceptual system based around a DNN. We note, however, that end-to-end computational models of human word recognition have been constructed using a recurrent neural network (e.g., Gaskell & Marslen-Wilson, 1997). This so-called distributed cohort model uses back-propagation to map from (artificially coded) speech segments to meaning. While this model is small in scale and unable to work with real speech input, recent progress in the use of neural networks for ASR suggest that this model could be developed further.

Perceptual learning in human and machine speech recognition

Perhaps the most significant challenge for machine speech recognition is that the identity of speech sounds is determined not only by the acoustic signal but also by the surrounding context (acoustic, lexical, semantic, etc.) in which those sounds occur and by the knowledge of the person who produced these sounds (their vocal tract physiology, accent, etc.). The optimal use of contextual information in recognition is not easily achieved by using either an HMM or a time-delay DNN for acoustic modelling in ASR systems. In both cases, only a relatively short period of prior acoustic context is encoded in the input to the acoustic models, and perceptual hypotheses for the identity of the current segment are determined (bottom-up) only on the basis of this acoustic input. For this reason, ASR systems defer decisions concerning the identity of specific speech segments until these sublexical perceptual hypotheses can be combined with higher-level information (such as knowledge of likely words or word sequences). As shown in Figure 10.1, identification of speech sounds in ASR systems arises through the combination of acoustic models with a lexicon and language model so that lexical and semantic/syntactic context can be used to support speech identification.

Human recognition shows similar lexical and sentential influences on segment identification. This has been shown by changes to phoneme categorization boundaries that favour real words or meaningful sentences. For example, a sound that is ambiguous between a /t/ and /d/ will be heard differently in syllables like "task" or "dark" (since listeners disfavour nonword interpretations like "dask" or "tark", i.e., the Ganong effect; Ganong, 1980). Furthermore, even when disambiguating information is delayed beyond the current syllable (as for an ambiguous /p/ and /b/ at the onset of "barricade" and "parakeet"), listeners continue to use lexical information to resolve segmental ambiguities in a graded fashion (McMurray, Tanenhaus, & Aslin, 2009). Sentence-level meaning that constrains word interpretation has also been shown to modify segment perception (Borsky, Tuller, & Shapiro, 1998). Thus, human listeners, like machine recognition systems, delay phonemic commitments until higher-order knowledge, including lexical and semantic information, can be used to disambiguate.

However, unlike human listeners, typical ASR systems do not change their subsequent identification of speech segments as a consequence of lexically or semantically determined disambiguation. As first shown by Norris, McQueen, and Cutler (2003; see Samuel & Kraljic, 2009, for a review), a process of perceptual learning allows human listeners to use lexical information to update or retune sub-lexical phoneme perception. That is, hearing an ambiguous /s/-/f/ segment at the end of a word like "peace" or "beef" that constrains interpretation leads to subsequent changes in the perception of an /s/ or /f/ segment heard in isolation. Human listeners infer that they are listening to someone who produces specific fricatives in an ambiguous fashion and change their interpretations of these sounds accordingly (see Eisner & McQueen, 2006; Kraljic & Samuel, 2006, for contrasting findings, however, concerning generalization among speakers).

Recent evidence suggests that for human listeners, perceptual learning arises only for ambiguous segments that occur towards the end of a word (Jesse & McQueen, 2011). Perceptual learning is thus absent for word-initial /s/-/f/ ambiguities even in strongly constraining contexts like "syrup" or "phantom", despite successful identification of the spoken words in these cases. Although human listeners can delay making commitments to specific phonemes in order to correctly identify words, they appear not to use these delayed disambiguations to drive perceptual learning. These observations suggest mechanisms for perceptual learning that are driven by prior knowledge of upcoming segments and not solely by word identification.

In combination, then, these learning effects point to a form of perceptual flexibility that is often critical for successful human speech recognition. Listeners are adept at using information gained from previous utterances to guide the processing of future utterances. In real-world listening situations, this learning process is most apparent when listeners hear strongly accented speech. Accented speech may contain multiple segments for which the form of perceptual learning described previously is required. Laboratory studies have shown rapid gains in the speed and accuracy of word identification following relatively short periods of exposure to accented speech (Clarke & Garrett, 2004; Adank & Janse, 2010).

One way of describing this process is as a form of (self-) supervised learning similar to that used in training deep neural networks (see Norris et al., 2003; Davis, Johnsrude, Hervais-Adelman, Taylor, & McGettigan, 2005). For human listeners, lexical identification provides knowledge of the segments that were presented in the current word. This knowledge is then used in a top-down fashion to modify the mapping from acoustic representations to segment identity such that a previously ambiguous acoustic input is more easily identified in future. While this process is similar to the supervised learning algorithms used in training DNNs, the neural networks in current ASR systems do not use such mechanisms during recognition. The procedures that are used to train the weighted connections in these systems require the batched presentation of large quantities of training data including (for discriminative training) external signals that supply frame-by-frame ground-truth labels of the phonemic content of speech signals. When these systems are used to recognise speech, they operate with these learning mechanisms disabled (that is, the weighted connections between units remain the same irrespective of the utterance that is being recognised).

One obstacle to including perceptual learning mechanisms in ASR systems is therefore that ASR systems would need to derive top-down supervisory signals without external guidance. That is, the system must not only recognise words but also determine whether recognition is sufficiently accurate to support changes to the mapping from acoustic vectors to segments (since it is better not to learn from incorrect responses). This introduces a further requirement – specifically that the system has an internally derived measure of confidence in its own recognition. At present, however, measures of confidence have not been used for this purpose (see Jiang, 2005, for a review of attempts to derive confidence measures from existing ASR systems). There is, however, some experimental evidence that recognition confidence may modulate the efficacy of human perceptual learning (see Zhang & Samuel, 2014; Drozdova, van Hout, & Scharenborg, 2015).

Mechanisms for adaptation to speaker-specific characteristics have, however, been incorporated into HMM-based machine recognition systems. These typically operate by including additional hyper-parameters that are associated with specific utterances or speakers heard during training (Woodland, 2001; Yu & Gales, 2007). Techniques such as Maximum a Posteriori (MAP) parameter estimation and Maximum Likelihood Linear Regression (MLLR) can then be used to adapt the trained model parameters or to establish hyper-parameters that optimize perception of utterances from a new speaker. These methods permit adaptation to a new speaker based on a more limited number of utterances than would otherwise be required. Similar maximum likelihood methods have also been used in accommodating speakers with different-length vocal tracts (which systematically change formant frequencies). However, a more straightforward frequency warping can also be used to adapt to novel speakers (Lee & Rose, 1998).

One distinction between machine and human adaptation that we wish to draw, however, is between machine recognition systems that adapt by using relevant past experience of similar speakers and human listeners who show rapid learning even when faced with entirely unfamiliar (fictitious) accents. For instance, in studies by Adank & Janse (2010), young listeners showed substantial improvements in their ability to comprehend a novel accent created by multiple substitutions of the vowels in Dutch (e.g., swapping tense and lax vowels, monopthongs and dipthongs, etc.). Improvements in comprehension were even more rapid when listeners were instructed to imitate the accented sentences (Adank, Hagoort, & Bekkering, 2010). These behavioural experiments point to a form of adaptation that can operate even when listeners have no relevant past experience of any similar accent. That this is a form of supervised learning is also apparent from research showing that accent adaptation is more rapid for listeners that receive supervisory information from concurrent written subtitles (Mitterer & McQueen, 2009).

Human listeners also show perceptual learning when faced with extreme or unnatural forms of degraded speech. For example, perceptual learning occurs when listeners hear speech that has been artificially time-compressed to 35% of the original duration (Mehler et al., 1993), or noise-vocoded to provide just a handful of independent spectral channels (vocoded speech, Davis et al., 2005), or resynthesized using only three harmonically unrelated whistles (sine wave speech, Remez et al., 2011). In all these cases, listeners rapidly adapt despite having had essentially no relevant prior exposure to other similar forms of speech. Once again, many of these forms of learning are enhanced by prior knowledge of speech content (e.g., written subtitles or clear speech presentations) that precede perception of degraded speech (e.g., Davis et al., 2005; Hervais-Adelman, Davis, Johnsrude, & Carlyon, 2008), further suggesting supervisory mechanisms involved in perceptual learning.

In sum, this evidence suggests that rapid and powerful learning processes contribute to the successful identification of accented and degraded speech in human listeners. It remains to be seen whether incorporating a similar form of self-supervised learning would enhance the performance of machine recognition systems. In explaining the abilities of human listeners, computational models of spoken word recognition have already been proposed that can adjust their internal processes to simulate perceptual learning of ambiguous speech segments (HebbTRACE: Mirman, McClelland, & Holt, 2006; Kleinschmidt & Jaeger, 2014). However, one interesting, and under-explored aspect of these models concerns the situations in which such rapid learning is possible. We have noted that accurate prior knowledge of the likely identity of upcoming speech segments is a necessary condition for perceptual learning to occur (cf. Davis et al., 2005; Jesse & McQueen, 2011). Predictive coding mechanisms may provide one proposal for how these findings can be accommodated in models of human speech recognition (Gagnepain, Henson, & Davis, 2012; Sohoglu, Peelle, Carlyon, & Davis, 2012): accurate predictions for upcoming speech signals are reinforced to drive perceptual learning, whereas speech signals that lead to large prediction errors provide a novelty signal to drive encoding of unfamiliar words.

Conclusion

This chapter has described the inner workings of machine speech recognition systems that have already transformed our day-to-day interactions with computers, smartphones, and similar devices. Improvements in the effectiveness and convenience of voice input seem set to continue; we imagine that our children will in time be amused at our generation's antiquated attachment to QWERTY keyboards. However, the ASR systems that we have described still fall short of human levels of recognition performance. Substantial improvements will be required if our communication with machines is to be as seamless as it is with our friends and family.

We have offered three distinct proposals for key aspects of human speech recognition that could inspire future developments in machine recognition systems. Specifically, we have proposed that it is worth exploring ASR systems that (1) relax the assumption that speech is comprised of a sequence of discrete and invariant segments (phonemes), (2) operate in an end-to-end fashion using neural network components, and (3) are able to learn from their own successes at recognition. We hope that these changes might allow for further progress in achieving accurate and robust machine speech recognition. However, we also acknowledge that existing systems are already good enough for day-to-day use by millions of people around the world. There is much for researchers to gain in human speech recognition from understanding the computational mechanisms that have achieved these successes. We hope that the overview of the underlying technology in the present chapter allows psycholinguists to learn from the successes of engineers and computer scientists working to improve ASR systems.

Notes

1 John West from Nuance's mobile group quoted at http://www.techweekeurope.co.uk/networks/voip/spinvox-faked-speech-transcription-service-and-broke-privacy-1451
2 Two further applications of research in human speech perception are to help listeners (1) who are hearing impaired (see Mattys et al., 2012) or are not native speakers (see Chen & Marian, Chapter 8 in this volume).

References

Adank, P., & Janse, E. (2010). Comprehension of a novel accent by young and older listeners. *Psychology and Aging, 25*, 736–740.

Adank, P., Hagoort, P., & Bekkering, H. (2010). Imitation improves language comprehension. *Psychological Science, 21*(12), 1903–1909. doi:10.1177/0956797610389192

Aimetti, G., ten Bosch, L., & Moore, R. K. (2009). Modelling early language acquisition with a dynamic systems perspective, 9th International Conference on Epigenetic Robotics. Venice.

Barker, J., Vincent, E., Ma, N., Christensen, H., Green, P., Barker, J., . . . Pascal, T. (2013). The PASCAL CHiME speech separation and recognition challenge. *Computer Speech & Language, 27*(3), 621–633.

Beaufais, F. (2015). The neural networks behind Google Voice transcription. Retrieved from http://googleresearch.blogspot.co.uk/2015/08/the-neural-networks-behind-google-voice.html

Bishop, C. M. (1995). *Neural networks for pattern recognition.* Oxford: Oxford University Press.

Borsky, S., Tuller, B., & Shapiro, L. (1998). "How to milk a coat:" The effects of semantic and acoustic information on phoneme categorization. *Journal of the Acoustical Society of America, 103*, 2670–2676.

Bourlard, H. A., & Morgan, N. (1994). *Connectionist Speech Recognition: A Hybrid Approach.* Boston: Kluwer.

Bourlard, H., Hermansky, H., & Morgan, N. (1996). Towards increasing speech recognition error rates. *Speech Communication, 18*, 205–231.

Cairns, P., Shillcock, R., Chater, N., & Levy, J. (1997). Bootstrapping word boundaries: A bottom-up corpus-based approach to speech segmentation. *Cognitive Psychology, 33*(2), 111–153. Retrieved from http://www.ncbi.nlm.nih.gov/pubmed/9245468

Carey, M. J., & Quang, T. P. (2005). A speech similarity distance weighting for robust recognition. Proceedings of Interspeech, Lisbon, Portugal, pp. 1257–1260.

Cho, K., van Merrienboer, B., Gulcehre, C., Bougares, F., Schwenk, H., & Bengio, Y. (2014). Learning phrase representations using RNN encoder–decoder for statistical machine translation. Conference on Empirical Methods in Natural Language Processing (EMNLP 2014).

Chorowski, J., Bahdanau, D., Cho, K. & Bengio, Y. (2014). End-to-end continuous speech recognition using attention-based recurrent NN: First results, pp. 1–10. Retrieved from http://arxiv.org/abs/1412.1602v1

Christiansen, M. H., Allen, J., & Seidenberg, M. S. (1998). Learning to segment speech using multiple cues: A connectionist model. *Language and Cognitive Processes, 13*(2–3), 221–268. doi:10.1080/016909698386528

Clarke, C. M., & Garrett, M. F. (2004). Rapid adaptation to foreign-accented English. *The Journal of the Acoustical Society of America, 116*(6), 3647–3658. doi:10.1121/1.1815131

Cooke, M., 2006. A glimpsing model of speech recognition in noise. *Journal of the Acoustical Society of America, 119*(3), 1562–1573.

Cutler, A., & Robinson, T., 1992. Response time as a metric for comparison of speech recognition by humans and machines. Proceedings of ICSLP, Banff, Canada, pp. 189–192.

Davis, M. H. (2003). Connectionist modelling of lexical segmentation and vocabulary acquisition. In P. Quinlan (ed.), *Connectionist Models of Development: Developmental Processes in Real and Artificial Neural Networks.* Hove, UK: Psychology Press, pp. 125–159.

Davis, M. H., Johnsrude, I. S., Hervais-Adelman, A., Taylor, K., & McGettigan, C. (2005). Lexical information drives perceptual learning of distorted speech: Evidence from the comprehension of noise-vocoded sentences. *Journal of Experimental Psychology: General, 134*(2), 222–241. doi:10.1037/0096–3445.134.2.222

Davis, M. H., Marslen-Wilson, W. D., & Gaskell, M. G. (2002). Leading up the lexical garden path: Segmentation and ambiguity in spoken word recognition. *Journal of Experimental Psychology: Human Perception and Performance, 28*(1), 218–244. doi:10.1037//0096–1523.28.1.218

Davis, S., & Mermelstein, P. (1980). Comparison of parametric representations for monosyllabic word recognition in continuously spoken sentences. *IEEE Transactions on Acoustics, Speech, and Signal Processing, 28*(4), 357–366. doi:10.1109/TASSP.1980.1163420

De Wachter, M., Matton, M., Demuynck, K., Wambacq, P., Cools, R., & Van Compernolle, D. (2007). Template based continuous speech recognition. *IEEE Transactions on Audio, Speech and Language Processing, 15*, 1377–1390, May.

Drozdova, P., van Hout, R., & Scharenborg, O. (2015). The effect of non-nativeness and background noise on lexical retuning. Proceedings of the International Congress of Phonetic Sciences, Glasgow, UK.

Eisner, F., & McQueen, J. M. (2006). Perceptual learning in speech: Stability over time. *The Journal of the Acoustical Society of America, 119*(4), 1950. doi:10.1121/1.2178721

Elman, J. (1990). Finding structure in time. *Cognitive Science*, *14*(2), 179–211. doi:10.1016/0364-0213(90)90002-E

Elman, J. L. (1993). Learning and development in neural networks: The importance of starting small. *Cognition*, *48*, 71–99.

Frankel, J. Linear dynamic models for automatic speech recognition. PhD thesis, The Centre for Speech Technology Research, Edinburgh University, April 2003.

Gagnepain, P., Henson, R. N., & Davis, M. H. (2012). Temporal predictive codes for spoken words in auditory cortex. *Current Biology: CB*, *22*(7), 615–621. doi:10.1016/j.cub.2012.02.015

Ganong, W. F. (1980). Phonetic categorization in auditory word perception. *Journal of Experimental Psychology: Human Perception and Performance*, *6*, 110–125.

Garofolo, J. S. (1988). Getting started with the DARPA TIMIT CD-ROM: An acoustic phonetic continuous speech database. Technical Report, National Institute of Standards and Technology (NIST).

Gaskell, M. G., & Marslen-Wilson, W. D. (1996). Phonological variation and inference in lexical access. *Journal of Experimental Psychology: Human Perception and Performance*, *22*, 144–158.

Gaskell, M. G., & Marslen-Wilson, W. D. (1997). Integrating form and meaning: A distributed model of speech perception. *Language and Cognitive Processes*, *12*(5–6), 613–656. doi:10.1080/016909697386646

Goldinger, S. D., & Azuma, T. (2003). Puzzle-solving science: The quixotic quest for units in speech perception. *Journal of Phonetics*, *31*(3–4), 305–320. doi:10.1016/S0095-4470(03)00030-5

Graves, A., & Jaitly, N. (2014). Towards end-to-end speech recognition with recurrent neural networks. *JMLR Workshop and Conference Proceedings*, *32*(1), 1764–1772. Retrieved from http://jmlr.org/proceedings/papers/v32/graves14.pdf

Greenberg, S. (1999). Speaking in shorthand: A syllable-centric perspective for understanding pronunciation variation. *Speech Communication*, *29*, 159–176.

Greenberg, S., Carvey, H., Hitchcock, L., & Chang, S. (2003). Temporal properties of spontaneous speech – A syllable-centric perspective. *Journal of Phonetics*, *31*, 465–485. d

Hawkins, S. (2003). Roles and representations of systematic fine phonetic detail in speech understanding. *Journal of Phonetics*, *31*(3–4), 373–405. doi:10.1016/j.wocn.2003.09.006

Hervais-Adelman, A., Davis, M. H., Johnsrude, I. S., & Carlyon, R. P. (2008). Perceptual learning of noise vocoded words: Effects of feedback and lexicality. *Journal of Experimental Psychology: Human Perception and Performance*, *34*(2), 460–474. doi:10.1037/0096-1523.34.2.460

Hilger, F., & Ney, H. (2006). Quantile based histogram equalization for noise robust large vocabulary speech recognition. *IEEE Transactions on Audio, Speech, and Language Processing*, *14*(3), 845–854.

Hinton, G. E. (2014). Where do features come from? *Cognitive Science*, *38*(6), 1078–1101.

Hinton, G., Deng, L., Yu, D., Dahl, G., Mohamed, A.-R., Jaitly, N., . . . Kingbury, B. (2012). Deep neural networks for acoustic modeling in speech recognition. *Signal Processing Magazine, IEEE*, *29*(November), 82–97. doi:10.1109/MSP.2012.2205597

Hinton, G. E., Osindero, S., & Teh, Y. (2006). A fast learning algorithm for deep belief nets. *Neural Computation*, *18*, 1527–1554.

Hochreiter, S., Bengio, Y., Frasconi, P., & Schmidhuber, J. (2001). Gradient flow in recurrent nets: The difficulty of learning long-term dependencies. In S. C. Kremer & J. F. Kolen (eds.), *A Field Guide to Dynamical Recurrent Neural Networks*. New York: IEEE Press.

Hochreiter, S., & Schmidhuber, J. (1997). Long short-term memory. *Neural Computation*, *9*(8), 1735–80. doi:10.1162/neco.1997.9.8.1735

Jakobson, R., Fant, G. M. C., & Halle, M. (1952). *Preliminaries to Speech Analysis: The Distinctive Features and their Correlates*. Cambridge, MA: MIT Press.

Jelinek, F. (1976). Continuous speech recognition by statistical methods. *Proceedings of the IEEE, 64*(4), 532–536.

Jesse, A., & McQueen, J. M. (2011). Positional effects in the lexical retuning of speech perception. *Psychonomic Bulletin & Review, 18*(5), 943–50. doi:10.3758/s13423–011–0129–2

Jiang, H. (2005). Confidence measures for speech recognition: A survey. *Speech Communication, 45*(4), 455–470. doi:10.1016/j.specom.2004.12.004

Juneja, A. (2012). A comparison of automatic and human speech recognition in null grammar. *Journal of the Acoustical Society of America, 131*(3), EL256–261.

Jurafsky, D., & Martin, J. H. (2009). *Speech and Language Processing: An Introduction to Natural Language Processing, Computational Linguistics, and Speech Recognition.* Prentice Hall Series in Artificial Intelligence (2nd ed.). Upper Saddle River, NJ: Prentice Hall.

King, S., & Taylor, P. (2000). Detection of phonological features in continuous speech using neural networks. *Computer Speech and Language, 14,* 333–353.

Kirchhoff, K. (1996). Syllable-level desynchronisation of phonetic features for speech recognition. Proceedings of Interspeech, pp. 2274–2276.

Kirchhoff, K. (1998). Combining articulatory and acoustic information for speech recognition in noisy and reverberant environments. Proceedings of ICSLP, pp. 891–894.

Kirchhoff, K. (1999). *Robust speech recognition using articulatory information*, PhD thesis, University of Bielefield, Germany.

Kirchhoff, K., Fink, G. A., & Sagerer, G. (2002). Combining acoustic and articulatory feature information for robust speech recognition. *Speech Communication, 37,* 303–319.

Kirchhoff, K., & Schimmel, S., (2005). Statistical properties of infant-directed versus adult-directed speech: Insights from speech recognition. *Journal of the Acoustical Society of America, 117*(4), 2238–2246.

Kleinschmidt, D. F., & Jaeger, T. F. (2014). Robust speech perception: Recognize the familiar, generalize to the similar, and adapt to the novel. *Psychological Review, 122*(2), 148–203. doi:10.1037/a0038695

Kraljic, T., & Samuel, A. G. (2006). Generalization in perceptual learning for speech. *Psychonomic Bulletin & Review, 13*(2), 262–268.

Lahiri, A., & Marslen-Wilson, W. D. (1991). The mental representation of lexical form: A phonological approach to the recognition lexicon. *Cognition, 38,* 245–294.

Lahiri, A., & Reetz, H. (2010). Distinctive features: Phonological underspecification in representation and processing. *Journal of Phonetics, 38,* 44–59.

Lee, L., & Rose, R. C. (1998). A frequency warping approach to speaker normalization. *IEEE Transactions on Speech and Audio Processing, 6*(1), 49–60.

Li, J., Deng L, Gong, Y., & Haeb-Umbach, R. (2014). An overview of noise-robust automatic speech recognition. *IEEE Transactions on Audio, Speech and Language Processing, 22*(4), 745–777.

Lippmann, R. P. (1989). Review of neural networks for speech recognition. *Neural computation, 1*(1), 1–38.

Lippmann, R. P. (1997). Speech recognition by machines and humans. *Speech Communication, 22*(1), 1–15. doi:10.1016/S0167–6393(97)00021–6

Livescu, K., Bezman, A., Borges, N., Yung, L., Çetin, Ö., Frankel, J. . . . Lavoie, L. (2007). Manual transcriptions of conversational speech at the articulatory feature level. Proceedings of ICASSP, Vol. 1, pp. 953–956.

Livescu, K., Glass, J. R., & Bilmes, J. A. (2003, September). Hidden feature models for speech recognition using dynamic Bayesian networks. *INTERSPEECH,* Vol. 4, pp. 2529–2532.

Marslen-Wilson, W., & Warren, P. (1994). Levels of perceptual representation and process in lexical access: Words, phonemes, and features. *Psychological Review, 101*(4), 653–675. Retrieved from http://www.ncbi.nlm.nih.gov/pubmed/7984710

Mattys, S. L., Davis, M. H., Bradlow, A. R., & Scott, S. K. (2012). Speech recognition in adverse conditions: A review. *Language and Cognitive Processes, 27*(7–8), 953–978.

McClelland, J. L., & Elman, J. L. (1986). The TRACE model of speech perception. *Cognitive Psychology, 18*(1), 1–86.

McClelland, J. L., & Rumelhart, D. E. (1986). *Parallel Distributed Processing: Explorations in the Microstructure of Cognition (Vol. 2: Psychological and Biological Models)*. Cambridge, MA: MIT Press.

McMillan, R. (2013). How Google retooled Android with help from your brain. *Wired Magazine*. Retrieved from http://www.wired.com/2013/02/android-neural-network/

McMurray, B., Tanenhaus, M. K., & Aslin, R. N. (2009). Within-category VOT affects recovery from "lexical" garden-paths: Evidence against phoneme-level inhibition. *Journal of Memory and Language, 60*, 65–91.

Mehler, J., Sebastian-Gallés, N., Altmann, G., Dupoux, E., Christophe, A., & Pallier, C. (1993). Understanding compressed sentences: The role of rhythm and meaning. In A. M. G. Paula Tallal, Rodolfo R. Llinas & Curt von Euler (eds.), *Temporal Information Processing in the Nervous System: Special Reference to Dyslexia and Dysphasia: Annals of the New York Academy of Sciences* (Vol. 682, pp. 272–282).

Meyer, B. T., Brand, T., & Kollmeier, B. (2011). Effect of speech-intrinsic variations on human and automatic recognition of spoken phonemes. *Journal of the Acoustical Society of America, 129*, 388–403.

Meyer, B., Wesker, T., Brand, T., Mertins, A., & Kollmeier, B. (2006). A human-machine comparison in speech recognition based on a logatome corpus. Proceedings of the workshop on Speech Recognition and Intrinsic Variation, Toulouse, France.

Miller, G. A., Heise, G. A., & Lichten, W. (1951). The intelligibility of speech as a function of the context of the test materials. *Journal of Experimental Psychology, 41*, 329–335.

Mirman, D., Estes, K. G., & Magnuson, J. S. (2010). Computational modeling of statistical learning: Effects of transitional probability versus frequency and links to word learning. *Infancy, 15*(5), 471–486. doi:10.1111/j.1532-7078.2009.00023.x

Mirman, D., McClelland, J. L., & Holt, L. L. (2006). An interactive Hebbian account of lexically guided tuning of speech perception. *Psychonomic Bulletin & Review, 13*(6), 958–965. doi:10.3758/BF03213909

Mitterer, H., & McQueen, J. M. (2009). Foreign subtitles help but native-language subtitles harm foreign speech perception. *PloS One, 4*(11), e7785. doi:10.1371/journal.pone.0007785

Mohamed, A. R., Dahl, G. E., & Hinton, G. E. (2009). Deep belief networks for phone recognition. Proceedings of the Neural Information Processing Systems Workshop on Deep Learning for Speech Recognition.

Moore, R. K. (2003). A comparison of the data requirements of automatic speech recognition systems and human listeners. Proceedings of Eurospeech, Geneva, Switzerland, pp. 2581–2584.

Moore, R. K., & Cutler, A. (2001). Constraints on theories of human vs. machine recognition of speech. In R. Smits, J. Kingston, T. M. Nearey, & R. Zondervan (eds.), Proceedings of the Workshop on Speech Recognition as Pattern Classification (pp. 145–150). Nijmegen: MPI for Psycholinguistics.

Nakatani, L. H., & Dukes, K. D. (1977). Locus of segmental cues for word juncture. *Journal of the Acoustical Society of America, 62*, 715–719.

Norris, D. (1990). A dynamic-net model of human speech recognition. In G. T. M. Altmann (ed.), *Cognitive Models of Speech Processing*. Cambridge, MA, MIT Press, pp. 87–103.

Norris, D., & McQueen, J. M. (2008). Shortlist B: A Bayesian model of continuous speech recognition. *Psychological Review, 115*(2), 357–395. doi:10.1037/0033-295X.115.2.357

Norris, D., McQueen, J. M., & Cutler, A. (2003). Perceptual learning in speech. *Cognitive Psychology*, 47(2), 204–238. doi:10.1016/S0010–0285(03)00006–9

Ostendorf, M. (1999). Moving beyond the 'beads-on-a-string' model of speech. Proceedings of IEEE ASRU Workshop, Keystone, Colorado, pp. 79–84.

Pearlmutter, B. A. (1995). Gradient calculation for dynamic recurrent neural networks: A survey. *IEE Transactions on Neural Networks*, 6, 1212–1228.

Pinker, S. (1994). *The Language Instinct: The New Science of Language and Mind*. New York: William Morrow.

Puurula, A., & Van Compernolle, D. (2010). Dual stream speech recognition using articulatory syllable models. *International Journal of Speech Technology*, 13(4), 219–230. doi:10.1007/s10772–010–9080–2

Remez, R. E., Dubowski, K. R., Broder, R. S., Davids, M. L., Grossman, Y. S., Moskalenko, M., . . . Hasbun, S. M. (2011). Auditory-phonetic projection and lexical structure in the recognition of sine-wave words. *Journal of Experimental Psychology: Human Perception and Performance*, 37(3), 968–977. doi:10.1037/a0020734

Robinson, A. J. (1994). An application of recurrent nets to phone probability estimation. *IEEE Transactions on Neural Networks*, 5(2), 298–305.

Rosenblatt, F. (1958). The perceptron: A probabilistic model for information storage and organization in the brain. *Psychological Review*, 65(6), 386–408.

Rumelhart, D. E., & McClelland, J. L. (1986). *Parallel Distributed Processing: Explorations in the Microstructure of Cognition (Vol. 1: Foundations)*. Cambridge, MA: MIT Press.

Rumelhart, D. E., Hinton, G., & Williams, R. J. (1986). Learning representations by back-propagating errors. *Nature*, 323, 533–536.

Salverda, A. P., Dahan, D., & McQueen, J. M. (2003). The role of prosodic boundaries in the resolution of lexical embedding in speech comprehension. *Cognition*, 90(1), 51–89. doi:10.1016/S0010–0277(03)00139–2

Samuel, A. G., & Kraljic, T. (2009). Perceptual learning in speech perception. *Attention, Perception & Psychophysics*, 71, 1207–1218.

Scharenborg, O. (2007). Reaching over the gap: A review of efforts to link human and automatic speech recognition research. *Speech Communication – Special Issue on Bridging the Gap between Human and Automatic Speech Processing*, 49, 336–347.

Scharenborg, O. (2010). Modeling the use of durational information in human spoken-word recognition. *Journal of the Acoustical Society of America*, 127(6), 3758–3770.

Scharenborg, O., Norris, D., Bosch, L., & McQueen, J. M. (2005). How should a speech recognizer work? *Cognitive Science*, 29(6), 867–918. doi:10.1207/s15516709cog0000_37

Scharenborg, O., Wan, V., & Moore, R. K. (2007). Towards capturing fine phonetic variation in speech using articulatory features. *Speech Communication*, 49, 811–826.

Schuppler, B., van Doremalen, J., Scharenborg, O., Cranen, B., & Boves, L. (2009). Using temporal information for improving articulatory-acoustic feature classification. Proceedings of the IEEE Automatic Speech Recognition and Understanding Workshop, Merano, Italy, pp. 70–75.

Shatzman, K. B., & McQueen, J. M. (2006a). Segment duration as a cue to word boundaries in spoken-word recognition. *Perception, & Psychophysics*, 68, 1–16.

Shatzman, K. B., & McQueen, J. M. (2006b). The modulation of lexical competition by segment duration. *Psychonomic Bulletin & Review*, 13, 966–971.

Siniscalchi, S. M., & Lee, C.-H. (2014). An attribute detection based approach to automatic speech recognition. *Loquens*, 1(1). Retrieved from http://dx.doi.org/10.3989/loquens.2014.005

Sohoglu, E., Peelle, J. E., Carlyon, R. P., & Davis, M. H. (2012). Predictive top-down integration of prior knowledge during speech perception. *The Journal of Neuroscience:*

The Official Journal of the Society for Neuroscience, 32(25), 8443–8453. doi:10.1523/JNEUROSCI.5069–11.2012

Sroka, J. J., & Braida, L. D., 2005. Human and machine consonant recognition. *Speech Communication, 45,* 401–423.

Vincent, E., Barker, J., Watanabe, S., Le Roux, J., Nesta, F., & Matassoni, M. (2013). The second "CHiME" speech separation and recognition challenge: An overview of challenge systems and outcomes. 2013 IEEE Workshop on Automatic Speech Recognition and Understanding, ASRU 2013 – Proceedings, pp. 162–167. doi:10.1109/ASRU.2013.6707723

Waibel, A., Hanazawa, T., Hinton, G., Shikano, K., & Lang, K. (1989). Phoneme recognition using time-delay neural networks. *IEEE, Transactions on Acoustics, Speech, and Signal Processing, 37*(3), 328–339.

Wester, M., 2003. Syllable classification using articulatory-acoustic features. Proceedings of Eurospeech, Geneva, Switzerland, pp. 233–236.

Woodland, P. C. (2001). Speaker adaptation for continuous density HMMs: A review. Proceedings ISCA Workshop on Adaptation Methods for Speech Recognition, pp. 11–19.

Young, S. J. (1996). A review of large-vocabulary continuous-speech recognition. *IEEE Signal Processing Magazine, 13*(5), 45–57.

Yu, K., & Gales, M. J. F. (2007). Bayesian adaptive inference and adaptive training. *IEEE Transactions on Audio, Speech and Language Processing, 15*(6), 1932–1943. doi:10.1109/TASL.2007.901300

Zhang, X., & Samuel, A. G. (2014). Perceptual learning of speech under optimal and adverse conditions. *Journal of Experimental Psychology: Human Perception and Performance, 40*(1), 200–217.

INDEX